COGNTIVE 2017

The Ninth International Conference on Advanced Cognitive Technologies and Applications

February 19 - 23, 2017

Athens, Greece

COGNITIVE 2017 Editors

Vincent Gripon, IMTA / Lab-STICC, France

Olga Chernavskaya, Lebeved Physical Institute, Moscow, Russia

Paul Smart, University of Southampton, UK

Tiago Thompsen Primo, Samsung Research Institute, Brazil

Printed from e-media with permission by:

Curran Associates, Inc.
57 Morehouse Lane
Red Hook, NY 12571

Some format issues inherent in the e-media version may also appear in this print version.

Printed by Curran Associates, Inc. (2017)

International Academy, Research, and Industry Association (IARIA)
412 Derby Way
Wilmington, DE 19810

Phone: (408) 893-6407
Fax: (408) 527-6351

petre@iaria.org

Additional copies of this publication are available from:

Curran Associates, Inc.
57 Morehouse Lane
Red Hook, NY 12571 USA
Phone: 845-758-0400
Fax: 845-758-2633
Email: curran@proceedings.com
Web: www.proceedings.com

Table of Contents

COGNITIVE 2017

Forward

The Ninth International Conference on Advanced Cognitive Technologies and Applications (COGNITIVE 2017), held between February 19-23, 2017 in Athens, Greece, continued a series of events targeting advanced concepts, solutions and applications of artificial intelligence, knowledge processing, agents, as key-players, and autonomy as manifestation of self-organized entities and systems. The advances in applying ontology and semantics concepts, web-oriented agents, ambient intelligence, and coordination between autonomous entities led to different solutions on knowledge discovery, learning, and social solutions

The conference had the following tracks:

- Brain information processing and informatics
- Emotions in Artificial Cognitive Systems
- Neuroinspired Informatics
- Human Behavior in Digital Education
- Artificial intelligence and cognition
- Cognition and the Web

We take here the opportunity to warmly thank all the members of the COGNITIVE 2017 technical program committee, as well as all the reviewers. The creation of such a high quality conference program would not have been possible without their involvement. We also kindly thank all the authors that dedicated much of their time and effort to contribute to COGNITIVE 2017. We truly believe that, thanks to all these efforts, the final conference program consisted of top quality contributions.

Also, this event could not have been a reality without the support of many individuals, organizations and sponsors. We also gratefully thank the members of the COGNITIVE 2017 organizing committee for their help in handling the logistics and for their work that made this professional meeting a success.

We hope that COGNITIVE 2017 was a successful international forum for the exchange of ideas and results between academia and industry and to promote further progress in the area of cognitive technologies and applications. We also hope that Athens, Greece provided a pleasant environment during the conference and everyone saved some time to enjoy the charm of the city.

COGNITIVE 2017 Committee

COGNITIVE 2017 Steering Committee

Po-Hsun Cheng, National Kaohsiung Normal University, Taiwan
Jose Alfredo F. Costa, Federal University - UFRN, Brazil

COGNITIVE 2017

Committee

COGNITIVE Steering Committee

Po-Hsun Cheng, National Kaohsiung Normal University, Taiwan
Jose Alfredo F. Costa, Federal University - UFRN, Brazil
Om Prakash Rishi, University of Kota, India
Kazuhisa Miwa, Nagoya University, Japan
Olga Chernavskaya, Lebeved Physical Institute, Moscow, Russia
Paul Smart, University of Southampton, UK
Ryotaro Kamimura, Tokai University, Japan
Olivier Chator, Ecole Nationale Supérieure de Cognitique, France

COGNITIVE 2017 Industry/Research Advisory Committee

Jayfus Tucker Doswell, The Juxtopia Group, Inc., USA
Tiago Thompsen Primo, Samsung Research Institute, Brazil
Galit Fuhrmann Alpert, computational neuroscientist, Israel

COGNITIVE 2017 Technical Program Committee

Witold Abramowicz, University of Economics and Business, Poland
Thomas Agotnes, University of Bergen, Norway
Jose Alfredo F. Costa, Federal University - UFRN, Brazil
Piotr Artiemjew, University of Warmia and Masuria, Poland
Petr Berka, University of Economics, Prague, Czech Republic
Ateet Bhalla, Independent Consultant, India
Peter Brida, University of Zilina, Slovak Republic
Dilyana Budakova, Technical University of Sofia - Branch Plovdiv, Bulgaria
Albertas Caplinskas, Vilnius University, Lithuania
Francesco Carlo Morabito, University Mediterranea of Reggio Calabria, Italy
Yaser Chaaban, Leibniz University of Hanover, Germany
Olivier Chator, Ecole Nationale Supérieure de Cognitique, France
Po-Hsun Cheng, National Kaohsiung Normal University, Taiwan
Olga Chernavskaya, Lebeved Physical Institute, Moscow, Russia
Sunil Choenni, Dutch Ministry of Security & Justice / Rotterdam University of Applied Sciences, Netherlands
Helder Coelho, Universidade de Lisboa, Portugal
Leonardo Dagui de Oliveira, University of São Paulo, Brazil
Darryl N. Davis, University of Hull, UK
Jayfus Tucker Doswell, The Juxtopia Group, Inc., USA
António Dourado, University of Coimbra, Portugal

Mounîm A. El Yacoubi, Telecom SudParis, France
Galit Fuhrmann Alpert, computational neuroscientist, Israel
Mauro Gaggero, National Research Council of Italy, Italy
Franck Gechter, Université de Technologie de Belfort Montbéliard - UBFC, France
Alessandro Giuliani, University of Cagliari, Italy
Vincent Gripon, Institut Mines-Télécom, France
Foteini Grivokostopoulou, University of Patras, Greece
Fikret Gürgen, Bogazici University, Turkey
Jianye Hao, Tianjin University, China
Ioannis Hatzilygeroudis, University of Patras, Greece
Marion Hersh, University of Glasgow, UK
Koen Hindriks, Delft University of Technology, Netherlands
Tzung-Pei Hong, National University of Kaohsiung, Taiwan
Zhisheng Huang, Vrije University, Netherlands
Ryotaro Kamimura, Tokai University, Japan
Jozef Kelemen, Institute of Computer Science - Silesian University, Opava, Czech Republic
Ruggero Donida Labati, Università degli Studi di Milano, Italy
Minho Lee, Kyungpook National University, Republic of Korea
Hai (Helen) Li, University of Pittsburgh, USA
Sheng Li, Northeastern University, Boston, USA
Yaliang Li, SUNY Buffalo, USA
Hakim Lounis, Universite du Quebec a Montreal (UQAM), Canada
Prabhat Mahanti, University of New Brunswick, Canada
Angel Alejandro Maldonado-Ramírez, CINVESTAV Campus Saltillo, Mexico
Giuseppe Mangioni, DIEEI - University of Catania, Italy
Francesco Marcelloni, University of Pisa, Italy
Franova Marta, CNRS, LRI & INRIA, France
Kathryn Merrick, University of New South Wales, Canberra, Australia
John-Jules Charles Meyer, Utrecht University, Netherlands
Kazuhisa Miwa, Nagoya University, Japan
Carlos Alberto Ochoa Ortiz, Juarez City University, Mexico
Yoshimasa Ohmoto, Kyoto University, Japan
Yiannis Papadopoulos, University of Hull, UK
Andrew Parkes, University of Nottingham, UK
Enrico Pontelli, New Mexico State University, USA
Mengyu Qiao, South Dakota School of Mines and Technology, USA
J. Javier Rainer Granados, Universidad Internacional de la Rioja, Spain
Julia Taylor Rayz, Purdue University, USA
Om Prakash Rishi, University of Kota, India
Alexandr Ryjov, Lomonosov Moscow State University, Russia
Fariba Sadri, Imperial College London, UK
Abdel-Badeeh M. Salem, Ain Shams University Abbasia, Cairo, Egypt
Nazha Selmaoui-Folcher, PPME University of New Caledonia, New Caledonia
Paulo Jorge Sequeira Gonçalves, Instituto Politecnico de Castelo Branco, Portugal

Copyright Information

The Hippocampus According to the Ouroboros Model, the "Expanding Memory Index Hypothesis"

Knud Thomsen PSI
Paul Scherrer Institut
NUM Forschung mit Neutronen und Muonen
CH-5232 Villigen PSI, Switzerland
e-mail: knud.thomsen@psi.ch

Abstract—**Understanding information processing in the brain demands more than one approach or method. Combining well-established and diverse novel experimental findings from neuroscience, connectionist approaches, and artificial intelligence, the perspective of the recently proposed cognitive architecture of the Ouroboros Model offers an integrative view on the functional role of the mammalian hippocampus: it is hypothesized to implement a rapidly laid down index, first establishing, contributing to binding, and then retrieving together memory entries, thus iteratively expanding the overall cognitive system in an autocatalytic process.**

Keywords - Cognition; schema; iterative processing; discrepancy monitoring; hypercycle; hash table; extreme learning machine.

I. INTRODUCTION

The hippocampus is a central neural structure on top of the processing hierarchy in mammalian brains. Homologous structures have been found in reptiles and birds. Widely and reciprocally connected to cortical areas, in mammals the hippocampus is comprised of several distinct main regions: Dentate Gyrus (DG), CA3, and CA1; see Fig. 1. These appear to implement successive stages of processing: DG as the input stage has been implicated in pattern separation whereas CA3 is best understood as a content-addressable auto-association memory providing pattern completion, as explained in some detail below [1]. A hippocampal memory indexing theory has been proposed 30 years ago, and it has fared quite well over time [2][3].

The paper is structured as follows. In section II, the gist of the Ouroboros Model is presented in just a few words, and in section III, a coarse conceptual sketch of an expanded dynamic indexing view is outlined. Conclusions and future work are indicated in Section IV.

II. TH E OUROBOROS MODEL IN TWO WORDS

The Ouroboros Model offers a cognitive architecture aiming at an encompassing account [4]. Cognition in general is explained as resulting from two fundamental building blocks: a memory structured into cohesive chunks called schemata, and a cyclic process termed 'consumption analysis', which "cultivates" consistency by monitoring for discrepancies and thereupon directing attention and also triggering memory storage according to demand.

A key tenet of the Ouroboros Model, in particular, is that novel memory entries are laid down as kind of "snapshots" linking all prevalent cortical activations at occasions marked as important by the outcome of consumption analysis [5]; this most efficiently includes distinct index records.

III. THE EXPANDING MEMORY INDEX HYPOTHESIS

Mapping structures of the Ouroboros Model to living brains, it has been hypothesized in various previous accounts that the hippocampus embodies an index to features in distributed representations over widely spread specialized cerebral cortex areas [2][3][6].

Arguing that there are diverse requirements on different forms of human memory it has been proposed that these can best be addressed with two memory systems: a limited fast, one-shot, component based in the hippocampus, and another with vast capacity and with some essential features slower but gradually improving, in the cerebral cortex [7].

Memorizing new episodes in the form of complete activation-images, demands fast and encompassing storage, exactly as has been described for the hippocampus [5][7]. (Almost) all activity in the entire brain is effectively bound together because the hippocampus sits on top of many diverse processing areas [8].

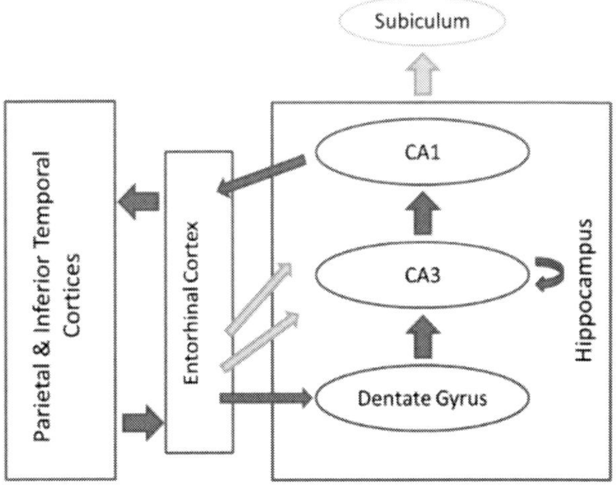

Figure 1. Principal stages for the hippocampus, with dark arrows indicating the links mentioned in the text [8].

Later, during remembering, when trying to reestablish an overall activation in the cortex, hippocampus acts as driver providing effective index-entries and bringing to bear efficient pointers to the distributed cortical representations.

The hippocampus thus can be understood as a top "convergence-divergence zone", which receives convergent projections from the sites whose activity is to be recorded, and which sends divergent projections to these same areas, similar to a proposal by Damasio [9]. The here proposed account is distinct from more standard conceptualizations of memory stressing clearly separated components, i.e., short- and long-term stores or more constricted situation-specific control processes like in the Atkinson–Shiffrin model [10].

Following the ideas of [2] and [7], memories according to the Ouroboros Model are stored in a partly redundant way: linked via the hippocampus and also, definitively after some consolidation over time (and slow wave sleep), permanently bound cortical representations. No 'transfer', in the sense of completely erasing hippocampal traces, normally takes place; cortex entries just become more independent with use.

Some type of two-pronged memory implementation appears indispensable for meta-cognition and meta-memory, which naturally enable an agent to assess her status of memory (-retrieval). Prominent examples in this context are the tip-of-the-tongue phenomenon and dèjá vu.

The hippocampal complex is hypothesized to work as an effective hash-table; index values are established from the activity distributions they code for in a given context, and, in turn, their activation later allows addressing and combining the detailed entries spread over widely dispersed cortex areas. At both storage sites, pattern completion is effective, enabling full retrieval from only a fraction of the features, efficiently implementing content-addressable memory.

During encoding, as well as for retrieval, the two repositories reinforce each other mutually. This constellation can be described as a minimum-hypercycle comprising only two main sub-stages [11][12]. These are distributed over the cerebral cortex and, on the other end, the CA3 section of the hippocampus. (For very important memories, e.g., ones containing strong (aversive) emotions, an additional structure is regularly involved, i.e., the amygdala, which allows for particularly fast reactions in already encoded contexts.)

Entries in the hippocampus, like in local neocortex areas, are laid down in patches of orderly maps. Sufficiently different contexts have been shown to lead to remapping in the hippocampus [13]. Specificity is taken to be ensured by well-separated attractor states in CA3 due to its prominent recurrent connections, while CA1 recoding for the output can preserve matched correspondence with cortical areas; see Fig.1. Different schemata as generalizations of place-cell maps would correspond to specific hippocampal mappings. Dynamically, these associations are seen as manifest in theta oscillations, which originate mainly in the hippocampus and cingulate cortex, and phase-locked high gamma oscillations in neocortex [14].

Due to the auto-association capabilities of the CA3 region, full activations can be provoked already when only part of their constituents are available first. In order to avoid disturbing overlap between distinct memories, a random component in the assignment from the DG, which effects very powerful input to CA3 storage, has been proposed [1].

An efficient additional way of minimizing collisions, i.e., preventing the overloading of a neural associative network, would be to add new neurons in the distributing stage as new (index) entries are required. After decades, in which the dogma "no new neurons in the adult brain" was accepted as valid, it has been found that the dentate gyrus in the hippocampal formation is one of two regions in the adult human brain where new neurons are continually developing and functionally integrated into working brain circuitry [15]. Contributions to better pattern separation and memory resolution have been suggested as main function of these added neurons [16][17]. There is ample evidence for their enhanced generation and survival when demand for new representational resources is presumably high, i.e., they are boosted by physical exercise in enriched environments, accompanied by significant improvement of previously impaired hippocampal long-term potentiation and cognitive performance in a mouse model [18].

It is important to note that index values are most useful if distinct. "Continuous" versions seem adequate within limits, but requirements for very fine-scaled representations and smooth transitions might more efficiently be taken care of by some general-purpose interpolator as has been argued to be the function of the cerebellum [19].

For the hippocampus, it is further proposed to investigate the idea how the observed addition of newborn neurons in living brains can be understood as a version of an extreme learning machine (ELM), a recent neural network lay-out featuring the random addition of hidden neurons, which yields spectacular improvements in learning rate compared to standard learning routines [20]. It has been shown that randomly introducing neurons and then selecting the ones which work best can further enhance the efficiency of ELMs compared to versions without pruning [21].

Following the Ouroboros Model, newborn neurons are inserted in living brains in a manner "better than random", i.e., their number and timing being controlled by the demand for finer differentiation in the already existing network of schemata [5][18]. This would actually fit nicely with hopscotch hashing, where additional entries are added demand-oriented for resolving hash collisions and inserted locally in the relevant neighborhood ensuring quick retrieval.

New and uncommitted neurons are most useful in the separation stage (DG) with initial high and rather localized sensitivity, and their weights constrained by neighbors, possibly not only for better discriminating and stabilizing but later also for condensing and compactifying (sparse) activity, which was before distributed more widely and implementing some type of population-code, all in tight interaction with the linked cortex representations and also inducing similar tuning, and likely also including pruning, there.

IV. Conclusion and Future Work

It is claimed that the Ouroboros Model sheds some light on the requirement and implementation of a continually expanding index to representations distributed over the cortex in mammalian brains: new entries are rapidly laid down as "snapshots" concatenating all concurrent activity upon a trigger by consumption analysis. The mammalian hippocampus is thus hypothesized to serve a fundamental role for relatively quickly establishing and also reliably retrieving distinct entries in episodic memory as well as for episodic simulation employing exactly that schema-type, which is claimed to form the ever-expanding basis for efficient cognition. Request-oriented storage of index entries in tight interplay with detailed cortical records thus efficiently implements autocatalytic learning and growth. This appears to be a significant step towards explaining how information is processed in vertebrate brains.

The Expanding Memory Index Hypothesis of the Hippocampus:

- The hippocampus provides an index to wide-spread cortical representations.
- Content-addressable at both repositories, memories can most efficiently be retrieved from partial keys.
- Entries in the hippocampus and in the cerebral cortex mutually endorse each other and thus form a hypercycle.
- Memory separation/orthogonalization capability for the unique indexing of novel episodes is greatly enhanced by adding adult-born neurons in the DG.
- This is somewhat similar to the addition of hidden units in Extreme Learning Machines (ELMs).
- All of this fits nicely with the Ouroboros Model.

A further piece of the puzzle will be to elucidate the link of the hippocampus with another central (control) structure, i.e., anterior cingulate cortex, ACC, which has been shown recently to possess direct monosynaptic connections to CA3 and CA1 regions [22]. With the hippocampus and the ACC in the center together, and including general cerebral cortex as well as subcortical structures, the neuronal basis for extensive cyclic iterative processing can be outlined.

Work on the Ouroboros Model in general and also on the role of the hippocampus and its connections is in progress. Following a fundamental self-reflective and self-consistent approach, a first schematic sketch will be filled-in with more fine-grained and quantitative details in subsequent iterations; collaborations to this end are most welcome.

ACKNOWLEDGMENT

A number of insightful comments and very helpful suggestions for improvements by several reviewers are gratefully acknowledged.

REFERENCES

[1] E. T. Rolls, "The mechanisms for pattern completion and pattern separation in the hippocampus," Frontiers in Systems Neuroscience, vol. 7, pp. 1-21, 2013.

[2] T. J. Teyler and P. DiScenna, "The hippocampal memory indexing theory," Behavioral Neuroscience, vol 100(2), pp. 147-154, 1986.

[3] T. J. Teyler and J. W. Rudy, "The hippocampal indexing theory and episodic memory: updating the index," Hippocampus, vol. 17, pp. 1158-1169, 2007.

[4] K. Thomsen, "The Ouroboros Model in the light of venerable criteria," Neurocomputing, vol. 74, pp. 121-128, 2010.

[5] K. Thomsen, "Concept formation in the Ouroboros Model," Third Conference on Artificial General Intelligence, Lugano, Switzerland, Proceedings of AGI 2010, pp. 194-195.

[6] K. Thomsen, "Ouroboros Model mapped to Brain," 8th IBRO World Congress of Neuroscience, Florence, Italy, 2011.

[7] J. L. McClelland, B. L. McNaughton, and R. C. O'Reilly, "Why there are Complementary Learning Systems in the Hippocampus and Neocortex: Insights from the Successes and Failures of Connectionist Models of Learning and Memory," Psychological Review 102, pp. 419-457,1995.

[8] T. Nakashiba, J. Z. Young, T. J. McHugh, D. L. Buhl, and S. Tonegawa, "Transgenic Inhibition of Synaptic Transmission Reveals Role of CA3 Output in Hippocampal Learning," Science vol. 319, 1260-1264, 2008.

[9] A. Damasio, "Time-locked multiregional retroactivation: A systems-level proposal for the neural substrates of recall and recognition," Cognition 33, pp. 25-62, 1989.

[10] R. C. Atkinson and R. M. Shiffrin, "Human memory: A proposed system and its control processes," in K. W. Spence and J. T Spence, The psychology of learning and motivation (Volume 2). New York: Academic Press, pp. 89-195, 1968.

[11] M. Eigen and P. Schuster, "The Hypercycle, A Principle of Natural Self-Organization, Part A, Emergence of the Hyper-cycle," Naturwissenschaften, vol. 64, pp. 541-565, 1977.

[12] M. Eigen and P. Schuster, "The Hypercycle, A Principle of Natural Self-Organization, Part B, The Abstract Hypercycle," Naturwissenschaften, vol. 65, pp. 7-41, 1978.

[13] J. K. Leutgeb, S. Leutgeb, M.-B. Moser, and E. I. Moser, "Pattern Separation in the Dentate Gyrus and DCA3 of the Hippocampus," Science, vol. 315, pp. 961-966, 2007.

[14] R. T. Canolty et al., "High Gamma Power is Phase-Locked to Theta Oscillations in Human Neocortex," Science, vol. 313, pp. 1626-1628, 2006.

[15] P. S. Eriksson et al., "Neurogenesis in the adult human hippo-campus," Nature Medicine, vol. 11, pp. 1313-1317, 1998.

[16] A. Sahay, D. A. Wilson, and R. Hen, "Pattern separation: a common function for new neuros in hippocampus and olfactory bulb," Neuron, vol. 70, pp. 582-588, 2011.

[17] J. B. Aimone, W. Deng, and F. H. Gage, "Resolving new memories: a critical look at the dentate gyrus, adult neurogenesis, and pattern separation," Neuron, vol. 70, pp. 589-596, 2011.

[18] M. E. Sakalem et al., "Environmental Enrichment and Physical Exercise Revert Behavioral and Electrophysiological Impairments Caused by Reduced Adult Neurogenesis," Hippocampus 27, pp. 36-51, 2017.

[19] K. Thomsen, "The Cerebellum according to the Ouroboros Model, the 'Interpolator Hypothesis'," Journal of Communication and Computer, vol.11, pp. 239-254, 2014.

[20] G. B. Huang, Q. Y. Zhu, and C. K. Siew, "Extreme learning machine: theory and applications," Neurocomputing, vol. 70, pp. 489-501, 2006.

[21] G. B. Huang and L. Chen, "Enhanced random search based incremental extreme learning machine," Neurocomputing, vol. 71, pp. 3460-3468, 2008.

[22] P. Rajasethupathy et al., "Projections from the neocortex mediate top-down control of memory retrieval," Nature 526, 653-659, 2015.

Performance of Neural Clique Networks Subject to Synaptic Noise

Eliott Coyac, Vincent Gripon, Charlotte Langlais, and Claude Berrou

Electronics Department
IMT Atlantique
Brest, France
email: name.lastname@telecom-bretagne.eu

Abstract—**Artificial neural networks are so-called because they are supposed to be inspired from the brain and from the ways the neurons work. While some networks are used purely for computational purpose and do not endeavor to be a plausible representation of what happens in the brain, such as deep learning neural networks, others do. However, the question of the noise in the brain and its impact on the functioning of those networks has been little-studied. For example, it is widely known that synapses misfire with a significant probability. We model this noise and study its impact on associative memories powered by neural networks: neural clique networks and Hopfield networks as a reference point. We show that synaptic noise can in fact slightly improve the performance of the decoding process of neural clique networks by avoiding local minima.**

***Keywords*–associative memories; neural clique networks; synaptic noise**

I. Introduction

There are multiple sources of noise in the brain. Indeed, they can be molecular [1], [2] or due to external neurons [2]. Other factors include synaptic noise, the intermittent failure of synapses, which seem to have a role outside of being just noise [1], [2]. In this paper, we explore this particular type of noise in details.

There are a lot of models of neural networks, which either aim at modeling what happens in the brain or simply focus on efficiency at their specific purpose. The study of the impact of noise on such artificial neural networks focusing on performance is only relevant in the context of electronical components, but that is obviously not the case when considering neural networks that strive to be biologically plausible. Such neural networks should not react adversely to noise to be considered biologically plausible. In this paper, we consider artificial neural networks that aim both at providing efficient solutions to real-world problems but also try to remain plausible as a possible way the brain works, and study the impact biological noise has on them. We focus on neural networks working as associative memories [3]–[6], and study how noise impacts their inner workings and performance. Studies have already been conducted on the impact of noise when implementing such neural networks on unreliable hardware circuits [7], where the noise is caused by unreliable components.

In this paper, we consider noise internal to the network, and more specifically synaptic noise. We show how it can be seen as an higher abstraction level than molecular noise and that it can be easily modelled. The impact of synaptic noise has been theoreticized in biological neural networks [8], but never studied with regard to artificial neural networks that are used for practical applications in computer science.

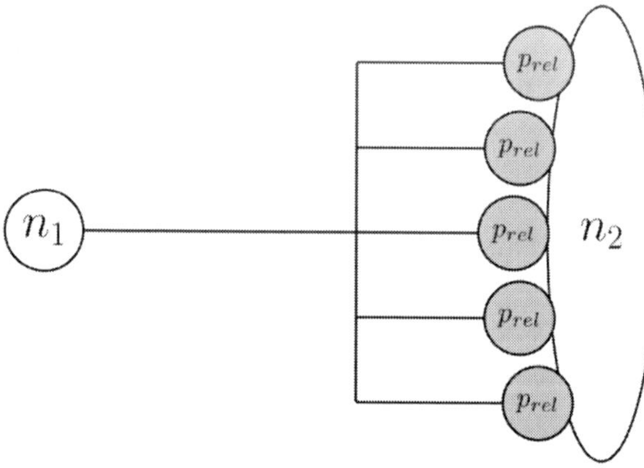

Figure 1. Example of neuronal transmission from one neuron n_1 to another n_2 with $\mathbf{n_{syn}} = \mathbf{5}$. Each synapse has a probability $\mathbf{p_{rel}} = \mathbf{0.5}$ of stimulating n_2 when n_1 is activated.

The outline of the paper is as follows. We first study how synaptic noise can be represented in Section II. In Section III, we introduce neural clique networks and discuss their biological plausibility and applications. Finally, in Section IV, we study the impact of synaptic noise on neural clique networks, both theoretically and by running simulations. We also briefly depict the impact of synaptic noise on Hopfield networks, a classical form of neural network behaving as an associative memory, for reference.

II. Synaptic noise in the brain

In the brain, each neuron has numerous inputs from other neurons and a single axon, which then branches to reach a multitude of other *target* neurons. Even then, there is not a single point of contact between the neuron and a target neuron, but several. The axon not only branches to reach multiple neurons, it also branches off in several synapses reaching the same target neuron.

Generally, the connection between two neurons is comprised of 5 to 25 synapses [9]. One may ask why there are so many synapses for a simple connection between two neurons. Having a few is understandable for redundancy, but there can be several tens of synapses. In fact, synapses are not reliable [9], [10], and the probability of them working typically ranges from 0.2 to 0.8 [9]. Such a configuration of synapses can help functioning when stressed under high frequency of neuronal activation by spreading the load over the different synapses [11], [12].

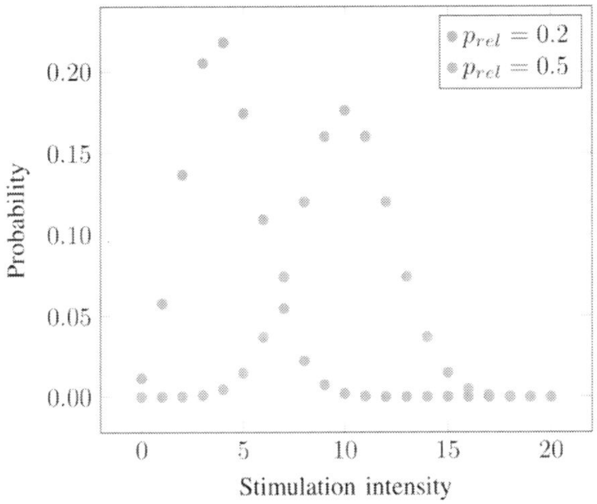

Figure 2. Probabilities for different stimulation instensities with $n_{syn} = 20$. Values for n_{syn} and p_{rel} fall within the model and are discussed at the end of the paper.

In this paper, we consider the way failing synapses affect the connection between two neurons, and then we show how it translates to artificial neural networks. To make things simpler, we consider that each connection between two neurons has n_{syn} synapses of the same strength, normalized to 1, and that they each have the same probability p_{rel} of working, independently one from another. p_{rel} is named as such as it represents the probability of releasing neuro-transmitters when stimulated by the axon. The connection between two neurons n_1 and n_2 is represented in Fig. 1. With this model, the stimulation a neuron receives from another follows a binomial law $B(tries, p_{success})$ with the parameters n_{syn} and p_{rel} as shown in Fig. 2,.

III. Neural Clique Networks

Neural clique networks are associative memories with error-correcting properties. They store binary patterns and use binary connections. They have a high capacity, comparable to binary storage. They also strive to achieve biological plausibility.

A. Minicolumns and clusters

The smallest unit in a neural clique network is a *fanal* and is based on a cortical minicolumn [13], which is a pattern comprising around 100 neurons. This pattern has been observed in humans and several other species. These fanals are organized in *clusters*, and only one fanal can be active at the same time in the same cluster, replicating the widely-used *winner-takes-all* law and alleviating concerns of energy efficiency.

A neural clique network is made of χ clusters containing ℓ fanals each.

B. Storage

A message is stored as a group of several fanals belonging to different clusters. A connection is established between two fanals if they both belong to the same message, following Hebb's law [14]. A fanal can belong to a multitude of messages. It is the connections between the fanals that define the messages and contain the information. Thus, each message is represented by a fully interconnected group of fanals, called a *clique*. In full neural clique networks, the number of fanals c making up a clique is equal to χ, the number of clusters in the network. As such, each clique contains one fanal from each cluster. As an example, a full neural clique network containing 3 messages is shown in Fig. 3.

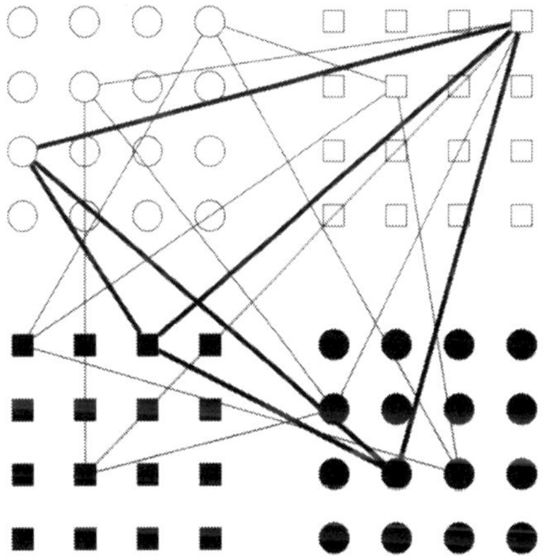

Figure 3. Storing procedure illustration. The pattern to store (with thick edges) connects units from 4 clusters of 16 units each (filled circles, filled rectangles, rectangles and circles).

In sparse neural networks, we have $1 < c < \chi$. Stored messages do not use all avalaible clusters.

C. Retrieval and performance

There are two forms of message retrieval. The network can be asked if a message exists already, which is a simple matter of testing if the fanals representing the message are fully interconnected. If a message was stored, the network will always say so, but false positives can be generated if two many messages sharing fanals in common overlap.

The second form of message retrieval is providing a partial message to the network with erasures (and possibly errors) and retrieving the full message. The algorithm for retrieving the full message simply consists of finding the fanals with the most connections to the known fanals, at most one per cluster.

As far as performance goes, the network needs a binary storage capacity of $(\chi \cdot \ell)^2/2$ bits to store the connections between the different fanals, the adjacency matrix of the graph representing the network. As shown in the examples further in this paper, a full network of 8 clusters of 256 fanals can retrieve 15000 half-erased messages with an error rate of less than 2%. The binary storage needed for storing all the messages without any error correcting mechanism would be 120 kB, and the neural network uses 260 kB of storage for the adjacency matrix, so the storage efficiency compared to raw binary is 46%, but with large resistance to message erasures.

D. Decoding algorithm

The algorithm that we use is suitable for retrieving partially erased messages. Other algorithms can be applied first to filter out irrelevant inputs or with other purposes. However, that is not our concern here.

1) Full networks: Each fanal gets a score, which is the number of other activated fanals connected to it. The fanals with the highest score in each cluster are activated for the next iteration, all the others are deactivated. Known fanals from the partially erased message are already provided with a high score at each iteration so they are always the only fanal activated in their own cluster. If there are several fanals with the same highest score in a cluster, they all are activated for the next iteration. The algorithm stops after several iterations, which are enough to reach a stable state with the *memory effect* introduced below. When the algorithm stops, one activated fanal is picked from each cluster, at random if there are several fanals activated.

A memory effect γ can be added, which increases performance in the case of noise-free networks. It consists of adding γ to the score of a fanal if it was activated the previous iteration. Generally, $\gamma = 1$ is used, simulating each fanal being connected to themselves. It is interpreted as an already active fanal being easier to activate than an inactive fanal of the same cluster.

2) Sparse networks: Sparse networks follow the same principle as full networks. The difference is that only a few clusters are to have a fanal activated for the next iteration amongst all the clusters. There are two algorithms in order to choose those activated clusters, the *c-global-winners-take-all* and *global-winners-take-all*. The *c-global-winners-take-all* takes the clusters with the highest score (determined by the score of the fanal with the highest score inside the cluster) until c clusters are chosen, with c being the size of the message. Then it takes all the clusters that tie the chosen cluster with the lowest score. All the chosen clusters are activated for the next iteration.

The *global-winners-take-all* just stops at taking c clusters. If several clusters have the same score, it only takes as many as it needs to have c clusters, at random. The *c-global-winners-take-all* is known to have better performance.

E. Applications

Neural clique networks have been used in various application cases. In electronics, Boguslawski et al. [15] use them to handle power management in multicore processors, showing significant improvements in energy usage compared to existing solutions. In [16], the authors propose to use neural clique networks to accelerate search in databases. They provide a fully hardware implementation of their solution using memristors, and obtain reduced energy consumption and delays compared to classical solutions.

In [17], the authors propose to use neural clique networks in combination with product quantization in order to accelerate search in visual descriptors of images. The result is a gain of a factor of about 100 in comparison to exhaustive search. Similar work has been proposed in [18].

IV. Neural Clique Networks with unreliable connections

We study the impact of unreliable connections due to synaptic noise on neural clique networks. Assuming messages are independently and uniformly distributed, we propose a full mathematical analysis of the retrieval of a partially erased pattern after one iteration, which corresponds to the second form of message retrieval previously discussed. For multiple iterations, due to the complexity of the problem and the multitude of variables we can only provide simulations, which show us the retrieval rates with or without synaptic noise.

A. One iteration

We consider the probability of finding the correct version of a partially erased message after one iteration.

1) Full network: Let's consider a full neural clique network (each cluster is used for each message). Let M be the number of messages in the network. When we try to recover a message in the network, let c_k the number of known clusters and c_e ($c_e = c - c_k$) the number of erased clusters. The density of the network, that is the probablity of a connection existing between any two fanals, is [7]:

$$d = 1 - \left(1 - \frac{1}{\ell^2}\right)^M \tag{1}$$

Let's consider an erased cluster. Let s_0 be the correct fanal, n_{s_0} its score, s be an incorrect fanal, and n_s its score. The score of a fanal is the number of synapses connected to it that released neurotransmitters. So a fanal connected to i other fanals can get a score between 0 and $i \cdot n_{syn}$. The correct fanal s_0 is obviously connected to the other c_k known correct fanals. So for x from 0 to $n_{syn} \cdot c_k$ we have

$$P(n_{s_0} = x) = P\left(B(n_{syn} \cdot c_k, p_{rel}) = x\right) \tag{2}$$
$$= pmf(x, n_{syn} \cdot c_k, p_{rel}) \tag{3}$$

We noted pmf the probability mass function of the binomial law B. The incorrect fanals of the erased cluster can have between 0 and c_k connections to the known correct fanals. First, we need to determine $P_E(i)$, the probability that an incorrect fanal has i connections to known correct fanals. In theory, existence of connections are not independent events, which may lead to difficult mathematical analysis [19]. In order to simplify the proofs, we make the assumption they are independent, which has been reported to be a fair approximation [6]. We find

$$P_E(i) = \binom{c_k}{i} d^i (1-d)^{c_k - i}. \tag{4}$$

Indeed, the probability of not being connected to any of the known fanals is $(1-d)^{c_k}$ and the probability of being connected to all the known fanals is d^{c_k}. The probability of being connected to only a specific known fanal is $(1-d)^{c_k-1}d$, and to be solely connected to any one of the known fanals is $c_k \cdot (1-d)^{c_k-1}d$.

And with that, we can deduce the probability of an incorrect fanal getting a score x_0 for any $0 \leq x_0 \leq n_{syn} \cdot c_k$:

$$P(n_s = x_0) = \sum_{i=0}^{c_k} P_E(i)\ pmf(x_0, n_{syn} \cdot i, p_{rel}) \tag{5}$$

$$P(n_s \leq x_0) = \sum_{x=0}^{x_0} \sum_{i=0}^{c_k} P_E(i)\ pmf(x, n_{syn} \cdot i, p_{rel}) \tag{6}$$

Now that we have this, we can write the probability that the correct fanal is amongst the fanals with the highest scores:

$$P_{succ}(s_0) = \sum_{x_0=0}^{n_{syn}\cdot c_k} P(n_{s_0} = x_0)P(n_s \leq x_0)^{\ell-1}. \quad (7)$$

The global probability of success, i.e., the probability that in all erased nodes the correct node is amongst the winner is $P_{succ} = P_{succ}(s_0)^{c_e}$. The error rate is $1 - P_{succ}$.

That approach is too lax, however. In practice, when looking for a message of size c, we want c symbols as the output of the network, not a set of size s ($s \geq c$) containing the c correct symbols. This means that if we have several fanals with the highest score in the same cluster, we need to pick only one of them. We then have a chance $\frac{1}{k+1}$ of picking the correct fanal in ambiguous cases, where k is the number of incorrect fanals sharing the highest score with the correct fanal.

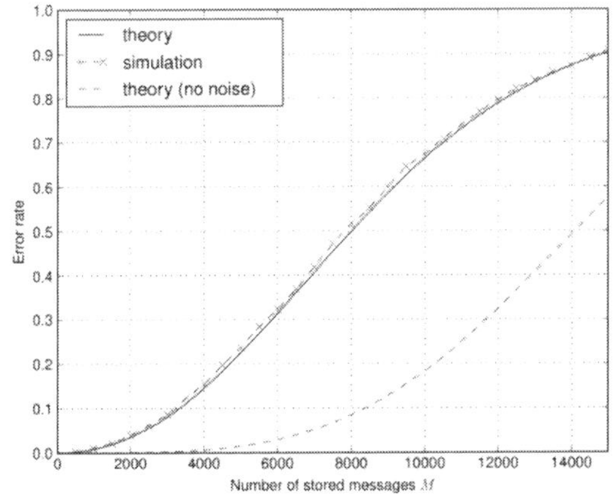

Figure 4. Analytical and simulated results with $c = 8, c_k = 4, \ell = 256, n_{syn} = 10, p_{rel} = 0.5$.

To take that into account, $P_{succ}(s_0)$ is rewritten. First, we create the probability of success for the correct fanal if its score is x_0:

$$P_{succ}(s_0, n_{s_0} = x_0) = \sum_{k=0}^{\ell-1} \frac{1}{k+1}\binom{l-1}{k} P(n_s = x_0)^k P(n_s < x_0)^{(\ell-1-k)} \quad (8)$$

and

$$P_{succ}(s_0) = \sum_{x_0=0}^{n_{syn}\cdot c_k} P(n_{s_0} = x_0)P_{succ}(s_0, n_{s_0} = x_0) \quad (9)$$

The results are shown on Fig. 4.

2) Sparse networks: Sparse networks are harder to tackle, due to the problem of spurious clusters. While what happens in each cluster with a correct fanal doesn't concern the other clusters, all the correct fanals belonging to the erased clusters must have a score higher than all the fanals of the erased clusters and incorrect clusters.

It is possible to formalize this second relationship, a.k.a. the lowest score of the correct fanals must be higher than the highest score of the incorrect fanals. If we consider χ the total number of clusters and c the size of a message, if $\chi >> c$ then we only need to consider that second relationship. As if each correct fanal has a score higher than the highest fanals of the $\chi - c$ incorrect clusters, then the probability that they have the highest score in their own cluster is close to 1.

Using the same logic as before, taking into account the c_e correct fanals and the $(\chi - c)\ell$ fanals belonging to incorrect clusters, we obtain the formula. First, we change $P_{succ}(s_0, n_{s_0} = x_0)$ into $P_{succ}(\ell_c, \ell_i | n_{s_0} = x_0)$, being the probability that given that l_c correct fanals have a score x_0 and the other correct fanals a higher score, all the correct fanals are chosen. We denote $\ell_i = (\chi - c)\ell$.

We get

$$P_{succ}(\ell_c, \ell_i | n_{s_0} = x_0) = \sum_{k=0}^{\ell_i} \frac{1}{\binom{k+\ell_c}{\ell_c}}\binom{\ell_i}{k} P(n_s = x_0)^k P(n_s < x_0)^{\ell_i - k} \quad (10)$$

and

$$P_{succ} = \sum_{x_0=0}^{n_{syn}\cdot c_k} \sum_{j=1}^{c_e} \binom{c_e}{j} P(n_{s_0} = x_0)^j P(n_{s_0} > x_0)^{c_e - j} P_{succ}(j, n_{s_0} = x_0) \quad (11)$$

B. Multiple iterations

In the case of multiple iterations, we are unable to provide a detailed mathematical analysis. But we can use simulations to study the impact of synaptic noise.

1) Parameters: The first question we have to answer is how do we know we have a solution. There's no perfect stable state due to the noise, so how do we determine when we stop the algorithm? We chose to keep a maximum of 100 iterations, in order to limit the execution time. Then, we stop if the result is stable after n_{it} iterations, n_{it} being a parameter that varies. Fig. 5 shows such a test on a full network, with n_{it} ranging from 2 to 4. From that graph we chose $n_{it} = 3$ as the best iteration number. For very low error rates, $n_{it} = 4$ is better, then $n_{it} = 3$ until an error rate of around 20%, then $n_{it} = 2$. The reason $n_{it} = 2$ becomes a better solution for higher error rates is probably because it is harder to keep a stable state then, making the algorithm reach 100 iterations before reaching a stable state with $n_{it} = 3$ or $n_{it} = 4$.

For sparse networks, experimentation has shown that $n_{it} = 2$ is a better choice.

There is also the question of the *memory effect*. The *memory effect* is known to be beneficial for networks when

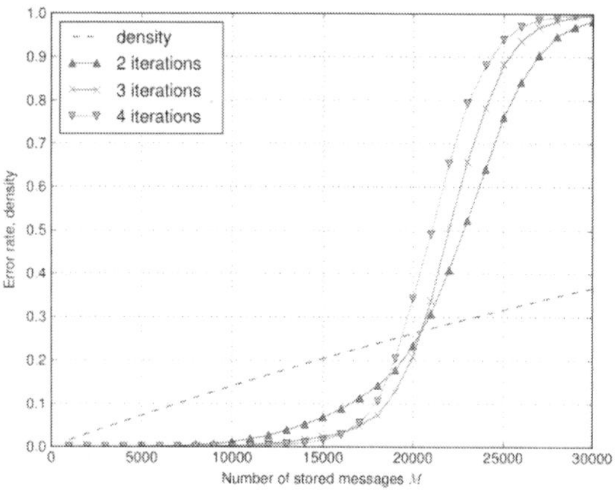

Figure 5. Error rate for a full neural clique network of parameters $c = 8$ and $\ell = 256$, with $n_{syn} = 10$, $c_k = 4$ and $p_{rel} = 0.5$. The decoding process is stopped after 2, 3 or 4 stable iterations.

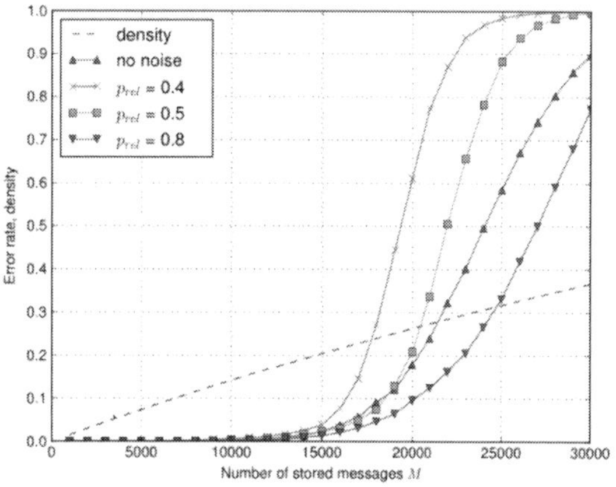

Figure 6. Error rate for a full neural clique network of parameters $c = 8$ and $\ell = 256$, with $n_{syn} = 10$, $c_k = 4$ and p_{rel} ranging from 0.4 to 1.

noise is not involved, but as noise is involved it is more beneficial to not have any memory effect. As shown on Fig. 4, the error rate after one iteration in a noisy network is important even for a low number of messages, and the memory effect would carry those mistakes onto further iterations. In order to avoid that, a memory effect of $\gamma = 0$ is chosen for noisy networks.

2) Results: As can be seen from Fig. 6 and Fig. 7, the binomial noise seems to have more beneficial effects on full networks than on sparse networks. For $p_{rel} = 0.5$, there's even a better capacity than with no noise for error rates inferior to 10%. For $p_{rel} = 0.8$, the capacity seems better for virtually all error rates.

Concerning sparse networks, a significant degradation of performance is observed for $p_{rel} \leq 0.5$ compared to when there is no noise. We observe a reduction of the capacity of the network of approximately 20% to 30% for error rates ranging from 2% to 10%, which is still a good result considering the

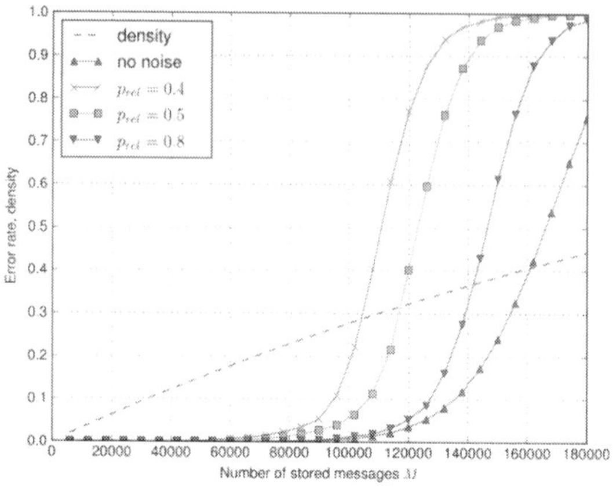

Figure 7. Error rate for a sparse neural clique network of parameters $\chi = 100$ and $c = 12$, with $n_{syn} = 10$, $c_k = 9$ and p_{rel} varying.

unreliability of the network.

Those results can be attributed to avoiding local mimima while still keeping a low deviation, with a principle loosely similar to simulated annealing. The reason full networks give better results than sparse networks would be that even if the noise can send the decoding algorithm off track, it still keeps to the same clusters in full networks.

C. *Impact on Hopfield Networks*

Hopfield networks [3] are artificial recurrent networks functioning as associative memories. They are made up of N neurons and can store binary messages of N bits, but the connection weights are not binary. The number of messages they can store is $\mathcal{O}(N/\log(N))$ [20]. Each pattern stored is an attractor, and when inputting data it shifts to the closest pattern stored.

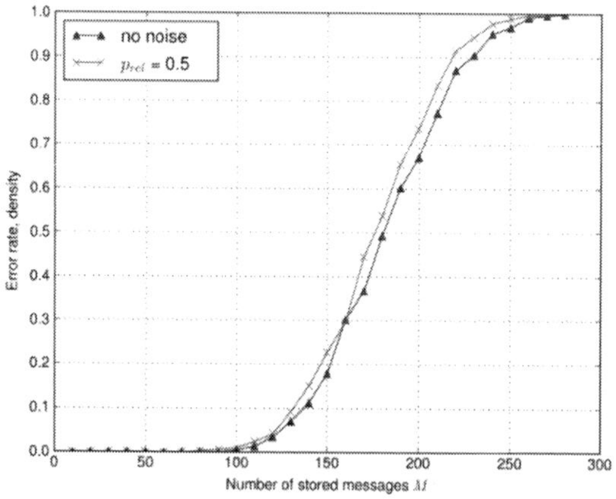

Figure 8. Error rate for an Hopfield network of 2048 neurons, with or without noise, and $\frac{1}{4}$ of the input erased.

We ran a simulation on Hopfield networks to see how such a model with precise synaptic weights would react to the large fluctuations introduced by the unreliable connections.

Fig. 8 shows the behavior of an Hopfield network in similar conditions to before, with $\frac{1}{4}$ of the input erased, 2048 neurons, and 10 synaptic contacts at each connection with each a probability of release of 0.5. The simulation stops when a stable state over two iterations is reached.

We can see that there is only a minor increase in the error rate. We can surmise that this is due to the high number of nodes active at the same time, averaging the effects of the binomial noise. Compared to full neural clique networks, which can take advantage of the noise, Hopfield networks seem to suffer a little decrease in performance.

V. Discussion

The analysis in this paper was based on the supposition of having 10 synaptic contacts per connection and a probability of release of the neurotransmitters of exactly 0.5 for each synaptic contact at each iteration, independently of the previous iterations.

The number of synaptic contacts per connection was chosen to be $n_{syn} = 10$, but simulations show a much lower error rate after one iteration for $n_{syn} = 20$, which is also a realistic number.

As said in [9], synaptic contacts adapt with the help of feedback, so it is wise to consider whether the release probability could exceed 0.5 where strong connections are concerned. Moreover, it is difficult to imagine that in the case of repeated stimulation of a synaptic contact, the probability of release of neurotransmitters each time is independent from the previous occurences. It makes sense that it is more probable for a synapse to release neurotransmitters if it did not with the previous stimulation, as it would be more ready. As such, the variance of the probalistic law governing the stimuli would be reduced, making the biological architecture — the brain — more reliable.

VI. Conclusion

The contribution of this paper is twofold. First, we show the significance of the noise generated by unreliable synapses, which we refer to as *synaptic noise*, and model that noise. We see it introduces randomness with high variance in the stimulation a neuron receives from another neuron, which can be represented by a binomial law depending on the number of synapses n_{syn} the connection is made of and the neurotransmitter release probability p_{rel}. We then study the impact of this noise on associative memories that strive on biological plausibility, to show if the models we have of neural networks in the brain survive scrutiny. In particular, we show the impact of synaptic noise on neural clique networks and Hopfield networks.

Suprisingly, we see that with the correct parameters such synaptic noise can in fact increase the retrieval rate of partially erased messages in neural clique networks. It is due to the noise allowing the network to overcome the local minima in its decoding process. Regarding Hopfield networks, on which a simulation is run as a reference, synaptic noise decreases performance only very slightly. As such, both associative memories sustain the test of synaptic noise and neural clique networks even benefit from it. As a future work, it would be interesting to see the impact of this kind of noise on feedforward neural networks, as they emulate the way the visual cortex works.

Acknowledgement

This work was funded in part by the European Research Council under the European Union's Seventh Framework Programme (FP7/2007-2013)/ERC grant agreement n° 290901. It was also funded in part by the CominLabs project Neural Communications and the Future & Rupture program.

References

[1] J. A. White, J. T. Rubinstein, and A. R. Kay, "Channel noise in neurons," Trends in neurosciences, vol. 23, no. 3, pp. 131–137, 2000.

[2] A. A. Faisal, L. P. Selen, and D. M. Wolpert, "Noise in the nervous system," Nature reviews neuroscience, vol. 9, no. 4, pp. 292–303, 2008.

[3] J. J. Hopfield, "Neural networks and physical systems with emergent collective computational abilities," Proceedings of the national academy of sciences, vol. 79, no. 8, pp. 2554–2558, 1982.

[4] D. J. Willshaw, O. P. Buneman, and H. C. Longuet-Higgins, "Non-holographic associative memory," Nature, pp. 960–962, 1969.

[5] D. H. Ackley, G. E. Hinton, and T. J. Sejnowski, "A learning algorithm for boltzmann machines," Cognitive science, vol. 9, no. 1, pp. 147–169, 1985.

[6] V. Gripon and C. Berrou, "Sparse neural networks with large learning diversity," Neural Networks, IEEE Transactions on, vol. 22, no. 7, pp. 1087–1096, 2011.

[7] F. Leduc-Primeau, V. Gripon, M. Rabbat, and W. Gross, "Cluster-based associative memories built from unreliable storage," in ICASSP, pp. 8370–8374, May 2014.

[8] A. Zador, "Impact of synaptic unreliability on the information transmitted by spiking neurons," Journal of Neurophysiology, vol. 79, no. 3, pp. 1219–1229, 1998.

[9] T. Branco and K. Staras, "The probability of neurotransmitter release: variability and feedback control at single synapses," Nature Reviews Neuroscience, vol. 10, no. 5, pp. 373–383, 2009.

[10] C. Allen and C. F. Stevens, "An evaluation of causes for unreliability of synaptic transmission," Proceedings of the National Academy of Sciences, vol. 91, no. 22, pp. 10380–10383, 1994.

[11] M. Fauth, F. Wörgötter, and C. Tetzlaff, "The formation of multi-synaptic connections by the interaction of synaptic and structural plasticity and their functional consequences," PLoS Comput Biol, vol. 11, no. 1, pp. e1004031, 2015.

[12] A. Figurov et al., "Regulation of synaptic responses to high-frequency stimulation and ltp by neurotrophins in the hippocampus," Nature, vol. 381, no. 6584, pp. 706–709, 1996.

[13] D. P. Buxhoeveden and M. F. Casanova, "The minicolumn hypothesis in neuroscience," Brain, vol. 125, no. 5, pp. 935–951, 2002.

[14] D. O. Hebb, The organization of behavior: A neuropsychological approach. John Wiley & Sons, 1949.

[15] B. Boguslawski, V. Gripon, F. Seguin, and F. Heitzmann, "Twin neurons for efficient real-world data distribution in networks of neural cliques: Applications in power management in electronic circuits," IEEE transactions on neural networks and learning systems, vol. 27, no. 2, pp. 375–387, 2016.

[16] H. Jarollahi et al., "A non-volatile associative memory-based context-driven search engine using 90 nm cmos mtj-hybrid logic-in-memory architecture," Journal on Emerging and Selected Topics in Circuits and Systems, vol. 4, pp. 460–474, 2014.

[17] D. Ferro, V. Gripon, and X. Jiang, "Nearest neighbour search using binary neural networks," in Neural Networks (IJCNN), 2016 International Joint Conference on. IEEE, pp. 5106–5112, 2016.

[18] C. Yu, V. Gripon, X. Jiang, and H. Jégou, "Neural associative memories as accelerators for binary vector search," in COGNITIVE 2015: 7th International Conference on Advanced Cognitive Technologies and Applications, pp. 85–89, 2015.

[19] V. Gripon, J. Heusel, M. Löwe, and F. Vermet, "A comparative study of sparse associative memories," Journal of Statistical Physics, pp. 1–25, 2015.

[20] R. McEliece, E. Posner, E. Rodemich, and S. Venkatesh, "The capacity of the hopfield associative memory," IEEE Transactions on Information Theory, vol. 33, no. 4, pp. 461–482, 1987.

The Implementation of Noradrenaline in the NeuCogAr Cognitive Architecture

Max Talanov, Mariya Zagulova, Salvatore Distefano
Boris Pinus, Alexey Leukhin

Kazan Federal Universtity
ITIS
Russia
Email: max.talanov@gmail.com, mazagulova@stud.kpfu.ru,
salvatdi@gmail.com, bvpinus@gmail.com,
alexey.panzer@gmail.com

Jordi Vallverdú

Universitat Autonoma de Barcelona, Catalonia
Spain
Email: jordi.vallverdu@uab.cat

***Abstract*—In this paper, we present a novel approach to model and re-implement the noradrenaline influence in a bio-plausible manner suitable for the modelling of emotions in a computational system. We have upgraded our previous bio-inspired architecture NEUCOGAR (Neuromodulating Cognitive Architecture) to capture a key aspect of cognitive processes: novelty detection and its evaluation. With our model, we can computationally implement a bioinspired cognitive architecture that uses neuromodulation as a mechanism to identify signals, as well as to evaluate them according to their novelty, taking into account the noradrenaline concentration dynamics. At the same time, the values thus generated are stored in the system using the same neurotransmitters model.**

Keywords–spiking neural networks; artificial emotions; affective computing.

I. Introduction

After the revolution provided by new neuroscientific tools, especially fMRI (functional magnetic resonance imaging), the studies on cognition changed drastically the understanding of the fundamental role of emotions [1]. When the sensorimotor and embodied approaches to cognition [2] were identified (even at robotic level [3]), the key functional role of emotions was still unexplored. Artificial cognitivists specializing in machine cognition started to consider the design and implementation of emotional architectures [4], as well as initiated the fields of affective computing [5] or social robotics [6]. At that point, the interest was to capture human affective modes to implement them into machines, which humans should interact with. During this process, a very important question emerged: do machines need to have emotions, if we want to make them cognitively powerful? This is the question that triggered our research some years ago [7][8] and that oriented our research towards biomimetic models [9]. The neurotransmitter architecture of human brains controls the main cognitive and emotional processes, indeed, acting as a twofold mechanism [10]. Therefore, the role of emotions and their effect (only including inborn basic emotional reactions) in the mammalian cognition is considered to be significant by several researchers [11][12][13][14][15]. Even from the evolutionary perspective, the key role of emotions in social design is of no doubt [16], and also helps to explain moral behaviour [17].

For all the reasons above, the design of artificial architectures through emotional values attracted interests, aiming at providing the key to the existence of adaptive, creative, and multiheuristic artificial architectures, by mimicking the most successful characteristics of human cognition. Several attempts to re-implement emotional aspects in artificial cognitive architectures have been performed as discussed in Section IV, but the work of [18] represents the fundamental internal approach to emotional robotics and AI (Artificial Intelligence). This way, we started with the assumption that it could be beneficial to re-implement basic emotional mechanisms in a computational system gaining the richness of emotional appraisal and behavioural strategies, as well as pain/pleasure reactions that could be used in reinforcement learning. Following Lövheim model of neurotransmitters [19], we propose a bio-inspired artificial architecture called NEUCOGAR that implements emotional-like mechanisms into machine data processing. In Section II, we point out the mismatch between computational resources available to current robotic systems and what is required for neuronal simulation, introducing our concept of a robotic system execution separated into day and night phases, in order to bridge the gap between robotic systems and supercomputers performing the simulation. In Section III, we introduce the notion of bisimulation to answer the questions of learning and mapping from realistic neural network to rules-based control system. Section IV provides the information about the actual topics in the field of affective computing, notable authors and research projects in this area. We sum up the ideas presented in the paper and discuss the arose questions in Section V.

II. The Approach

The key aspect for any living system is the skill to recognize external and internal signals and to evaluate them [20]. On top of this basic feature, more complex operations can be performed, such as the identification of novel signals [21][22]. The novelty can be considered as the discrepancy between what is known and what is discovered, by which activity and exploration of the environment are elicited. Creativity is also deeply related to this process [23].

Based on this consideration, we propose to implement emotional mechanisms to manage processes such as attention, resource allocation, goal setting, into our biomimetic architecture NEUCOGAR. These mechanisms seem to be beneficial for dealing with informational systems in general (such as living entities) and for AI and robotic systems in particular. Indeed, classical approaches tend to be computationally demanding, as well as current cognitive-based ones, while the

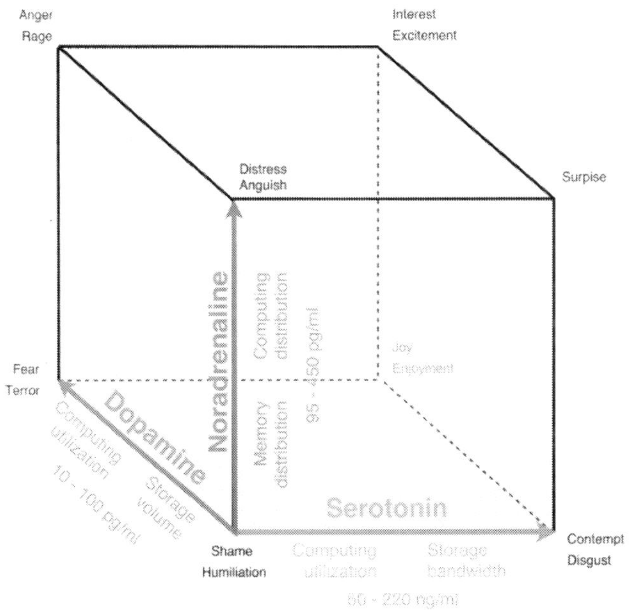

Figure 1. A three-dimensional space of three basic neuromodulators encapsulating basic emotions, mapped to computational system parameters.

proposed solution, NEUCOGAR, is quite promising, since it adopts a higher level, mammalian neurotransmitter-like model to implement a cognitive architecture for machine novelty-detection and evaluation. This way, to implement the phenomena related to emotions, we simulate the neurobiological processes underlying emotional reactions, basically through three neurotransmitters, which are active during brain cognitive processes: noradrenaline (NA), dopamine (DA) and serotonin (5HT). It is important to remark that several works identify the noradrenaline as the main driver of neural response to novelty, while this response is dampened by cholinergic transmission. Later responses to novelty emanating from the frontal cortex seem to be under the influence of the cholinergic system [24].

The selection of the neuro-plausible approach is based on the assumption that the main mechanisms of neuro-computations are similar to those of cellular level bio-chemical reactions. We do not limit our approach to neuro-plausible modelling, we established a link between psychological phenomena, neuro-biological mechanisms and computational processes. We started from the "cube of emotions" by Hugo Lövheim [19], bridging psychological phenomena of "affects" with neuro-biological phenomena of monoamines neuromodulation, i.e., using NA, DA and 5HT, see Figure 1. We have thus built a bio-plausible emulation of the dopamine pathways and managed to emulate the "fear-like" state of the computational system in [25][26]. Further developments include the emulation of serotonin and noradrenaline. This paper is focused on emulating the noradrenaline mechanisms through the neurobiological simulator NEST [27] to reproduce in a bio-plausible manner the psycho-emotional states identified by dopamine and noradrenaline.

As the neuropsychological base for our cognitive architecture, we used a three dimensional monoamines neuromodulators model called "Cube of emotions" created by Hugo Lövheim [19]. Three-dimensional space of three basic neuromodulators: noradrenaline (NA), serotonin (5HT) and dopamine (DA) encapsulates basic emotions or affects inherited from work by Silvian Tomkins [28]. We have extended it with mapping to computational system parameters: computing utilization, computing redistribution, memory redistribution, storage volume and storage, utilization.

III. THE EXPERIMENTS

The proposed noradrenaline concentration dynamics model is based on Izhikevich model for dopamine [29]. The state of each synapse is described by two variables: synaptic weight w and synaptic tag c, also called "eligibility trace". The eligibility trace is a parameter used to control the "memory" of the algorithm, associated with a given state, enabling the assignment of some values to the data under analysis [30][31]. From a biological perspective, it is either some enzyme activation, or another relatively slow process that happens in the synapse, if pre-synaptic and post-synaptic neurons fire by the spike-timing-dependent plasticity (STDP) rule. The eligibility trace can modify the synaptic weight, but only in the presence of extracellular neurotransmitter (noradrenaline), and only during the timeframe of a few seconds. During that time interval, the eligibility trace decays to zero. In a nutshell: the eligibility trace controls the data evaluation in learning processes and is directly involved in novelty detection, something that manages temporal difference learning [32][33]. In this process, the predictive role of dopamine is fundamental [34].

Consequently, we extend the Izhikevich equations for dopamine [29], referring to interesting approaches such as [35] or [36], to describe some governing equations and features in the model of a neural network by noradrenaline. The key aspect of this approach is that we are not just using some kind of existing neural network, but the one implementing a fundamental biomimetic model. Our approach allows to consider classic neural networks adding a biomimetic meaning and semantics to implement the mechanistic regulation operated by neurotransmitters, especially dopamine as a modulator of novelty detection and management [37].

We begin this process considering spiking network of quadratic leaky integrate-and-fire neurons [38]. The neuron ratio is distributed as follows: a) 80% excitatory neurons, and b) 20% inhibitory. The dynamics of each neuron is such that the membrane potential v of each neuron at each moment (new current potential $\dot{v}$) depends on abstract membrane recovery variable u (new current value $\dot{u}$) [39]:

$$\dot{v} = k(v - v_{rest})(v - v_{thresh}) - u + I \quad (1)$$

$$\dot{u} = a * b * (v - v_{rest}) - u \quad (2)$$

$$if(v >= 30[mV]) : \{v = -65[mV], u = u + 2[mV]\} \quad (3)$$

In our model, membrane voltage threshold v_{thresh} and resting potential v_{rest} are constant, and the synaptic current input I (the current flowing in a neuron) has an exponential shape. The spike occurs when the membrane potential is higher than -50 mV, and then the membrane potential recovers: v decreases to -65 mV, u increases by 2 mV. We set a to 0.02, b to 0.2, k to 1.

Following Izhikevich, the STDP model [40] does not change the synaptic weights directly, but instead it modulates weights through a temporal eligibility trace (as it will be shown in 6. The variation of the eligibility trace c (new current eligibility trace $\dot{c}$) is described as follows:

$$\dot{c} = -\frac{c}{\tau_c} + A^{+} e^{\frac{(t_{pre}-t_{post})}{\tau^{+}}} \delta(t-t_{post}) - A^{-} e^{\frac{(t_{pre}-t_{post})}{\tau^{-}}} \delta(t-t_{pre}) \quad (4)$$

where t_{pre} and t_{post} are the times of a pre- or post-synaptic spike, A^{+} and A^{-} are the amplitudes of the weight change, τ_{+} and τ_{-} are constant rates, $\delta(t)$ is the Dirac delta function that step-increases the variable c. The eligibility trace decays at the rate of τ_c.

The concentration of noradrenaline also impacts the modulation of synaptic weights [41][42], as shown in (6).

The noradrenaline concentration n decreases exponentially with time (natural fade rate is τ_n), and increases depending on salient, novel events:

$$\dot{n} = -\frac{n}{\tau_n} + p_{nov} n(\delta(t - t_n) p_{rew} + \delta(t - t_n) p_{pun}) \quad (5)$$

where p_{punish} is a punishment (stressor) event, p_{rew} is a reward event, p_{nov} is the probability of the event being novel and unexpected (salient). The noradrenaline concentration cannot go below zero: it increases with stressors, if p_{nov} is bigger than zero (a sudden stress), as well as with rewards, if p_{rew} is bigger than zero (a surprise reward).

The excitatory synaptic weight w (new current value $\dot{w}$) is not changed directly in the model. Instead, it is modulated proportionally to relative concentration of noradrenaline n (to its baseline level b_n), multiplied by eligibility trace c:

$$\dot{w} = c(n - b_n) \quad (6)$$

The model was tested on MATLAB with the following parameters:

- Network of 1000 leaky neurons with STDP;
- 100 synapses per neuron;
- Maximal synaptic strength = 5;
- Initial synaptic strength (w) = 0;
- Conduction delay = 1 [ms];
- Membrane ground potential (v) = -65 [mV];
- Coincidence interval for pre- and post-synaptic neurons = 20 [ms];
- Current level of NA concentration (n) = 0, as well as 5-HT and DA concentration;
- Initial eligibility trace (c) = 0;

The results thus obtained from simulation, shown in Fig. 2, demonstrate that:

1) Noradrenaline concentration was not affected whatsoever by predictable rewards with the novelty of zero. Meanwhile, serotonin and dopamine concentration were increased by reward - each of the three times in the interval of first 100 ms;
2) Noradrenaline concentration was almost not affected by predictable punishment with zero novelty while serotonin fade rate was vastly increased by it, which led to the serotonin concentration drop at the 90th ms of the simulation run;
3) Noradrenaline concentration was increased by every unpredictable event, proportionally to the level of the event's saliency - it went much higher at the 180th ms, when the reward's novelty was 0.75, than at 380th ms, when the reward's novelty was only 0.6. Same reaction was demonstrated for the punishments of different novelty, at the moments of 230 ms and 380 ms. However, dopamine and serotonin reaction to reward and punishment events did not depend on how unpredictable the events were: dopamine concentration was proportional to the frequency of the rewards (of whatever novelty), serotonin concentration - to both reward and punishment event frequency.

IV. RELATED WORK

Since the last decade of 20th Century the interest towards emotions and emotional representations in computational systems has been exponentially growing [43][44]. At the same time, the industrial applications that could relate humans and machines have required increased investments into Human-Robot Interaction (HRI) studies, covering a big array of topics [45][46][47], even ethical ones [48][49]. This rise of activity was based on understanding of the role of emotions in human intelligence and consciousness that was indicated by several neuroscientists [50][51].

Starting from the seminal ideas of bioinspired neural networks of Stephen Grossberg in the 1970's [8], in the following decade a new vision on computational emotional architectures was investigated by Aaron Sloman [52]. A few years later, affective computing was born thanks to the book by Rosalind Picard [5]. Social robotics was the natural evoluton of these new trends, also at MIT by Cynthia Breazeal [6].

We could identify two main directions in the new research field of affective computing: emotion recognition and re-implementation of emotions in a computational system, mostly for HRI purposes. There are several cognitive architectures that are capable of the re-implementation of emotional phenomena, starting from ACT-R [53] to modern BICA [54], among others. The interest in implementation of emotional mechanisms is based on the fundamental role of emotions in basic cognitive processes: colouring in appraisal, decision making mechanisms, and emotional behaviour, as Damasio showed in [1].

Our approach takes a step further on the road for neurobiologically plausible model of emotions [26]: Arbib and Fellous [55][56] created the neurobiological background for the direction to neurobiologically inspired cognitive architectures; appraisal aspects were analyzed by Marsella and Gratch researches [14][15], as well as in Lowe and Ziemke works [13][57], or temporal and reinforcement learning [58][59].

As it was mentioned earlier in this paper, the processing of the simulation took 4 hours of supercomputer's processing time to calculate 1000 milliseconds [60].

V. CONCLUSION AND FUTURE WORK

In our paper, we have described a new approach for augmentation of autonomous robotic systems with mechanisms of emotional revision and feedback. We have modelled novelty

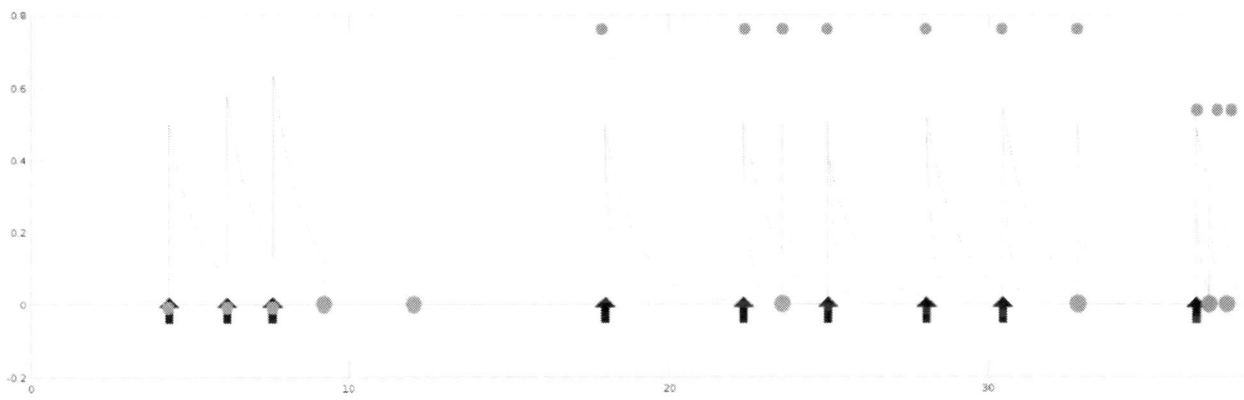

Figure 2. Transient evolution of eligibility trace c (cyan) and concentration of NA n (red), 5-HT (blue), DA (green), being exposed to reward (arrow) and punishment (red circle) events with different levels of saliency (grey circles).

recognition and evaluation skills, which are useful for a broad range of implementations: cognitive architectures, self-learning models, HRI, among other possibilities. The implementation of a biomimetic cognitive architecture that captures the basic neutrotransmitters roles (noradrenaline, dopamine and serotonin), as well the noradrenaline concentration dynamics model based on Izhikevich model for dopamine has made it possible for our NEUCOGAR model to build reliable ways to deal with cognitive novelty. This feature, novelty, is of the outmost importance for a cognitive system, because it selects and manages attention, modifies memory resources and data, stimulates responses, among other functions [61][62].

Despite of the good preliminary results, this research offers also some important questions: a) first of all, to define clearly the input formats for realistic neural network; b) secondly, the necessity of establishing reliable emotional revision thresholds; c) finally, the clarification of the way by which we capture and reproduce emotional equalizing (homeostasis) in a biomimetic way (for "average human" inspired architectures, as well as for bioinspired but open ones).

On the one hand, different answers to these questions allow us to adapt our model to a range of possible architectures of robots' control systems. These robotic architectures can follow several scenario-demanding conditions (responses optimized by velocity, approximation, low computing demand, etc.), which can be managed through the neurotransmitters biomimetic model. The fundamental aspect of our model is that it can follow human-like standard neurotransmitting mechanisms; or the mechanisms can be modified, in order to optimize other cognitive heuristics adapted to the real demands at that specific time. On the other hand, we consider that the best way to implement our model would be a software framework with several pluggable adapters to accommodate the most popular choices for robots' "brains". This can be achieved using an accepted programming language, at least for academics (the barriers that create diverse manufactures employing own languages are well known: ABB (Asea Brown Boveri Ltd.) has its RAPID language, KUKA (Keller und Knappich Augsburg) has KRL (Kuka Robot Language), Comau uses PDL2 (Process Design Language 2), Yaskawa Electric Corporation uses INFORM language, FANUC (Factory Automation NUmerical Control) uses Karel language, etc.) [63][64]. Our idea is that the power and simplicity of our model, as well as its accessibility (offering all our data at free repositories), can help to unify the field. The benefits of our bioinspired architecture are evident: it allows to connect and manage modular systems with a main but not dominant emotional architecture (like our NEUCOGAR model). It can be seen as a cognitive net that increases and empowers managing systems without the necessity of reprogramming the whole architecture: it is a thin global layer that coordinates sub-layers/modules activations, allowing even a multi-heuristic system adapt to fast changing demands.

ACKNOWLEDGMENTS

This work was funded by the subsidy of the Russian Government to support the Program of competitive growth of Kazan Federal University among world class academic centers and universities. This paper has been partially funded by Spanish Government DGICYT: Creatividad, revoluciones e innovacin en los procesos de cambio cientfico (FFI2014-52214-P).

REFERENCES

[1] A. Damasio, Ed., Descartes' Error: Emotion, Reason, and the Human Brain. Penguin Books, Jan. 1994.

[2] O. Vilarroya, "Sensorimotor event: an approach to the dynamic, embodied, and embedded nature of sensorimotor cognition," Frontiers in Human Neuroscience, vol. 7, 2014, p. 912.

[3] R. Pfeifer and J. C. Bongard, How the Body Shapes the Way We Think: A New View of Intelligence (Bradford Books). The MIT Press, 2006.

[4] A. Sloman, "Computational Modelling of Motive-Management Processes," in Proceedings of the Conference of the International Society for Research in Emotions, N.Frijda, Ed. Cambridge: ISRE Publications, 1994, pp. 344–348.

[5] R. W. Picard, Ed., Affective Computing. Massachusets Institute of Technology, 1997.

[6] C. Breazeal, Ed., Emotion And Sociable Humanoid Robots. Elsevier Science, 2002.

[7] J. Vallverdú, Creating Synthetic Emotions through Technological and Robotic Advancements. IGI Global, 2012, ch. Subsuming or Embodying Emotions?, pp. IX–XIV.

[8] J. Vallverdu, Ed., Handbook of Research on Synthesizing Human Emotion in Intelligent Systems and Robotics. Hershey, PA, USA: IGI Global, 2015.

[9] M. Talanov, J. Vallverdú, S. Distefano, M. Mazzara, and R. Delhibabu, "Neuromodulating Cognitive Architecture: Towards Biomimetic Emotional AI," in 2015 IEEE 29th International Conference on Advanced Information Networking and Applications, vol. 2015-April. IEEE, mar 2015, pp. 587–592. [Online]. Available: http://www.scopus.com/inward/record.url?eid=2-s2.0-84946224675&partnerID=tZOtx3y1 http://ieeexplore.ieee.org/lpdocs/epic03/wrapper.htm?arnumber=7098025

[10] M. R. Zarrindast, "Neurotransmitters and Cognition," EXS, vol. 98, 2006, pp. 5–39.

[11] A. Hyungil and R. Picard, "Affective Cognitive Learning and Decision Making: The Role of Emotions," in The 18th European Meeting on Cybernetics and Systems Research (EMCSR 2006), 2006.

[12] R. W. Picard, E. Vyzas, and J. Healey, "Toward Machine Emotional Intelligence: Analysis of Affective Physiological State," vol. 23, no. 10, 2001, pp. 1175–1191.

[13] T. Ziemke and R. Lowe, "On the Role of Emotion in Embodied Cognitive Architectures: From Organisms to Robots," Cogn Comput, 2009, pp. 104–117.

[14] S. Marsella, J. Gratch, and P. Petta, Computational Models of Emotion. Oxford: Oxford University Press, 2010, pp. 21–46.

[15] J. Gratch and S. Marsella, "Evaluating a Computational Model of Emotion," Autonomous Agents and Multi-Agent Systems, vol. 11, 2005, pp. 23–43.

[16] F. De Waal, "Putting the Altruism Back into Altruism: the Evolution of Empathy," Annu. Rev. Psychol., vol. 59, 2008, pp. 279–300.

[17] G. Rizzolatti and L. Craighero, "The Mirror-Neuron System," Annual Review of Neuroscience, 2004.

[18] M. Minsky, The Emotion Machine: Commonsense Thinking, Artificial Intelligence, and the Future of the Human Mind. Simon and Schuster, 2007.

[19] H. Lövheim, "A New Three-Dimensional Model for Emotions and Monoamine Neurotransmitters," Medical Hypotheses, vol. 78, no. 2, feb 2012, pp. 341–8. [Online]. Available: http://www.sciencedirect.com/science/article/pii/S0306987711005883

[20] R. H. Wiley, Signal Detection, Noise, and the Evolution of Communication. Berlin, Heidelberg: Springer Berlin Heidelberg, 2013, pp. 7–30.

[21] E. Mather, "Novelty, Attention, and Challenges for Developmental Psychology," Frontiers in Psychology, vol. 4, 2013, p. 491.

[22] S. J. and M. Meeter, "Short- and Long-Lasting Consequences of Novelty, Deviance and Surprise on Brain and Cognition," Neuroscience and Biobehavioral Reviews, vol. 55, 2015, pp. 268–279.

[23] A. J. Cropley, "Creativity and Cognition: Producing Effective Novelty," Roeper Review, vol. 21, no. 4, 1999, pp. 253–260.

[24] W. T. Blows, "Neurotransmitters of the Brain: Serotonin, Noradrenaline (Norepinephrine), and Dopamine," J Neurosci Nurs., vol. 32, no. 4, 2000, pp. 234–8.

[25] A. Leukhin, M. Talanov, I. Sozutov, J. Vallverdú, and A. Toschev, "Simulation of a Fear-Like State on a Model of Dopamine System of Rat Brain," vol. 449, 2016, pp. 121–126.

[26] J. Vallverdú, M. Talanov, S. Distefano, M. Mazzara, A. Tchitchigin, and I. Nurgaliev, "A Cognitive Architecture for the Implementation of Emotions in Computing Systems," Biologically Inspired Cognitive Architectures, 2015.

[27] M. Gewaltig and M. Diesmann, "NEST (NEural Simulation Tool)," Scholarpedia, vol. 2, no. 4, 2007, p. 1430.

[28] S. Tomkins, Affect Imagery Consciousness Volume III : the Negative Affects Anger and Fear. New York: Springer Publishing Company, 1991.

[29] E. M. Izhikevich, "Solving the Distal Reward Problem through Linkage of STDP and Dopamine Signaling," Cerebral Cortex, vol. 17, no. 10, 2007, pp. 2443–2452.

[30] K. Katahira, T. Cho, K. Okanoya, and M. Okada, "Optimal Node Perturbation in Linear Perceptrons with Uncertain Eligibility Trace," Neural networks : the Official Journal of the International Neural Network Society, vol. 23, no. 2, Mar 2010, pp. 219–25.

[31] M. Geist and B. Scherrer, "Off-Policy Learning with Eligibility Traces: A Survey," J. Mach. Learn. Res., vol. 15, no. 1, Jan. 2014, pp. 289–333.

[32] A. Adam and M. White, "Investigating Practical Linear Temporal Difference Learning," in Proceedings of the 2016 International Conference on Autonomous Agents and Multiagent Systems, ser. AAMAS '16. Richland, SC: International Foundation for Autonomous Agents and Multiagent Systems, 2016, pp. 494–502. [Online]. Available: http://dl.acm.org/citation.cfm?id=2936924.2936997

[33] C. Dann, G. Neumann, and J. Peters, "Policy Evaluation with Temporal Differences: A Survey and Comparison," Journal of Machine Learning Research, vol. 15, 2014, pp. 809–883. [Online]. Available: http://jmlr.org/papers/v15/dann14a.html

[34] W. Schultz, "Predictive Reward Signal of Dopamine Neurons," Journal of neurophysiology, vol. 80, no. 1, 1998, p. 1.

[35] H. M. Bayer and P. W. Glimcher, "Midbrain Dopamine Neurons Encode a Quantitative Reward Prediction Error Signal," Neuron, vol. 47, no. 1, Jul 2005, pp. 129–41.

[36] C. Yu, N.and Canavier, "A Mathematical Model of a Midbrain Dopamine Neuron Identifies Two Slow Variables Likely Responsible for Bursts Evoked by SK Channel Antagonists and Terminated by Depolarization Block," Journal of Mathematical Neuroscience, vol. 5, 2015, p. 5.

[37] M. Garcia-Garcia, I. Clemente, J. Domínguez-Borràs, and C. Escera, "Dopamine transporter regulates the enhancement of novelty processing by a negative emotional context," Neuropsychologia, vol. 48, no. 5, Apr 2010, pp. 1483–8.

[38] A. N. Burkitt, "Balanced Neurons: Analysis of Leaky Integrate-and-Fire Neurons with Reversal Potentials," Biological Cybernetics, vol. 85, no. 4, Oct 2001, pp. 247–55.

[39] T. Chou, L. D. Bucci, and J. L. Krichmar, "Learning Touch Preferences with a Tactile Robot Using Dopamine Modulated STDP in a Model of Insular Cortex," Frontiers in Neurorobotics, vol. 6, no. 6, Jul 2015.

[40] J. Lisman and N. Spruston, "Questions about STDP as a General Model of Synaptic Plasticity," Frontiers in Synaptic Neuroscience, vol. 2, 2010.

[41] P. A. Baumann and W. P. Koella, "Feedback Control of Noradrenaline Release as a Function of Noradrenaline Concentration in the Synaptic Cleft in Cortical Slices of the Rat," Brain research, vol. 189, no. 2, May 1980, pp. 437–48.

[42] J. Ludwig, M. Gerlich, T. Halbrügge, and K. H. Graefe, "The synaptic noradrenaline concentration in humans as estimated from simultaneous measurements of plasma noradrenaline and dihydroxyphenylglycol (dopeg)," Journal of Neural Transmission Supplementum, vol. 32, 1990, pp. 441–5.

[43] C. Breazeal, Designing Sociable Robots. MIT Press, 2004.

[44] R. W. Picard, What Does it Mean for a Computer to "Have" Emotions?, 2001.

[45] H. Admoni, "Nonverbal Communication in Socially Assistive Human-Robot Interaction," AI Matters, vol. 2, no. 4, 2016, pp. 9–10.

[46] A. Esposito and L. C. Jain, "Modeling emotions in robotic socially believable behaving systems," in Toward Robotic Socially Believable Behaving Systems (I), ser. Intelligent Systems Reference Library, A. Esposito and L. C. Jain, Eds. Springer, 2016, vol. 105, pp. 9–14. [Online]. Available: http://dx.doi.org/10.1007/978-3-319-31056-5

[47] J. Vallverdú and G. Trovato, "Emotional affordances for human-robot interaction," Adaptive Behaviour, no. 5, pp. 320–334.

[48] B. Lewandowska-Tomaszczyk and P. Wilson, Physical and Moral Disgust in Socially Believable Behaving Systems in Different Cultures, ser. Intelligent Systems Reference Library. Springer, 2016, vol. 105, pp. 105–132. [Online]. Available: http://dx.doi.org/10.1007/978-3-319-31056-5

[49] F. Operto, "Ethics in Advanced Robotics: ELS Issues in Advanced Robotics," IEEE Robotics and Automation Magazine, vol. 18, no. 1, 2011, pp. 72–78.

[50] A. Damasio, The Feeling of What Happens : Body and Emotion in the Making of Consciousness. New York, 1999.

[51] A. Murata, L. Fadiga, L. Fogassi, V. Gallese, V. Raos, and G. Rizzolatti,

"Object Representation in the Ventral Premotor Cortex (Area F5) of the Monkey," J Neurophysiol., vol. 78, no. 4, 1997, pp. 2226–30.

[52] A. Sloman and R. Chrisley, "Virtual Machines and Consciousness," Journal of Consciousness Studies, 2003.

[53] A. Harrison, "jACT-R: Java ACT-R," in Proceedings of the 8th Annual ACT-R Workshop, 2002.

[54] A. V. Samsonovich, "Modeling Human Emotional Intelligence in Virtual Agents," in AAAI Fall Symposium - Technical Report, vol. FS-13-03. AI Access Foundation, 2013, pp. 71–78.

[55] J. Fellous, "The neuromodulatory basis of emotion," The Neuroscientist, vol. 5, 1999, pp. 283–294.

[56] M. Arbib and J. Fellous, "Emotions: from Brain to Robot," Trends in Cognitive Sciences, vol. 8(12), 2004, pp. 554–559.

[57] R. Lowe and T. Ziemke, "The Role of Reinforcement in Affective Computation Triggers, Actions and Feelings," in IEEE Symposium on Computational Intelligence for Creativity and Affective Computing (CICAC), 2013.

[58] R. Sutton, "Learning to Predict by the Methods of Temporal Differences," Mach. Learn., vol. 3, no. 1, Aug. 1988, pp. 9–44.

[59] S. P. Singh and R. S. Sutton, "Reinforcement learning with replacing eligibility traces," Machine Learning, vol. 22, no. 1-3, 1996, pp. 123–158.

[60] V. Kugurakova, M. Talanov, and D. Ivanov, "Neurobiological Plausibility as Part of Criteria for Highly Realistic Cognitive Architectures," in Procedia Computer Science, vol. 88, 2016, pp. 217–223. [Online]. Available: www.scopus.com

[61] M. Kishiyama and A. Yonelinas, "Novelty Effects on Recollection and Familiarity in Recognition Memory," Memory and cognition, vol. 31, no. 7, 2003, pp. 1045–1051.

[62] T. Saigusa, T. Tuinstra, N. Koshikawa, and A. R. Cools, "High and Low Responders to Novelty: Effects of a Catecholamine Synthesis Inhibitor on Novelty-Induced Changes in Behaviour and Release of Accumbal Dopamine," Neuroscience, vol. 88, no. 4, 1999, pp. 1153–63.

[63] S. Calinon, "Robot Programming by Demonstration," in Springer Handbook of Robotics, 2008, ch. 59, pp. 1371–1394.

[64] R. L. Wexelblat, History of Programming Languages. Academic Press, 2014.

A Neurochemical Framework to Stress and the Role of the Endogenous Opioid System in the Control of Heart Rate Variability for Cognitive Load

Sergey Parin
Lobachevsky State University
Nizhny Novgorod, Russia
e-mail: parins@mail.ru
Anna Polevaia
Lobachevsky State University
Nizhny Novgorod, Russia
e-mail: a.dostoevskaya@gmail.com

Sofia Polevaia
Nizhny Novgorod State Medical Academy,
Lobachevsky State University
Nizhny Novgorod, Russia
e-mail: polevaia@ipfran.ru

Abstract— **This paper presents a complex analysis of the stress and shock phenomena. These specific reactions represent non-specific, protective, stepwise, multi-systemic, reduced psychophysiological responses to injury or threat. Finding psycho-physiological, neurochemical and patho-physiological mechanisms of stress and shock is an important task nowadays. It is relevant not only from the theoretical, but also from practical point of view, as every day thousands of people die from shock. At the beginning of 1980s, it has been suggested to look at stress and shock as processes based on similar mechanisms of hyperactivation of three neuro-endocrine systems: sympatho-adrenal system, hypothalamic-pituitary-adrenal axis and endogenous opioid system. The mechanisms of stress and shock are related to a significant reduction of regulatory mechanisms. On the basis of these theoretical concepts, we created an explicit psycho-physiological model of stress that describes in mathematical form, how neuro-endocrine input modulates cardiac responses during the first phase of stress reaction. Here, we give a comparative analysis of the heart-rate variability dynamics. This analysis was carried out for drug-addicts with reduction of endogenous opioid receptor apparatus, and for healthy volunteers in the context of cognitive loads of different levels. It is shown that such specific reactions as the reduction of the hart-rate autonomic regulation mode and the lack of adaptive variations in the heart-rate structure as response to the changing external information context, are typical for the examined drug-addicts.**

Keywords - stress; endogenous opioid system; heart rate variability; cognitive functions

I. Introduction

Stress (or general adaptive syndrome) is a nonspecific reaction to injury, according to the theory of H. Selye [1][2]. This theory was globally recognized over the past decades. However, many of its key points become questioned at the XXI century. E.g., the use of the term "adaptation" has led to confusion that any impact is stressor. Lack of attention to the results of researching the functions of the endogenous opioid system (EOS) has led to stagnation of studies of neurochemical stress mechanisms. Our methods include psycho-physiological, — Electro-encephalography (EEG), Event-Related Telemetry (ERT), Hart-Rate Variabitily (HRV), respirography, measurement of hemodynamic etc., — biochemical, radioimmunoassay, psychophysical (computer laterometry and campimetry), psychological, and mathematical approach. A total of 1850 animals (7 species) and 800 subjects participated in the studies.

Note that stress represents a simplified (reduced) reaction to an emergency, which provides decreasing individual deviations of psychological, physiological, biochemical, and other indicators from the normal value. This is the result of depleting the regulatory mechanisms: three neuroendocrine stress-protective systems have exclusive dominance. This standardization provides nonspecific protection that is optimal only in emergency situations [7].

It should be emphasized that the stress phenomenon itself appears to be wide-spread and rather normal for modern life. However, this actually represents a danger due to the possibility of stress-to-shock transition. Shock represents a special case of stress thus, they have similar physiological mechanisms [2][4]. However, the shock (in contrary to the stress) *always* leads to devastating and life-threatening consequences.

Stress is a basic extreme process. It may be the main component of the extreme condition, a forming factor, and a response to the extreme action. It is known that H. Selye had argued that the shock is an extreme degree of stress. It is widely believed, that the question about the mechanisms of extreme functional states has been studied in detail. But it is far from being true. E.g., for many decades, the basic physiologic mechanisms of stress (and particularly, shock) have traditionally been reduced to the emergency activation of two neuroendocrine complexes: the sympathetic-adrenal-medullary system (SAS) and hypothalamic-pituitary-adrenal (HPAS) system. No doubt, these two systems, providing various nonspecific patterns of psychic, motor, metabolic and visceral functions, form mainly the first two stages of stress: anxiety and resistance. At the same time, the mechanisms of the third stage of stress — the stage of exhaustion — were studied superficially. This is to a big extent connected with the "hypnosis" of the classic idea to treat it as a period of complete disintegration of regulatory and executive mechanisms. In contrast to this misconception, it has been proven convincingly that the stage of exhaustion is also a regulated process similar to the first two stages of stress [7]. The only difference is that EOS becomes the basic neuroendocrine control system providing minimization of the energy consumption and transfer of the organism to hypobiotic mode. Besides, EOS does work in all three stress stages with different extent of dominance. These statements were supported by the results of numerous experiments on animals, as well as by calculations within the neuron-like mathematical model. However, the researches by means of noninvasive methods of monitoring functional state of an individual in the condition of daily life (and primarily, under cognitive loads), are undoubtedly very important.

The paper is organized as follows. In Section II, the problem of strict formalization of the stress process is discussed. In Section III, we present the neuron-inspired model of stress-protective systems. In Section IV, we present a complex of methods, directed to the study of the dynamic aspects of EOS activity in the functional system. In Section V, the psycho-physiological markers of EOS activity during interactive communication with information images are determined. Further working perspectives are discussed in Section VI.

II. FORMALIZATION OF THE STRESS PHENOMENON

In spite of various studies of the problem, some very important points concerning the definition and marker of the stress process should be clarified.

A. *Definition of Stress*

Classic postulates (H.Selye) read: «Stress (general adaptation syndrome) is a non-specific response of the body to the physical or psychological effects of violating its homeostasis»; «Stress is a reaction based on the interaction of two regulatory stress reactive systems: SAS and HPAS»; «Stress is adaptive response»; «Stress response has three stages: alarm, resistance, and exhaustion stages» [1][2].

Our postulates are somewhat different: «Stress is a nonspecific phase systemic protective reduced psycho-physiological reaction to injury or threat»; «Stress is a systemic reaction based on the dynamical interplay of three regulatory neuroendocrine systems: SAS, HPAS, and, most important, EOS»; «Stress is not an adaptive, but protective response»; «Stress is a phasic response. Stages of stress are associated with considerable dominance of one of the stress-protection systems: alarm stage – SAS domination, resistance stage – HPAS domination, exhaustion stage – EOS domination» [6]-[8].

B. *Markers of Stress*

Classic postulate (H.Selye) reads: the endocrine markers of stress correspond to increased levels of cortisol, epinephrine, norepinephrine, Adrenocorticotropic Hormone (ACTH), Corticotropin Releasing Hormone (CRH), etc.

Our postulate reads: the endocrine markers of stress are increased levels of enkephalins, endorphins, dynorphins, etc.

Neurophysiological marker is simultaneous increase of the autonomic balance index and fall in the total power spectrum of HRV [4][6][7].

Below, the results of the measurement of cardiovascular reactivity and cognitive functions of the opiate-dependent patients are presented.

III. THE THREE-COMPONENT MODEL

The algorithm is based on the hypothesis of dynamic interaction between SAS, HPAS and EOS (Fig. 1) and realized via the neuron-likely network equations.

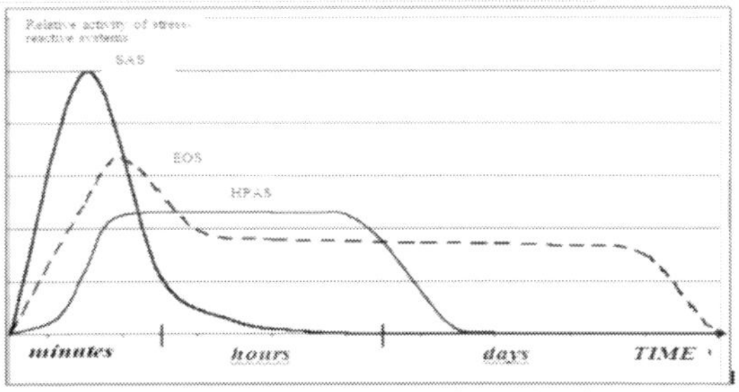

Figure 1. The qualitative characteristics of dynamics of the stress-protection systems (extracted from [6][7], short version).

In order to describe the neurochemical processes during the stress process, we use the model based on the neuron-likely network equations, which consists of four elements, representing SAS, HPAS and two components of EOS (quick and the slow ones), see Fig. 2. Model (1) has been realized as a discrete algorithm in the MATLAB environment; here:

M1 – SAS activity;
M2 – HPAS activity;
M3 – EOS slow component activity;
M4 – EOS quick component activity;
i – typical Mi activity period;
aji – the parameter indicating the influence of Mj on Mi;
Ti – the parameter of Mi self-excitation.

The activity of each Mi system is controlled by interaction with other three systems, and by the self-excitation. The values outside the interval are truncated to its ends.

The influence parameters aji and the typical periods i were chosen according to neurobiological data. In accordance with the activity attenuation and systems` depletion, the Ti parameters change with time.

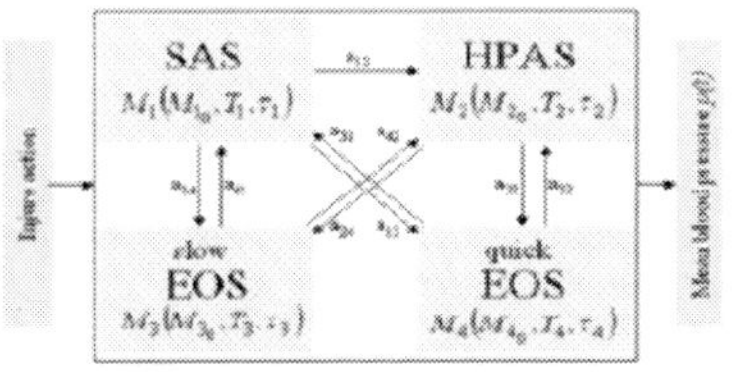

$$\tau_i \frac{\partial M_i}{\partial t} = -M_i + F\left[\sum_j a_{ji} M_j + T_i\right] \quad (1)$$

$$p(t) = p_0 + \sum_j ap_j \int_{t-\Delta t}^{t} \left(1 - \frac{(t-t')}{\Delta t}\right) M_j(t')\,dt' \quad (2)$$

a	M_1	M_2	M_3	M_4
M_1	0	0.4	0.2	0.9
M_2	0	0	0.5	0.6
M_3	-0.74	-0.965	0	0
M_4	-0.4	-0.45	0	0

Figure 2. The algorithm of functional system of stress.

The dynamics of R-R intervals in the stress process has been chosen as a test parameter for the model functioning. It is an integral characteristic of the functional state depending on the activity of the stress-protective systems. This parameter is used for indicating the severity of stress in experiments and clinical practice. The model calculations are in a good agreement with experimentally measured changes in R-R intervals during acute stress in healthy adults (Fig. 3).

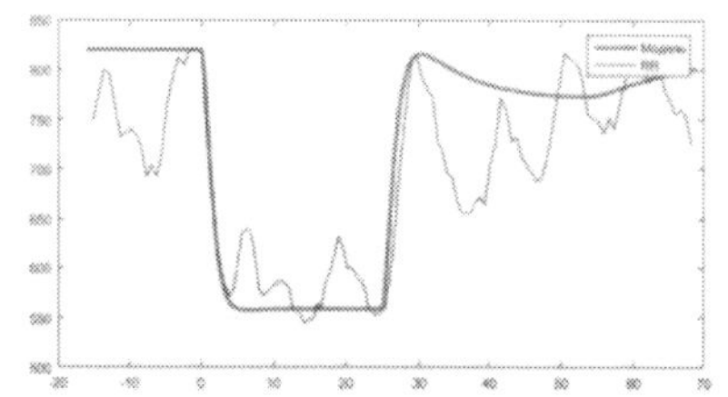

Figure 3. Examples of comparison of model calculation results (red line) with the experimental data during electrically induced pain stress.

These results were obtained within the neuron-based model suggested. It has been tested and proved to give stable results, which reproduce the interaction dynamics of neurochemical stress-protective systems, RR changes in stress and shock, and the elements of pharmacological correction of this integral body state. We hope that the suggested model can serve as a useful tool for further research of the neurobiological mechanisms of stress and shock at the system and cell level, and for finding the best methods for the extreme-states treatment.

IV. THE METHODS

Our information technology ERT provides long continuous collection, transmission, storage and preprocessing the time-synchronized recordings of heart-rate data and psycho-physiological test results [9][10] (Fig. 4). The optimum size and power consumption of the sensors of physiological signals, microprocessors and devices for radio signal reception and transmission were chosen. Data are transmitted to the Smartphone or personal computer via Bluetooth. Then, the data in processed form are transmitted via Global System for Mobile Communications (GSM) channels to a dedicated server system (StressMonitor WEB application) on the Internet. There, the preprocessing and spectral analysis of rhythmograms is performed in pseudo-time, allowing us to determine the initial point of the stress process with an accuracy of up to a few seconds. The result has the form of the spectrogram, which provides the possibility to determine automatically the place, time, and events associated with stress for a particular person in his everyday activity. Thus, the HRV spectral analysis corresponds to:

Total Power (0,015-0,6 Hz);

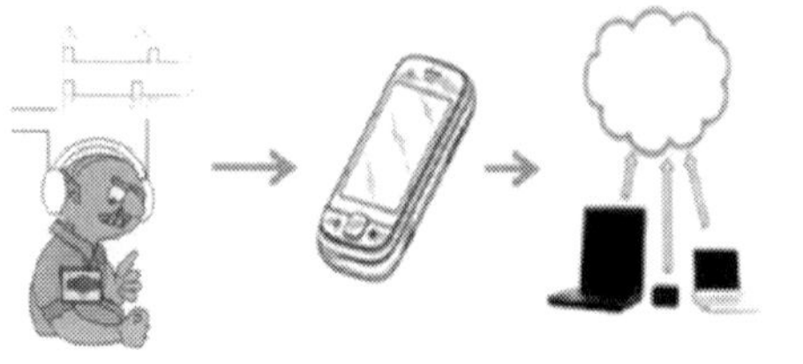

Figure 4. Mobile heart-rate telemetry system: WEB-application Stress Monitor.ru.

Low Frequency band (0,04-0,15 Hz) (LF);
High Frequency band (0,15-0,6 Hz) (HF); LF/HF ;
Very High Frequency band (0,6-2 Hz) [11]-[14].

For the purpose of the cognitive function study, a WEB-platform Apway.ru has been developed. It provides the universal framework for design and testing. Besides, a similar system has been constructed, with a computer being the source of the signal and current registrar (Fig. 5). The distortions and errors introduced by human into the managed attribute information on the image represent a characteristic of the cognitive system. The system includes a module for the stimulus formation in a wide range of amplitude-time values, a virtual measurement mode control panel, a module for registration of operator motor responses, a database, and a module for report generation in the form of tables and graphs. The efficiency of cognitive functions was estimated by the absolute and differential thresholds, and the sensorimotor coordination errors. We used the following computer tests: the computer laterometry, the computer campimetry, the Stroop task, the test "Clock face", the simple sensorimotor activity.

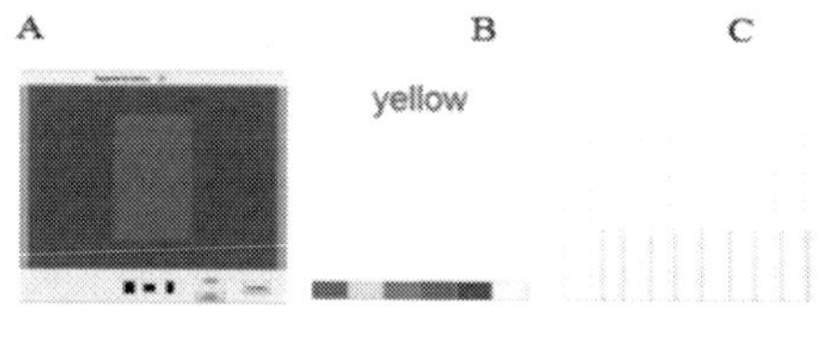

Figure 5. Cognitive simulator: WEB-platform Apway.ru: A - Color discrimination thresholds in shade (computer campimetry); B - Level of cognitive conflict (Stroop test); C - Tests for sensorimotor activity.

V. THE RESULTS

Two groups of subjects participated in the study: 54 opiate-dependent patients during opiate withdrawal (26 men and 28 women, with a mean age of 22.5 (±1.2)) and 25 healthy control participants (12 men and 13 women, with a mean age of 21.5 (±1.3)). An independent samples t-test revealed significant difference in frequency-domain indices of HRV ($p<.03$). The opiate dependent patients exhibited reduced LF, HF, TP (LFm=233.95; HFm=203.77; TPm=765.88) and increased LF/HF ratio (LF/HFm=1.87) in comparison with healthy control participants (LFm=447.37; HFm=700.94; TPm=1592.34; LF/HFm=0.98) in rest context. ANOVA (General Linear Models) revealed significant difference in frequency-domain indices of HRV between contexts different cognitive loads for healthy control participants (F=15.48, p<.05) but no this difference for opiate- dependent patients (F=1, p>.05) (Fig. 6).

The opiate-dependent patients respond to incentives with frequency 5 Hz without errors in tests for sensorimotor coordination. The healthy control participants respond without errors only to incentives with frequency no more 2.5 Hz.

However, the opiate-dependent patients demonstrated increased delay of motor component of reactions (p<0.01). The subjects could make an unlimited number of attempts during setting a predetermined time in the test "Clock face". They turned to the next task, when the error of the set time seemed satisfactory to them. Most opiate-dependent patients were satisfied by the error of the set time from 0 to 2 (74%). Most healthy control participants were satisfied with the error of the set time from 2 to 4 (76%).

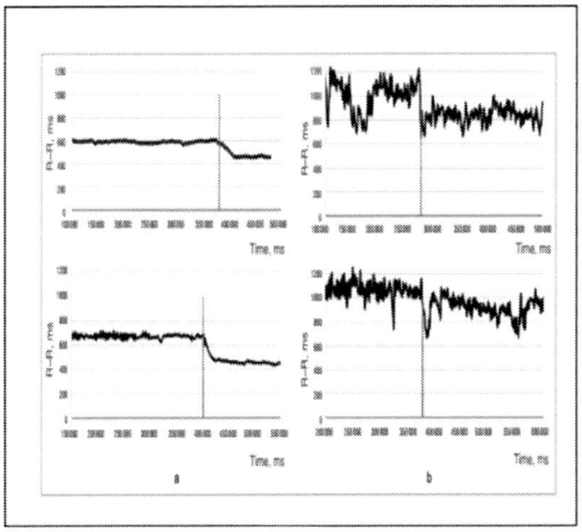

Figure 6. Reduction of autonomic regulation of heart rate in drug-addicts. Dynamics of RR-intervals for the tested drug-addicts (a) and healthy people (b); the beginning of orthostatic test is shown by a red marker.

The opiate-dependent patients are people with disorders of EOS. It is quite natural that the results of our study show cognitive and cardiovascular changes, which are associated with reduced activity of EOS.

VI. Conclusions

Summarizing all presented arguments, we can infer that:

- Stress is an integrative psycho-physiological response to injury or threat of injury. Its psychological component is assessment of the threat power and formation of protective strategies;
- Its physiological component provides the energy supply for cognitive and motor functions by enhancing the effect of regulatory systems SAS, HPAS, and EOS [3]-[5];
- Stress is a nonspecific reaction. It develops regardless of the type of stress factor and has the typical autonomic markers (e.g., the simultaneous increase in the autonomic balance index and decrease in the total power spectrum of HRV). This differs from a variety of specific regulation mechanisms for adequate load;
- Stress is not an adaptive response, but a protective reaction, in analogy with inflammation [6]. It is based not only on functional, but also on structural changes (e.g., the "Selye triad");
- Stress is a systemic response. It is based on the dynamic interaction of three stress-protection systems: SAS, HPAS, and (it is especially important) EOS;
- Stress is a three-step process. The stages of stress are associated with the dominance of one of the stress-protection systems: the alarm corresponds to the dominance of SAS, the resistance – HPAS, the exhaustion – EOS;

We believe that the proposed refinements (corrections) of the stress conception could provide rather clear understanding of the phenomenon and draw attention to the systemic aspects of the problem.

The proposed technology ERT has already proven its efficiency in a variety of natural, clinical and experimental contexts, — namely, in the study of the EOS role in control of HRV, in mapping stressful road infrastructure in metropolitan areas, in the study of spatial dynamics of stress in bus and private car drivers; in the study of autonomic regulation of patients with chronic headache; in the monitoring the stress of translators in course of simultaneous translating, etc.

We have shown that the disorders of EOS could result in:

- Increased operation speed in the case of simple sensorimotor reactions;
- Increased requirements to control accuracy;
- Decreased efficiency of central cardiac-rhythm-control system.

We can infer that the lack of adaptability of autonomic regulation during cognitive tasks is a specific feature of opiate-dependent patients. Thereby, EOS activity is represented in VHF component of HRV.

However, there are still the problems for further researches. In particular, it would be interesting to compare the results of our model with the stress\shock model presented by Chernavskaya [14].

Acknowledgment

This work was partially supported by the Russian Foundation for Humanities, grant 15-06-10894_a, grant 16-06-00133_a, and RFBR, grant 16-06-00501_a.

References

[1] H. Selye, "The general adaptation syndrome and the diseases of adaptation", J. Clin. Endocrinol Metab., vol. 6, pp. 117–230, 1946.

[2] H. Selye. The physiology and pathology of exposure to stress. Montreal: Acta Inc. Medical Publishing, 1950.

[3] E. V. Golanov, S. B. Parin, and V. V. Yasnetsov, "Effect of nalorphine and naloxone on the course of electronociceptive shock in rabbits", Bull. Exp. Biol. Med., vol. 93(6), pp. 765–767, 1982.

[4] E. V. Golanov, A. A. Fufacheva, and S. B. Parin, "Plasma β-endorphin-like immunoreactivity and its variations in baboons", Bull. Exp. Biol. Med., vol. 100(6), pp. 1653–1655, 1985.

[5] E. V. Golanov, A. A. Fufacheva, G. M. Cherkovich, and S. B. Parin, "Effect of ligands of opiate receptors on emotiogenic cardiovascular responses in lower primates", Bull. Exp. Biol. Med., vol. 103(4), pp. 478–481, 1987.

[6] S. B. Parin, "Humans and animals in emergency situations: neurochemical mechanisms, evolutionary aspect", Vestnik NSU, vol. 2(2), pp. 118–135, 2008.

[7] S. B. Parin, A. V. Bakhchina, and S. A. Polevaia, "A neuroc hemical framework of the theory of stress", International Journal of Psychophysiology, vol. 94, pp. 230–234, 2014.

[8] E. V. Runova et. al., "Vegetative correlates of arbitrary mappings of emotional stress", STM, vol. 5(4), pp. 69–77, 2013.

[9] S. Polevaia et al., "Event-related telemetry (ERT) technology for study of cognitive functions", International Journal of Psychophysiology, vol. 108, pp. 87–88, 2016.

[10] J. Taelman, S. Vandeput, E. Vlemincx, A. Spaepen, and S. Van Huffel, "Instantaneous changes in heart rate regulation due to mental load in simulated office work", Eur. J. Appl. Physiol., vol. 111(7), pp. 1497–1505, 2011.

[11] J. P. Headrick, S. Pepe, and J. N. Peart, "Non-analgetic effects of opioids: cardiovascular effects of opioids and their receptor systems", Curr. Pharm., vol. 18(37), pp. 6090–6100, 2012.

[12] J. F. Thayer, F. Ahs, M. Fredrikson, J. J. Sollers, and T. D. Wager, "A meta-analysis of heart rate variability and neuroimaging studies: implications for heart rate variability as a marker of stress and health", Neurosci. Biobehav. Rev., vol. 36, pp. 747–756, 2012.

[13] G. J. Taylor, "Depression, heart rate related variables and cardiovascular disease", Int. J. Psychophysiol., vol. 78, pp. 80–88, 2010.

[14] O. D. Chernavskaya and Ya. A. Rozhylo, "The Natural-Constructive Approach to Representation of Emotions and a Sense of Humor in an Artificial Cognitive System", IARIA Journ. of Life Sciences, vol. 8(3&4), pp. 184–202, 2016.

Two-Component Scheme of Cognitive System Organization: the Hippocampus-Inspired Model

Ekaterina D. Kazimirova
AO Kaspersky Lab
Moscow, Russia
e-mail: Ekaterina.Kazimirova@kaspersky.com

Abstract – **This paper presents a hypothesis on two-component principle of the cognitive system organization. We propose a biologically inspired architecture, which involves two subsystems, external and internal. Both subsystems are capable of compressing data by converting the images into symbols. They are connected at the symbol level, with necessary "relay" controlling their interaction. The External Subsystem reflects and processes the external image information. The Internal Subsystem reflects the internal states of the system and contains a "personal sense" of the external images; thus, it can be considered as a Library of Emotions. We propose a hypothesis that in living systems the role of a "relay" (a connector) between the external and internal libraries may be performed by the hippocampus. When applied to an artificial cognitive system, our hypothesis would imply the inclusion of certain modules (blocks), constructed in analogy with the hippocampus, into the system. This approach could be useful for designing self-regulatory systems that would account for both the external and internal factors. It may also be important for large industrial systems related to cyber-physical objects, which have hundreds of thousands of sensors; in this setting, decoupling the internal and external information may ensure efficient monitoring and protection. Technically, such two-component system could be represented as a block (modular) neural network.**

Keywords* - *emotion; symbol; cognitive architecture; hippocampus; industrial system

I. INTRODUCTION

Nowadays, robotic systems are growing more closely connected to humans. In the future, many of them may become an integral part of a human being for a certain time. A car equipped with an autopilot may be considered as an example of such integration. For such situations, simulation of "emotion" and "personal meaning" of events in artificial cognitive systems becomes very important.

Emotions are analyzed and interpreted within the framework of various scientific disciplines. Psychology is trying to define the basic mechanisms of emotions and their relation to personality. Neurophysiology explores the neural substrates of emotions (e.g., neural networks involved). Scientific efforts (both in robotics and in other domains) aimed at the development of General Artificial Intelligence seem to be especially active in the field of imitating human emotions. This includes the use of video recordings of human facial expressions for generating facial expressions of robots, mirroring human facial expressions, etc.

Obviously, the mere simulation of emotions is not enough, if we want an emotional unit to regulate the behavior of the robotic system. Thus, we need a certain understanding of the very essence and nature of emotions and we have to create an architectural solution in order to bring that understanding into reality.

There is a number of interesting attempts in this area. In some approaches, emotions are represented as noise [1]. In others, attention is drawn to the importance of the "mental states" of the intelligent agent [2], etc.

There are also efforts underway to draw parallels between the action of neurotransmitters in the living brain and the computational processes (in computers), such as computing power, memory distribution, learning and storage [3].

In this paper, we argue that a simple decoupling of any cognitive system into two subsystems could be useful for different disciplines. Such approach could advance our understanding of emotions as a reflection of internal states and regulation of behavior, both for robotic and living systems.

In this paper, we discuss the Symbol-Image model of cognitive system (Section II), present the two-component model (Section III), discuss the possible verification and application of the model (Section IV), and present conclusions and future perspectives (Section V).

II. SYMBOL-IMAGE MODEL OF COGNITIVE SYSTEM

First, we have to select a paradigm for solving the problem of emotion modeling. Let us examine the symbol-image model of the cognitive system [4]. The cognitive space consists of elements that can be described as symbols, images and attributes. The model describes our informational fields in terms of hierarchical structures of symbols and images. Previously, we have introduced the term "attribute" to describe the content of an image via the fields of attributes [5].

One of the important consequences of this simple model is that the attribute fields (different characteristics of the images) can overlap. In this model, symbols play a very important role, because they separate different images (the corresponding group of attributes). We propose that symbols represent the memory of such a cognitive system, because they prevent mixing of images and provide a possibility for storing the images as entire units.

Concerning the living brain, this arrangement implies that the encoding neuron-symbols should be located in the structures responsible for memory. One of the key memory-related structures in the living brain is the hippocampus, as its lesions lead to inability to form memory of recent events.

III. The Two-Component Model

A. *Internal and External Symbol Libraries*

We suppose that the system, which is responsible for acquiring images from the external world, is only a part of the living cognitive system. Another part of the cognitive system has to encode its own inner states (see mental states, [2]). Here, we put forward a hypothesis that there are two cognitive subsystems – "external" and "internal". Our idea is that the basic principles of the organization of these systems may be similar. We assume that both of them contain images compressed into symbols.

Obviously, those subsystems have to be interconnected. Actually, it is this connection that provides appropriate reactions to external events, forms behavioral patterns and allows making predictions (forecasts). This interaction between the subsystems can be indirect – for example, through the decision-making unit – but it still has to be present.

In artificial systems, we can also try generating two subsystems – external and internal – and connecting them. This would constitute a simple architectural solution. Furthermore, we assume that, in the artificial cognitive systems, the internal subsystem may parallel (be analogous to) the emotional component of the live cognitive system. It is "emotional", because it automatically reflects some kind of "personality meaning" of the external images and because it forms a basis for generating prognoses and forming behavioral strategies.

We propose that the two cognitive subsystems are connected at the level of symbols.

B. *Is the Internal Library an Emotional Library?*

In a living organism, formation of such two-component system is a result of a life experience. It can serve as a basis for connection between the internal and external environments, for generating prognoses and forming behavioral patterns and strategies. Thus, a favorable context and images of external environment will correspond to "positive" internal images and symbols, while negative external events and images will correspond to "negative" internal images and symbols.

We may consider the "internal" library as an "emotional library", because it summarizes and reflects the internal states and the personal meanings of the external events and images.

C. *Specific Role of the Hippocampus*

Let us consider the arguments in favor of the idea that the hippocampus could play the role of a "relay", i.e., a connector between two subsystems, the external and internal symbols' libraries.

1) The hippocampus is connected with both, the cortex (that receives information from the outside world), and the limbic structures (that receive information from the internal organs and are responsible for emotions).

2) The hippocampus is involved in the memory consolidation [6]. We can assume that the hippocampus is the very place where the symbols are stored. The activation of the neuron-symbol stored in the hippocampus activates the image associated with that symbol in the cerebral cortex.

3) Neurogenesis (production of new neurons) was observed in the adult hippocampus [7] and was not detected in most of the other brain structures. We propose that new neurons may be required for marking (labeling) new images.

Taken together, these arguments make us suggest the hypothesis that the hippocampus is an integrator of the two (internal and external) subsystems in the brain at the symbol's level.

D. *A Two-Component Hippocampus-Inspired Model*

We propose a simple model of the cognitive system, which consists of two subsystems. One of them is responsible for processing and compressing the external information. The second one relates to internal information. They are connected by means of a "relay". In the living systems, the hippocampus could play the role of such a relay. This implies that everything that we see, hear, feel, and perceive via our sensory systems, results in formation of images in the brain cortex. This is similar to the appearance of images in a kaleidoscope. Later on, the images are to be converted into symbols.

At the same time, the internal system of receptors records the actual indices of the organism, its hormonal, physical, biochemical state, etc.

There are two information flows. One of them reflects the external stimuli, while another one reflects the internal changes.

The brain, in order to perform its functions effectively, has to process these two information flows simultaneously (subject to certain time intervals). The hippocampus appears to be a plausible candidate for coordinating these two data streams, since it is a key element connecting the cortex with the limbic system. Through the limbic system, the hippocampus is connected with the thalamic neural block, which is responsible for controlling the internal states.

Thus, in the artificial cognitive systems that are based on the emotional management model (e.g., [8]), it is possible to reproduce this type of data separation and integration. The internal state of the intelligent agent (IA) is described by data from the internal state sensors. This information has to be combined with the data obtained from the outside world. Thus, the external data acquire personal meaning in terms of the internal states of IA.

IV. Possible Verification and Applications

Our hypothesis is that there are links between internal states of the system and corresponding external images. This assumption can be verified by explaining some psychological phenomena.

Let us consider a case of post-traumatic stress disorder, when a person throws himself into a ditch at a certain sound, e.g., a sound resembling a shell blast. According to our model, such behavior could be explained by activation of a single attribute and (selectively, despite the context) of the related symbol that means the "mortal danger" in the Internal Library.

In another example, an external image is ambiguous, i.e., it plays positive and negative roles simultaneously. So, it activates contrasting states (images) in the Internal Library of Images. In psychology, such situation is called a "double bind". E.g., if mother's attitude towards a child switches from overly affectionate to overly strict, it may lead to nervous and mental disorders up to schizophrenia. The Double Bind theory was described by Gregory Bateson and his colleagues in the 1950s [9]. The phenomenon of divarication (e.g., identical commands lead to different processes) in the artificial neuro-semantic graph is described in [10].

In the artificial cognitive system based on the Symbol-Images Cognitive Architecture (SICA), the absence or presence of instability (like divarication of images described above) or hyperstability may serve as a diagnostic factor. This implies that appearance of such double patterns could be treated as the indicator of anomaly.

Being applied to the goal of monitoring the state of industrial system, the model results in conclusion that certain set (sequence) of processes in the physical part of the system should correspond to a certain (identical) set of operator's commands. The observed divarication may be an indicator of a hacker's intrusion into the system.

V. Conclusions and Future Work

Since the robotic systems become more and more closely connected with humans, the importance of the intelligent systems that provide "personal sense" of the information, or the "emotional response" is constantly growing. However, modern neural networks, as a rule, do not provide any "personal interpretation" of the data received.

We propose a simple two-component hippocampus-inspired model of a cognitive system, which could fill that gap. In the artificial cognitive systems, this concept corresponds to embedding a certain module (block), which should be constructed to perform the main functions of the hippocampus.

The model has explanatory power for a range of psychological phenomena and is to be developed further. Furthermore, our hypothesis can be applied to industrial system for enhanced monitoring and protection.

Acknowledgments

The author is grateful to Sergey Sadovnikov, Andrey Lavrentyev, and Alexander Kharlamov for the fruitful discussions.

References

[1] O. D. Chernavskaya et al., "An architecture of the cognitive system with account for emotional component," Biologically Inspired Cognitive Architectures, vol. 12, pp. 144–154, 2015.

[2] A. V. Samsonovich, "Emotional biologically inspired cognitive architecture," Biologically Inspired Cognitive Architectures, vol. 6, pp. 109-125, 2013.

[3] M. Talanov, J. Vallverdú, S. Distefano, M. Mazzara, and R. Delhibabu, "Neuromodulating cognitive architecture: towards biomimetic emotional AI," IEEE 29th International Conference on Advanced Information Networking and Applications, pp. 587-592, 2015.

[4] O. D. Chernavskaya, D. S. Chernavskii, V. P. Karp, A. P. Nikitin, and D. S. Shchepetov, "An architecture of thinking system within the Dynamical Theory of Information," Biologically Inspired Cognitive Architectures, vol. 6, pp. 147--158, 2013.

[5] E. D. Kazimirova, "Elements of the symbol-image architecture of cognition and their parallelism to certain linguistic phenomena," "Нейрокомпьютеры" ("Neurocomputers"), vol. 4, pp 35-37, 2015. Available from: http://www.radiotec.ru/catalog.php?cat=jr7&art=16364 2017.02.06

[6] L. R. Squire, L. Genzel, J. T. Wixted, and R. G. Morris, "Memory consolidation," Digital Object Identifiers (DOIs): 10.1101/cshperspect.a021766 Available from: https://www.ncbi.nlm.nih.gov/pubmed/?term=26238360 2017.02.06

[7] J. T. Gonçalves, S. T. Schafer, and F. H. Gage, "Adult Neurogenesis in the Hippocampus: from Stem Cells to Behavior," Cell., vol. 167(4), pp. 897–914, 2016.

[8] S. M. Sadovnikov, S. V. Moiseev, and E. D. Kazimirova, "Utility function of intellectual agent and its self regulation," pp. 152—153, 2013 (in Russian). Available from: http://nd-cogsci.iapras.ru/2013/img/ND-2013.pdf 2017.02.06

[9] G. Bateson, D. D. Jackson, J. Haley, and J. Weakland, "Towards a Theory of Schizophrenia," Behavioral Science, vol. 1, pp. 251–264, 1956.

[10] A. B. Lavrentyev, "Neurosemantic approach and free energy minimization principle," The Sixth International Conference On Cognitive Science, pp. 68-70, 2014.

On the Possibility to Interpret Aesthetic Emotions and the Concept of Chef-D'oeuvre in an Artificial Cognitive System

Olga Chernavskaya
Lebedev Physical Institute (LPI)
Moscow, Russia
E-mail: olgadmitcher@gmail.com

Yaroslav Rozhylo
BICA Labs
Kyiv, Ukraine
E-mail: yarikas@gmail.com

Abstract— **The problem of interpretation and simulation of the Aesthetic Emotions (not inspired by a pragmatic goal, but by impression of Artwork, natural phenomena, etc.) is considered under the Natural-Constructive Approach to modeling the cognitive process. The designed cognitive architecture is represented by the complex multilevel combination of various types of neuroprocessors, with the whole system being composed of two subsystems, by analogy with the two hemispheres of the human brain. Only one subsystem involves mandatory random component (noise), and the noise-amplitude variation controls the subsystem activity representing the emotional responses. A peculiar feature of the architecture is the fuzzy set at the lowest ("image") hierarchy level. This neuroprocessor contains images of the objects recorded by weak ("grey") connections that reflect personal (unformulated) experience. It is shown that individual aesthetic preferences arise at the border of image (fuzzy set) and symbolic internal information. The concept of Chef-d'oeuvre is associated with the "paradox of recognition", which is caused by ambiguous impression (familiar and unusual simultaneously) induced by the Artwork. These impressions could be accompanied by small oscillation (trembling) of the noise amplitude around a normal value that represents an analogue to the human "goosebumps".**

Keywords – emotions; neuroprocessor; noise; paradox; ambiguity; weak connections.

I. Introduction

This paper represents a sequel to the series of works [1]–[4] on modeling intrinsic human cognitive features — intuition, emotions, individuality, etc., — in an artificial cognitive system. This problem is considered within the Natural-Constructive Approach (NCA) elaborated just for human-like cognition modeling on the base of Dynamical Theory of Information (DTI) [5][6], Neuroscience [7][8] and Neuropsychology [9] data, and Neurocomputing [10][12] (though based on the dynamical-formal-neuron concept, [1]). Among other popular approaches to modeling the cognitive systems, such as Active Agent models [13], Brain Re-Engineering [14][15], etc, NCA is somewhat similar to the Deep Learning paradigm [16][17] though it involves several important distinctive features.

The Natural-Constructive Cognitive Architecture (NCCA) designed under NCA represents a combination of two linked subsystems, in analogy with two cerebral hemispheres, the right (RH) and the left (LH) ones. Each subsystem represents a complex multi-level hierarchical structure of the two-type neuroprocessors. One subsystem (RH) is responsible for processing of new information and learning, while the other one (LH) refers to the processing of well-known information (recognition, forecast, etc.).

Being biologically inspired, NCCA (as well as each neuromorphic model) inevitably faced the problem of Explanatory Gap [18]. This implies that despite the huge amount of experimental information on brain neurons ("Brain" area) and on psychological reactions and rational thinking ("Mind" area), the main challenge is to reveal the mechanism of transition from neural ensemble to the consciousness and self-appraisal. It concerns rational, as well as emotional aspects of the cognitive process.

Note that one of the basic elements of NCA is DTI, the theory of information origin. It seems to be the most relevant tool to analyze the Explanatory Gap problem, since information itself represents the dual-nature object: it has material, as well as virtual nature. According to Quastler's definition [19], information is the "*memorized random choice of one option among several similar ones*". *Objective* (material) information is the choice made by Nature; it does not depend on individuality and refers to the "Brain" approach. *Subjective (conventional)* information represents the choice made by living subjects (people, animals, neurons) as a result of interaction within their community, which refers to the "Mind" sphere. Thus, NCA includes inherently the possibility to bridge the Gap.

The problem of incorporating the "emotio" and "ratio" in a unified cognitive (artificial) system attracts now great attention and evokes a lot of studies (see, e.g., [20]–[30]). However, the variety (great number) of different approaches itself indicates that the problem is far from being solved.

Under NCA, emotions are considered as a product of interaction of two different-nature variables. One belongs to the "Brain" representation and corresponds to the aggregated composition of neurotransmitters. The other refers to the "Mind" representation and corresponds to variation of the random-element (noise) amplitude. The activity of two subsystems is controlled by the emotional manifestation expressed via the noise-amplitude derivative. In this process, negative emotions (nervousness, fear) evoke RH activation, while positive ones (relaxation, relief, satisfaction) activate LH.

Note that the problem of integration of emotions and rational reasoning could be formulated and even solved, as far as so-called "pragmatic" emotions (those that are associated with certain goal) are concerned. In this case, quite obvious reasons should play the main role: achieving the goal results in positive emotions, and vice versa [2]. But what are the reasons for so-called Aesthetic Emotions (AE), i.e., those that are evoked by Nature phenomena (sunrise, rainbow, fire, water cascade, etc.), Artwork, Music, etc.? In this case, the very concept of "positive\negative" does not work, and one could soon speak about formed preferences. These emotions are strictly individual, with the reasons for personal sympathy and antipathy being often unclear for the person himself/herself.

Seemingly, there are no rational motives for personal sympathies and preferences, and that is why formalization and simulation of AE (i.e., interpreting in terms of neurons and their interactions) represents the most difficult problem. Moreover, this area is traditionally attributed not to natural sciences, but to the Humanities and Art study. Nevertheless, this work represents an attempt to reveal possible mechanisms that could cause AE.

The paper is organized as follows. Section II is focused on the formulation of the AE problem. In Section III, the main peculiar features of NCCA are discussed. In Section IV, the hypothesis on the mechanism of AE is presented. Summary and discussion of further working perspectives are presented in Section V.

II. Formalization of AE Problem

The problem of revealing the AE nature and mechanisms should be solved again from the "Brain" and "Mind" positions together. This implies that one has to take into account neurophysiology, as well as psychology and personal experience motives.

A. *General considerations*

Apparently, it is the cultural context that does play a very important role here. Indeed, something quite unknown, like, e.g., Japanese music for European people, could hardly evoke sincere emotions (may be academic interest only).

The other first-glance reasons for AE (see, e.g., [31]) could be connected with:

- childish vague impressions;
- personal fuzzy associations;
- the influence of cultural mini-media (family, messmates, etc.).

Actually, all these factors produce *subjective associations*, and this is the very mechanism of the Art perception. Indeed, the lack of clear goal that could provide "rational" emotions (i.e., those that could be explained by evident reasons) should be compensated by certain excitation caused by personal indirect (i.e., fuzzy, vague) associations. Surely, they are strictly individual, and this provides the explanation of personal impression.

Note that the Art perception, being quite subjective, could be measured objectively: really deep impression produces a "*goosebumps*" (horripilation), and this feeling is quite sincere and could not be shammed. Of course, one could express admiration remaining quite indifferent, but the "goosebumps" could not be felt if there are none.

But then, the question arises: what is the "masterpiece", or *Chef-D'oeuvre* (ChD)? Why a certain piece of Art is perceived as ingenious by almost the whole community? Surely, there is a great influence of the mass media (fashion). Generally speaking, there is a great temptation to define ChD as a "*product of convention in the society expressed in monetary ($) equivalent*". This factor actually works, but it cannot explain the phenomenon. There should be something inherent to the ChD itself, that does distinguish the ingenious creation from a solid professional work. In other words, what factors could provide the difference between Mozart and Salieri? And is it possible to explain personal Art preferences and the phenomenon of ChD from the positions of neuromorphic cognitive modeling? This problem is the subject of the present paper.

B. *Physiology & psychology*

Any piece of Art is perceived as sensor information, which is obtained by sensory organs. For example, any Painting represents (roughly speaking) a color pattern. It is well known from physiology that human beings differently perceive the excitations in different parts of the color spectrum. The visual perception is most sensitive in the *green* part of spectrum where the greatest number of various shades could be distinguished [32]. Vice versa, the red part of the spectrum awakes nervousness and involuntary fear (may be associated with the dangerous fire).

As far as the music is considered, its physical effect on the human organism is obvious. Indeed, the music, — from ancient times up to nowadays, — produces a rhythmic impact that does interfere with proper rhythms of the human brain (see, e.g., [24][33]). It is well known that only a part of the acoustic spectrum is pleasant for the human ear and could be perceived as music [33][34]. Some other frequencies (including the ultrasonic and infrasonic regions) do produce a strong but destructive effect on human psychical state, with the most "soft" manifestation being the uncontrolled nervousness and fear [24].

Perhaps, these peculiarities of human perception originated from the process of evolutionary adaptation to the Environment: certain really dangerous phenomena (e.g., earthquake) are accompanied by rare and unusual visual and acoustic effects, and this circumstance is sewn in the genetic memory of human beings. However, these reasons do not explain *individual* preferences concerning normal (pleasant) spectrum region.

Finally, what about the Literature? It does produce a significant effect on many people, but is not directly related with "raw" sensory perception. Thus, only the "Brain" representation cannot explain the AE enigma.

C. *Art Study*

The Art study seems to be more relevant to the problem under consideration. First of all, it does take into account the role of cultural context and the mentality of a given society. This partly explains why the recognition of some Artwork's ingenuity often does not come immediately but requires certain time: the society has to be *ready* to admit the pattern. In economy, the term "competence" is used to describe the social readiness to certain innovations. But the very mechanism of the competence occurrence is not clear and even considered.

However, the Art study is also divided into separated branches where specific regularities (common features) had been revealed.

1) Painting, Sculpture and Architecture: From the Leonardo times, they were studied even mathematically (the concepts of "Golden Section", "3D-perspective", etc.). However, such painting schools as *primitivism* (Pirosmani, Henry Russo) and *surrealism* (Salvatore Dali) do neglect the perspective, but some their patterns are nonetheless admitted as ChD.

2) Music: European and Eastern (Japanese and China) music representations (harmony) do differ essentially, with only a small number of people paying tribute to both musical patterns. European Music School is based on the concepts of *consonance* and *dissonance,* which correspond to different and definite ratio of the note frequencies within one chord. It appears that the consonance is pleasant for perception, and vice versa. However, great (ingenious) musical compositions from Mozart, Beethoven, Chopin, etc. do involve as consonances, as well as a quote of dissonances. Moreover, the patterns of *major* and *minor* music (well defined by the frequency ratios) produce different and again individual effect. Several studies (see [23][24]) have shown that the *major* music, in spite of its *bravura* character, often is not admitted, while the *minor* music, despite its somewhat tragic shadow (like the "Funeral March" of Chopin, or "Lacrimosa" of Mozart, or "Casta Diva" of Bellini), produces strong and rather *light* emotions.

3) Literature: This is the most mysterious Art, since it does not appeal directly to any organs of sense, but does produce strong impression to the majority of people. This process requires active *cooperation* of the author and the reader, since the effect could be produced only in the case if the reader would reproduce the situation described in the literature using the elements of his own personal experience. Hence, the key words here are *imagination* and *empathy.* However, these processes should be initiated by verbal information. But what is the mechanism of such effect?

Under NCA, all these problems could be formulated and even solved in terms of neurons and their connections.

III. NATURAL-CONSTRUCTIVE COGNITIVE ARCHITECTURE (NCCA)

Let us recall briefly the main features of the architecture NCCA developed in our previous works [1][2].

A. *Schematic representation of NCCA*

The schematic representation of NCCA is shown in Figure 1. The whole system represents complex multilevel block-hierarchical combination of the Hopfield [10] and Grossberg [11] type neuroprocessors. According to DTI principles [6], as well as neuropsychology data [9], the system is combined of two coupled subsystems, the right Hemi-system (RH) and the left Hemi-system (LH) by analogy to the cerebral hemispheres of human brain. One of them (RH) is responsible for learning the *new* information, the other (LH) does process the *well-known* information.

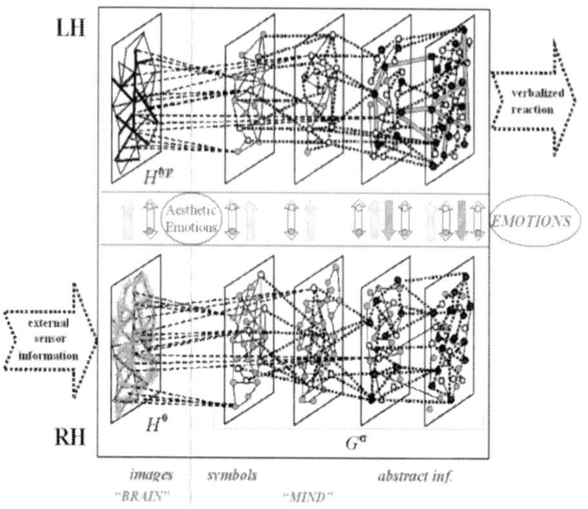

Figure 1. Schematic representation of NCCA.

This functional specialization is secured by three factors:

- the random component (noise) present in RH only;
- different training rules in the two subsystems: Hebbian principle [8] of frequently-used connection amplification in RH (providing the *choice*), and Hopfield's principle [10] of selecting relevant connections ("redundant cut-off") in LH;
- the "connection-blackening" principle of self-organization: well-trained images in RH are replicated in LH (see below).

According to these factors, the whole system does evolve by self-development (in Figure 1 — from the left to the right). The ground (zero) level is represented by two ***H***-type processors receiving the external information directly from the organs of sense. These "raw" images of real objects presented to the system are recorded in the form of certain *chain of neurons* (pure distributed memory).

All other levels $\sigma = 1,\ldots N$ are presented by ***G***-type processors carrying the *symbolic* information. It is necessary to stress that each generated symbol carries out all the information about its image in a compressed form [12]. Each symbol G^{σ} is linked by *semantic* connections $\Psi^{(\sigma-1)}$ with its "parent" image at the previous level and $\Psi^{(\sigma+1)}$ with its "child" symbol at the next level $\sigma+1$. Besides, it is linked with its neighbors by cooperative connections (which create that "current" image at the σ level).

Note that increasing level's number corresponds to increasing degree of "abstraction", that means the weaker relation with the neurons-progenitors (those directly connected with the organs of sense). The high-level symbols correspond to *abstract concepts*, which are not based on any raw image of real object, — such as *consciousness, conscience, love*, etc. It should be stressed that internal abstract symbol information can be *verbalized*, i.e., associated with the *words* by means of common *language*, and this stage represents the highest level of the system's evolution [33]. These very levels correspond to developed human consciousness that refers to the "Mind" sphere.

However, these high-level symbols could be excited from outside by words and then, decomposed to lower-level image-of-symbols down to the lowest image level. This process represents the mechanism of imagination.

B. *Mathematics &Phylosophy*

The mathematical grounds for the architecture presented in Figure 1 were discussed in details in the works [1][2][4]. Let us recall the key points and present the math basis in generalized form:

$$\frac{dH_i^0(t)}{dt} = \frac{1}{\tau_i^H}[\Im_H\{H,\beta_i(G^R{}_{\{i\}})\} + \sum_{i\neq j}^{n}\Omega_{ij}^{Hebb}H_j^0 + \sum_k \Psi_{ik}G_k{}^{R,1} - \Lambda(t)\cdot H_i^{typ}] + Z(t)\xi_i(t), \quad (1)$$

$$\frac{dH_i^{typ}(t)}{dt} = \frac{1}{\tau_i^H}[\Im_H\{H,\beta_i(G^L{}_{\{i\}})\} + \sum_{i\neq j}^{n}\Omega_{ij}^{Hopf}\cdot H_j^{typ} + \sum_k \Psi_{ik}\cdot G_k{}^{L,1} + \Lambda(t)\cdot H_i^0], \quad (2)$$

....

$$\frac{dG_k^{R,\sigma}}{dt} = \frac{1}{\tau_G}[\Im_G\{G_k,\alpha^\sigma{}_k(\{\Psi_{ik}^{R,(\sigma-1)}\},G^{\sigma+v})\} + \hat{Y}\{G_k^{R,\sigma},G_l^{R,(\sigma+v)}\} - \Lambda(t)\cdot G_k^{L,\sigma}] + Z(t)\cdot\xi(t), \quad (3)$$

$$\frac{dG_k^{L,\sigma}}{dt} = \frac{1}{\tau_G}[\Im_G\{G_k,\alpha^\sigma{}_k(\{\Psi_{ik}^{L,(\sigma-1)}\},G^{L,(\sigma+v)})\} + \hat{Y}\{G_k^{L,\sigma},G_l^{L,(\sigma+v)}\} + \Lambda(t)\cdot G_k^{R,\sigma}], \quad (4)$$

$$\frac{dZ(t)}{dt} = \frac{1}{\tau^Z}\cdot[a_{Z\mu}\cdot\mu + a_{ZZ}\cdot(Z-Z_0) + F_Z(\mu,Z) + X\{\mu,G_k^{R,\sigma}\} + \{\chi\cdot(D-\omega\cdot dD/dt) - \eta\cdot\delta(t-t_{D=0})\}], \quad (5)$$

$$\frac{d\mu}{dt} = \frac{1}{\tau^\mu}\cdot[a_{\mu\mu}\cdot\mu + a_{\mu Z}\cdot(Z-Z_0) + F_\mu(\mu,Z)], \quad (6)$$

$$\Lambda(t) = -\Lambda_0\cdot th\left(\gamma\cdot\frac{dZ}{dt}\right). \quad (7)$$

Here, variables H and G refer to purely "cognitive" components, which are associated with neocortex structures. The functionals $\Im_H$ and $\Im_G$ describe internal dynamics of corresponding neurons; the functionals $Y^R\{G_k^R\}$ and $Y^L\{G_k^L\}$ describe interaction of symbols at various levels.

The bottom block of equations (5)–(7) refers to representation of emotions. The variable $\mu(t)$ represents purely "emotional" component produced by sub-cortical ("Brain") structures; it represents the effective composition of neurotransmitters (the difference between stimulants and inhibitors). The variable $Z(t)$ represents the amplitude of random (stochastic) component presented in RH only. The functional $X\{\mu,G_k^{R\sigma}\}$ refers to the process of new symbol formation; the discrepancy $D(t)$ describes the difference in RH and LH records of the same real object.

The variable $\Lambda(t)$ refers to the cross-subsystem connections, which provide the dialog between two subsystems. Here, $\Lambda = +\Lambda_0$ corresponds to RH→LH transfer, while $\Lambda = -\Lambda_0$ corresponds to LH→RH. Note that this is the only variable present in each of the seven equations, thus *sewing* all the components together.

This system of equations is complete (in math sense), since all the variables are determined via their mutual interactions. The first two equations refer to the lowest (zero) level of hierarchy, while the next (G^σ variables) describe $\sigma=1,\ldots N$ symbolic levels. Note that the dotted line between two first equations and the other equations indicates the analogy with the dotted line in Figure 1. This line symbolizes the virtual border between the "Brain" and the "Mind". Indeed, the *H*-plates (zero-level of the hierarchy) containing only the "raw images", serve to represent the sensory information received from the organs of sense. This information is (roughly speaking) objective, and this level belongs to the "Brain".

The first level (σ=1) corresponds to the symbols of typical images. It already belongs to the "Mind", since any symbol represents not objective, but conventional, i.e., *subjective* and *individual* (for a given system) information. The same is true for all other hierarchy levels, up to the highest level associated with the abstract information. Hence, any symbolic information refers to the "Mind".

Thus, we can infer that the phenomena appearing at the transition from the "Brain" to the "Mind" occur at the virtual border between zero and first levels.

C. *Formation of Two Basic Levels of NCCA*

Let us consider in more details the small fragment of the architecture NCCA — the lower (basic) levels corresponding to σ = 0, 1 (see Figure 2). The *H*-type plates (σ=0) are responsible for recording the raw sensory information in the form of distributed memory. This implies that each external real object presented to the system excites

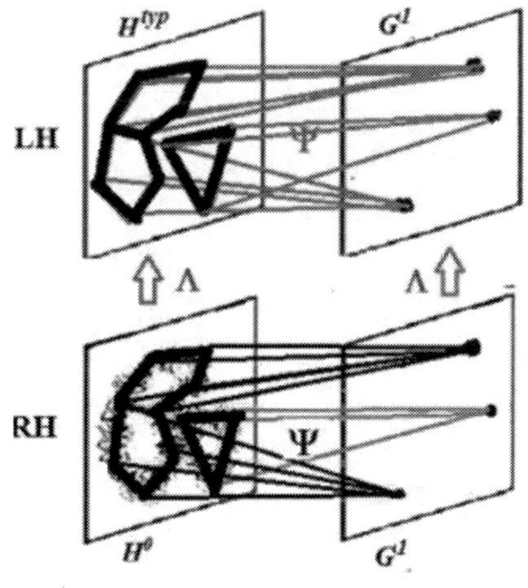

Figure 2. A fragment of two basic levels of NCCA.

a chain of neurons, which is called the "*image*". The *choice* of those neurons (i.e., generation of information) proceeds in RH with required participation of the noise. Then, the connections in the chain are to be trained according to Hebb's principle of amplifying the frequently-used connection (see Figure 3a).

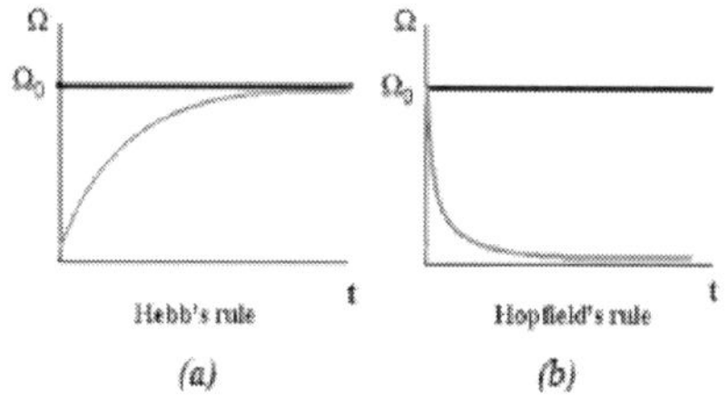

Figure 3. Dynamics of neuron's connection *Ω(t)* training for (a) Hebb's rule and (b) Hopfield's rule.

The plate H^0 contains maximum information on each object whenever presented to the system, i.e., all generated connections, as weak ("grey"), as well as strong ("black") ones. Let us clarify this point.

Note that each presentation of the same object results in activation of slightly different set of neurons. Let us introduce the notions:

- "*Core*" neurons — the neurons that are excited at each presentation of the given object. These neurons form strong ("black") connections between them, thus providing the "*typical image*" of the object, representing its *typical attributes.*
- "*Halo*" neurons — a part (and by far not a small one) of neurons that are excited relatively rarely, at some *atypical* presenting and/or reflect *atypical* (inessential) *attributes* of the given object. The connections between them and core neurons are weaker ("grey"), so that they surround the core neurons forming a grey "halo" *blurring* the typical image (that is why H^0 was called the *fuzzy* set).

The "connection-blackening" principle implies that when the main bulk of connections between the core neurons become strong enough, i.e., achieve the level of so called "black" connections Ω_0, the image is treated as learned (well-known) or "typical" one. Such images are transferred (by the direct one-to-one cross-subsystem Λ connections) to the plate H^{typ} in LH for memorization and storage. Then, all connections in LH are trained according to the Hopfield's rule that corresponds to *selection* of relevant connections at the "black" level of Ω_0, with diminishing other (redundant) connections (see Figure 3b).

The next step of the system's self-organized evolution consists in conversion of the image into symbol. It was shown in [1][4] that in NCCA, this procedure corresponds to generation of the *conventional* (*subjective*) information. After the typical image (the chain of core neurons) is transferred to the plate G^1 in RH, the free *choice* of a single neuron-symbol occurs as a result of the competitive interaction (see Figure 2). Then again, according to the connection-blackening principle, after the *semantic* connections Ψ^R (one-to-many) between the chosen symbol and its image became strong ("black") enough, the symbol is replicated in LH. Here, it forms its semantic connections Ψ^L with the typical image according to Hopfield's training principle of selecting relevant connections.

Let us stress that only the core neurons are involved into the typical image of the given object. Under NCA, these core neurons are modified to be excited directly by corresponding symbol. Moreover, at relatively high (verbalized) levels of hierarchy, the typical images could be excited by means of corresponding *words*.

The halo neurons, in spite of their participation in the training process, are not connected with any symbol (and thus, with any word), hence they could not be controlled by the "Mind". The information on the halo neurons together with their gray connections is stored in the *fuzzy set* H^0 only and could be activated just occasionally (by chance); this very process represents the "*insight*".

Finally, it is very important to stress that in the process of transition from H^0 to H^{typ}, a part of associative connections between the raw images also could be lost. In Figure 2, bottom part (RH), all the presented images are connected associatively. In the upper part (LH), one image appears to be quite separated from two others (connected objectively), since its connections with them were mediated only by the halo-neurons.

Thus, the fuzzy set plays a very important and enigmatic role in the cognitive process. Actually, it could be treated as the *sub-consciousness* filled with personal subjective associations and motives. Returning to possible reasons of AE listed above — namely, childish vague impressions, personal fuzzy (indirect) associations, etc., — we can infer that the source of AE is hidden just in the fuzzy set H^0.

Note that hidden (latent) information appears also at the higher levels of hierarchy. Generalized images, i.e., images created by a set of symbols, also involve their core neuron-symbols, as well as halo-symbols that are presented in RH only and not transferred to the corresponding level in LH. Hence, this part of latent information (auxiliary and individual for a given system) representing its casual (episodic) experience could be associated with the *intuition.* These halo-symbols refer to not so deeply hidden information and could be activated by certain (again occasional) *words.* These triggering words may have no relation to the current problems, but could switch on the chain of indirect (personal) association and thus, lead to unexpected (intuitive) solution also looking like insight.

Thus, we infer that the motives for AE are connected with the halo-neurons (including halo-symbols).

IV. Approaches to AE Nature and Phenomenon of Chef-D'oeuvre

Any cognitive process is based on the *recognition* of an object\phenomenon\situation and its *trend*, i.e., the *anticipation* (forecast). And the forecast is based on the first impressions in the process of recognition. In the presence of a rational goal, this process always is accompanied by pronounced emotions. Under NCA, emotional manifestation is directly connected with the noise-amplitude derivative

dZ/dt defined by (6), which controls the subsystem activity (Λ). According to (6)–(7), negative emotions (nervousness, fear) correspond to incorrect recognition ($dZ/dt>0$) and activation of RH ($\Lambda<0$), consequently. Vice versa, correct recognition and prognosis results in decreasing noise amplitude ($dZ/dt<0$) with switching on LH ($\Lambda>0$), which is accompanied by relaxation, satisfaction, etc. Let us consider certain details of these processes.

A. Recognition & Prognosis

The procedures of recognition and prognosis were considered in details in our works [3][4]. It was shown that recognition goal can be achieved by means of the low levels $\sigma=0$ ("images") and $\sigma=1$ (typical-image symbols). The examinee object is recorded in H^0 and compared with known (learned) typical images in H^{typ}. Further procedure is controlled by the value of discrepancy $D_0(t)$ between the **RH** and **LH** zero-level records, which can be defined as:

$$D_{\sigma=0}(t) \equiv \sum_i \left\| H_i^{typ} - H_i^0 \right\|, \qquad (8)$$

where summation proceeds over excited neurons.

There are several typical regimes.

- The examinee object is well-known to the system, i.e., its image completely coincides with one of typical images, so that $D(0)=0$. Then, it is associated with corresponding symbol in LH, and RH does not participate further in the process. Emotional manifestations are absent ($dZ/dt=0$).
- The examinee object is *similar* to one of the known typical images (fits its "attracting area"), $D(0)\neq 0<D_{cr}$. Then, it is treated as an already known object: it has its typical image together with the corresponding symbol G^{L1}. Here, however, the recognition accuracy requires verification. For this purpose, the symbol should be transferred to RH for decomposition, and the result is compared with the examinee image. Here, the discrepancy provokes repeating, and the procedure should pass over several iterations. This corresponds to dumping oscillation of the noise amplitude dZ/dt (see Figure 4a) representing the emotional fluctuations.
- The examinee object is unknown to the system ($D>D_{cr}$). This provokes the recognition failure, that is accompanied (depending on the final goal) by either zero, or negative emotion manifestations. Then, the full procedure of new image formation and recording to H^{typ} is to be performed.

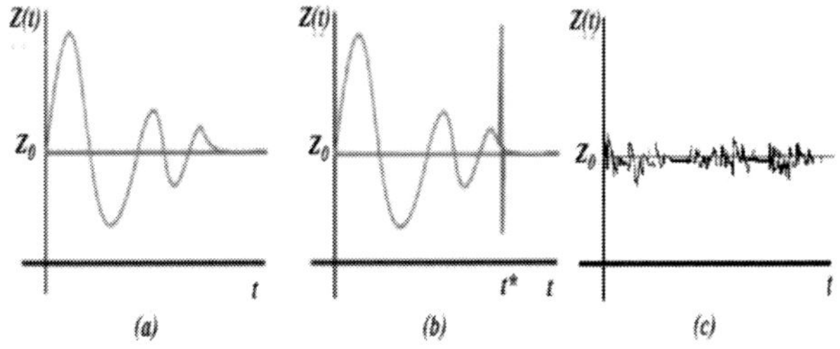

Figure 4. Typical patterns of the noise amplitude $Z(t)$ behavior in the cases of (a) recognition procedure; (b) incorrect prognosis with sense of humor manifestation, and (c) Aesthetic Emotions ("goosebumps").

The *prognosis* represents the recognition of time-dependent process and proceeds in a similar way. Special case of incorrect prognosis, which activates the sense of humor has been discussed in [3][4]. It appears when examinee process seems familiar up to some moment t^*, but the next bulk of information appears to be once unexpected, but still well-known. This switches the recognition process to the other, also familiar pattern. This corresponds to the specific reaction of the system, — namely, sharp up-down jump ("spike") in the noise amplitude, which could be associated with human *laughter* (see Figure 4b).

B. Interpretation of AE: "Recognition Paradox"

Perception of any Artwork represents a particular case of recognition-and-anticipation procedure (see, e.g., [24]). Contrary to everyday life, when recognition is a part of behavioral program and connected with obvious and rational goal, the Artwork does not require any actions, so that the goal of such anticipation is not pragmatic, but rather latent. It could be connected with certain dissatisfaction, i.e., *ambiguous impression* produced by the piece of Art, which does not allow to put it in line with any known symbol (and consequently, with a certain word). Differently speaking, AE arise when the impression cannot be formulated and explained.

According with the above consideration, AE appear if the examinee object\phenomenon does excite the *halo neurons* in RH. Since they are *not* connected with any specific symbol and thus, such impressions remain unconscious, this gives rise to a "vague effect" that could not be formalized or verbalized; these very impressions produce tingling sensations called the "goosebumps" (or "horripilation"). This also implies that the discrepancy $D(t)$ defined by (8) could never come to zero since information on halo neurons is absent in LH**,** but its value is small. Hence, the "goosebumps" correspond to small vibration (*trembling*) of $Z(t)$ around the normal value (Figure 4c).

According to this hypothesis, strong AE, which can be treated as personal impression produced by the masterpiece (ChD), could be caused by the "*recognition paradox*". This phenomenon can take place in at least two cases.

1) Recognition paradox #1: It appears if the Art object is very similar to something well known, despite some minor and even *unconscious* (by the first glance) difference (light *inaccuracy),* which involves the halo-neurons only. Then, $D(0)=D(t)\neq 0$, but this discrepancy could not be comprehended and explained by words. The most pronounced example of such painting ChD is the "Black Square" of Malevich, which appears to be neither square, nor monotone black. This pattern contains actually small (and even invisible) deviations in lines and color, and these differences could be measured objectively. Hence, the eyes (i.e., the "Brain", not the "Mind") do actually notice this inaccuracy, and this provides some ambiguous impression of dissatisfaction producing AE. Speaking picturesquely, this feeling may be expressed by the formula "*to see invisible*".

Thus, in this case, the paradox consists in the fact that small and incomprehensible deviations of ChD from the ordinary pattern emphasize its individuality.

2) Recognition paradox #2: ChD looks like *several* familiar patterns simultaneously, so it could not be recognized as any of them. It could be linked with all of them by associative *"grey"* connections in RH (via the "halo"-neurons), while in LH, all these patterns with corresponding symbols are separated. Such type of ChD activates fuzzy subjective associations, which were stored in RH but lost in LH. In other words, the "Brain" does know it, but the "Mind" cannot formulate and comprehend.

Perception of such ChD is to a large extent similar to manifestation of the sense of humor, but in this case, the incorrect (ambiguous) prognosis cannot be turned to a new familiar symbol and the corresponding word, i.e., again cannot be formulated and explained.

Striking examples of such type ChD are the great musical compositions of Mozart, Beethoven, Chopin, Wagner, etc., which have something insensibly in common with each other (classical), as well as with the older traditional (often folk) music (see, e.g., [33]).

Speaking picturesquely, this impression could be formulated as *"to unite unconnectable"*.

3) General formula of ChD: In both these cases of recognition paradox, LH could not perform alone the recognition task, so that RH should be activated. This is the mechanism of AE appearance. Both these pathways lead to the feeling of ChD and realize the formula: "*to see invisible, to unite unconnectable*". Accounting for participation of the halo-neurons, we may rephrase this formula as "*the "Brain" does already know, while the "Mind" still cannot realize*".

Let us point out to the interesting consequence of the "halo-neuron hypothesis". It implies that halo-neurons do accompany the corresponding *core* neurons. It means that the system actually has recorded and memorized similar (but not identical) patterns. In other words, the system has its own experience with the patterns of a given type and hence, has sufficiently large *repertoire* (expertise) in such area. Nevertheless, relatively inexperienced ("green") system could perceive ChD, but only in those parts, which are familiar to the system itself. This effect corresponds to the formula "*each person has its own vision of ChD*".

Note that the presented hypothesis provides a key to the explanation of another enigma: why the pleasure of favorite Art patterns does not lose its luster after multiple acts of perception? In contrast to a joke, which provides the impression due to an element of unexpectedness and its subsequent resolution, the recognition paradox has *no resolution:* an ambiguous feeling arises whenever this Artwork is presented.

V. Conclusion and Further Work

Thus, it is shown that NCCA contains inherent possibility to reveal the mechanism of Aesthetic Emotions (AE) appearance. The whole architecture represents a combination of two multilevel subsystems, in analogy with two hemispheres of human brain. One of them (RH) processes any new, unexpected or ambiguous information. The other one is dealing with familiar (well known), i.e., clearly formulated information. The role of each subsystem in solving the current problem should be controlled by *emotions* (in particular, AE).

It is shown that the AE reasons are stored at the ground ("image") level of the architecture in the RH subsystem, which is called the *fuzzy set* $\boldsymbol{H^0}$. This neuroprocessor contains the whole information whenever recorded. In particular, it involves insignificant (at the first glance) information stored in weak ("grey") connections between so-called "halo" neurons, which correspond to *atypical* (inessential) attributes of real objects. This information is hidden in RH only and is transferred neither to LH nor to the high (symbolic) hierarchy levels of RH, hence could be neither formulated nor comprehended.

According to our main hypothesis, the mechanism of AE consists in excitation of personal subjective (may be *vague*) *associations* provided by weak connections via halo neurons. These associations could not be formulated and verbalized, thus, comprehended. Within NCCA, these excitations correspond to small oscillation ("trembling") of the noise amplitude $Z(t)$ that could be treated as analogy to human feeling of "goosebumps".

This hypothesis provides the possibility to explain several *enigmas* connected with AE*:*

- This explains the individuality of AE;
- This involves all the intuitively obvious reasons for AE listed above — childish vague impressions, fuzzy associations, indirect influence of micro-society, etc.
- Deep AE, i.e., personal feeling of ChD could be caused by the *recognition paradox*, which arises when the Artwork seems *familiar* and *unusual* simultaneously, with this impression being not formulated and explained.
- In aphoristic form, the feeling of ChD can be presented as "*to see invisible, to unite unconnectable*".
- Perception of any Artwork requires proper personal *repertoire* (competence, erudition, etc.) stored as in episodic (RH), as well as in semantic (LH) memory. Otherwise, the system remains quite indifferent to any piece of Art including ChD. This explains the "enigma of blind and deaf".
- The mechanisms providing sense of humor and AE actually have something in common. However, the sense of humor is caused by *unexpectedness* (surprise), which could be still recognized immediately. But AE arise in the case of *ambiguous* (*paradoxical*) impression that remains unformulated (hence, unrecognized) even in the long run. That is why a joke, repeated twice, does not cause a specific reaction (laughter), while favorite Artwork (ChD) always causes another specific reaction ("goosebumps").

Returning to the Explanatory Gap challenge, we can infer that the study of AE, being seemingly not a scientific problem (rather Humanities and Art study), actually provides the possibility to "*open a gate*" to the gap between "Brain" and "Mind". It is shown that AE emerge (as indicated in Figure 1) at that virtual border. Then, general formula "to see invisible, to unite unconnectable" could be expressed in more constructive (still aphoristic) form:

"Brain does already know, while Mind cannot still realize". And this very ambiguity provides the feeling of ChD.

Let us emphasize that all these reasons are inherently connected with NCA grounds. This is DTI that point out the role of *conventional* (*subjective*) information as a whole, and the role of a symbol as a *representative* of this information in particular. According to NCA viewpoint, the symbol is the very first object that, being relied on the "Brain" area, represents a "molecule of the Mind". And this is the technique of nonlinear differential equations that enable us to describe the procedure of symbol formation and the point where weak ("grey") connections appear to be lost.

It should be stressed that all these arguments represent not an instruction for ChD production, and not the method to estimate the value of ChD. The study represents only an attempt to understand the *mechanisms of perception* of the Art as a whole and ChD in particular. Nonetheless, this study can be used in social surveys, highly targeted advertising, and other social actions.

However, we have not discussed here the phenomenon of "socially accepted ChD" — why the significant part of society (not only certain persons) does feel a "goosebumps" caused by certain (ingenious) piece of Art? The mechanism could be similar, but this problem requires further work.

REFERENCES

[1] O. D. Chernavskaya, D. S. Chernavskii, V. P. Karp, A. P. Nikitin, and D. S. Shchepetov, "An architecture of thinking system within the Dynamical Theory of Information," BICA, vol. 6, pp. 147—158, 2013.

[2] O. D. Chernavskaya et al., "An architecture of the cognitive system with account for emotional component," BICA, vol.12, pp. 144—154, 2015.

[3] O. D. Chernavskaya and Ya. A. Rozhylo, "On the Possibility to imitate the Emotions and "Sense of Humor" in an Artificial Cognitive System," The Eighth Int. Conf. on Advanced Cognitive Technologies and Applications (COGNITIVE), IARIA, March 2016, pp. 42—48, 2016; ISBN: 978-1-61208-462-6.

[4] O. D. Chernavskaya and Ya. A. Rozhylo, "The Natural-Constructive Approach to Representation of Emotions and a Sense of Humor in an Artificial Cognitive System," IARIA Journal of Life Sciences, vol. 8(3&4), pp. 184—202, 2016.

[5] H. Haken, Information and Self-Organization: A macroscopic approach to complex systems. Springer, 2000.

[6] D. S. Chernavskii, Synergetics and Information. Dynamical Theory of Information. Moscow, URSS, 2004 (in Russian).

[7] J. Panksepp and L. Biven, The Archaeology of Mind: Neuroevolutionary Origins of Human Emotions. N.Y.: Norton, 2012.

[8] D. O. Hebb, The organization of behavior. John Wiley & Sons, 1949.

[9] E. Goldberg, The new executive brain. Oxford University Press, 2009.

[10] J. J. Hopfield, "Neural networks and physical systems with emergent collective computational abilities," PNAS, vol. 79, p. 2554, 1982.

[11] S. Grossberg, Studies of Mind and Brain. Boston: Riedel, 1982.

[12] T. Kohonen, Self-Organizing Maps. Springer, 2001.

[13] J. E. Laird, The Soar cognitive architecture. MIT Press, 2012.

[14] L. F. Koziol and D. E. Budding, Subcortical Structures and Cognition. Implications for Neurophysiological Assessment. Springer, 2009.

[15] K. Doya, "Complementary roles of basal ganglia and cerebellum in learning and motor control," Current Opinion in Neurobiology, vol. 10, pp. 732—739, 2000.

[16] Y. Bengio and Y. LeCun, Scaling learning algorithms towards AI. In: Large Scale Kernel Mashines, L. Botton, O. Chapelle, D. DeCoste, and J. Weston (Eds.), MIT Press, 2007.

[17] Y. LeCun, Y. Bengio, and G. Hinton, "Deep Learning," Nature, vol. 521, pp. 436–444, 2015.

[18] J. Levin, "Materialism and Qualia: The Explanatory Gap," Pacific Philosophical Quarterly, vol. 64(4), pp. 354–361, 1983.

[19] H. Quastler, The emergence of biological organization. New Haven: Yale University Press, 1964.

[20] A. Samsonovich, "Emotional biologically inspired cognitive architecture," BICA, vol. 6, pp. 109—125, 2013.

[21] E. Hudlyka, "Affective BICA: Challenges and open questions," BICA, vol. 7, pp. 98—125, 2014.

[22] M. I. Rabinovich and M. K. Muezzinoglu, "Nonlinear dynamics of the brain: emotions and cognition," Physics-Uspehi, vol. 53, pp. 357—372, 2010.

[23] J. Schmidhuber, "Simple algorithmic theory of subjective beauty, novelty, surprise, interestingness, attention, curiosity, creativity, science, music, jokes," Journal of Science, vol. 48 (1), pp. 21—32, 2009.

[24] D. Huron, Sweet Anticipation: music and physiology of expectation. MIT Press, 2006.

[25] C. L. Dancy, "ACT-R<PHI>: A cognitive architecture with physiology and affect," BICA, vol. 6, pp. 40—45, 2013.

[26] E. M. Izhikevich and G. M. Edelman, "Large-scale model of mammalian thalamocortical systems," PNAS, vol. 105 (9), pp. 3593—3598, 2008.

[27] O. Larue, P. Poirier, and R. Nkambou, "The emergence of (artificial) emotions from cognitive and neurological processes," BICA, vol. 4, pp. 54—68, 2013.

[28] M. Sellers, "Toward a comprehensive theory of emotion for biological and artificial agents," BICA, vol. 4, pp. 3—26, 2013.

[29] J. Valerdu et al., "A cognitive architecture for the implementation of emotions in computing systems," BICA, vol. 15, pp. 34—40, 2016.

[30] R. Kushiro K., Y. Harada, and J. Takeno, "Robot uses emotions to detect and learn the unknown," BICA, vol. 4, pp. 69—78, 2013.

[31] R. Solso, Cognitive psychology (5th ed.). Needham Heights, MA: Allyn & Bacon, 1998.

[32] V. L. Bianki, "Parallel and sequential information processing in animals as a function of different hemispheres," Neuroscience and Behavioral Physiology, vol. 14 (6), pp. 497-501, 1984.

[33] M. Korsakova-Kreyn and W. J. Dowling, "Emotional Processing in Music: Study in Affective Responses to Tonal Modulationin Controlled Harmonic Progressions and Real Music," Psychomusicology: Music, Mind and Brain, vol. 24(1), pp. 4—20, 2014.

[34] T. W. Deacon, The symbolic species: the co-evolution of language and the brain. N.Y.: Norton, 1997.

Enhancing Learning Objects for Digital Education

Tiago Thompsen Primo
Samsung Research Institute
Campinas, Brazil
Email: tiagoprimo@gmail.com

Abstract—**This research presents a method to describe Learning Objects as Semantic Web compatible Ontologies. The proposed method divides the Ontologies among three layers. The first is composed of the knowledge domain, the second by the Learning Objects (LOs) and their relations, and the third is responsible for knowledge inference and reasoning. As study case, we present the Ontologies of Learning Object Metadata (LOM) and Brazilian Metadata for Learning Objects (OBAA) metadata standards as part of the Layer One. The Layer Two composed by the description of sample Learning Objects based on the properties and restrictions defined by the Layer One ontologies. Layer Three describes the knowledge inference axioms, which we defined as Application Profiles. Our current results can summarize a contribution to Ontology Engineering for Semantic Web applied to Digital Education.**

Keywords–Digital Education; Adaptive Learning; Computational Intelligence; Mobile Computing; Smart Environments.

I. Introduction

Technology Enhanced Learning has the purpose of easing the knowledge retention and improve the learning performance in formal, non-formal or informal environments. Researchers and companies are always exploring new educational methodologies and artificial intelligence algorithms seeking to find the "secret recipe" to help teachers increase the educational performance of their students.

Despite current achievements, [1], [2], [3], are skeptic regarding formal learning in classrooms. According to these authors, there is no clear evidence that the usage of technology in classroom environments can increase the learning retention. We believe that there are two main causes for that: (i)the lack of standardized technological artifacts (Learning Objects) for sharing of educational content between students and educators [4], [5], [6] and (ii) the focus on the role of technology as support to current pedagogical models, provide class statistical analysis[7], [8] and enhance ludic experiences. This research will focus on the item (i).

Nowadays, we have a plethora of alternatives to access information. Television, the Internet, and mobile devices are platforms that ease the access to several kinds of educational contents. Many of them are hard to reuse [9]. The challenge resides in designing Learning Objects that are standardized, easy to share and able to leave a trace of performance measures among its application in different educational domains.

To deal with such complex domain that involves variables such as usage context, academic profile, cognitive styles, among many others, we believe that the technologies of the Semantic Web [10] and the Knowledge Representation and Reasoning [11] seem to be promising.

The contributions for educational systems can be classified in three areas [12]: (1) Information Storage and Retrieval; (2) Autonomous Agents and Artificial Intelligence Inference and (3) Communication and Information Persistence over time. In this research, we are focusing on Information Storage and Retrieval.

Considering this, we must comply with variables that are related to the learning progress of a student. It is perceived from many perspectives (e.g., Pedagogy, Philosophy, Psychology, Human Computer Interaction) [13]. It became necessary to design a flexible and interoperable approach to model the Learning Object and those variables inside educational environments [14], [15], [16]. We believe that this is the first step to achieving large-scale personalization [17], [18] in educational systems.

Therefore, we propose a method to use the standards and technologies of Semantic Web associated with ontological representations to describe Learning Objects. Also, we present our findings and experiences developing and deploying Semantic Web Learning Objects.

The rest of the paper is structured as follows. Section II presents detailed information regarding the built Knowledge Representation; Section III discusses the challenges and opportunities to explore this work further and, in Section IV, we provide our concluding remarks and future work.

II. Building the Knowledge Representation

The users in educational domains can be classified according to their roles. They can be teachers, students, tutors, administrators, between several other classifications; Learning Objects are digital or non-digital; and the relationships between the user(s) × Learning Object and user × user, have several associated properties. For example, Learning Objects can be associated with content relation; users can be related to authorship or activity like assessment, sharing or reading.

There are alternatives in the Knowledge representation and reasoning area to represent this kind of domain. We choose to use Ontologies due to their popularity and availability of design tools for Semantic Web. Web Ontology Language (OWL) ontologies were the most nature choice since it is based on description logics. This representation allows to cope with incomplete information and also to manage consistency check of the students profile during information updates.

The proposed ontologies are divided into three layers. The Layer One is composed of ontologies that describe metadata schemas, for instance, the Learning Object Metadata (LOM) Ontology; Layer Two ontologies describes a User Profile, Learning Objects or their relationships with properties from a Layer One Ontology; and Layer Three Ontologies comprehend the description of Applications Profiles that will provide reasoning over the Layer One and Layer Two.

To describe the method we use several key terms of OWL ontologies: **Class:** describe concepts of a domain, a structure that can encompass a set of Data Properties or Object Properties and individuals; **Properties:** is a binary relation on individuals; **Object Properties:** relations between individuals; **Data Properties:** relationships among individuals and an eXtensible Markup Language (XML) Schema Datatype value or a literal; **Axiom:** a premise or a point to begin the reasoning process; **Range:** links a property to either a class description or a data range; **Domain:** it is used to link a property to a class description; **Cardinality:** it is a restriction, defines the maximum or minimum number of individuals to link with a property; **Individuals:** represent the objects in the domain that we are interested in.

A. Describing Layer One Ontologies

The first thing to consider is the application domain: A Standard for User Profile representation; an educational metadata standard; a relationship standard; among other possible top layer descriptions.

The Layer One ontologies are used to describe classes and properties that are used to represent individuals in the Layer Two ontologies. This layer stores ontology with the semantics of a metadata schema, considering: cardinality; data ranges; association properties; and the necessary axioms to describe the application domain.

For example, Layer One ontologies can comprehend LOM Metadata Standard [19]; Brazilian Metadata for Learning Objects (OBAA) metadata standard [20] or Friend of a Friend (FOAF) metadata standard. The nature of those ontologies regards properties to describe a context, a domain or their members.

To design Layer One ontologies, we propose the following set of practices: Metadata classes became OWL Class and OWL Subclass; Metadata Properties became OWL Data Properties and OWL Object Properties according to their semantic; We describe the semantics of metadata as restriction axioms.

Building Layer One Ontologies regards the definition of the properties that are necessary to describe the Layer Two individuals and the Layer Three ontologies Application Profiles.

We define a few steps to follow to describe this kind of ontology:

- Study and understand the whole standard;
- define the set of Classes and Properties exactly like the standard incorporating their Ranges and Cardinalities;
- choose a Reasoner to test the ontology;
- provide a Universal Resource Identifier (URI) to publish the ontology.

To exemplify the design of Layer One Ontology, we will use as case study the LOM Metadata Standard for three reasons: LOM is considered an international standard to describe Learning Objects [21]; It is commonly used by researchers in educational technology, and, there is an opportunity to describe a standardized LOM OWL ontology.

LOM is a massive educational standard. We will define some classes and properties. The chosen LOM group (LifeCycle) is sophisticated enough (cardinality restrictions, domain, and range restriction) to demonstrate our method. The LOM ontology is available to reuse through the following URI [22].

We choose to present the study case using the LOM LifeCycle group because of its characteristics. It is relatively small but preserves the semantic complexity of the larger groups, such as General or Educational. Following we present the Classes and Properties described according to our ontology engineering approach. The LifeCycle group shows the LOM metadata Standard group 2.

a) Defining the Classes: Each metadata from LifeCycle group becomes a class and a subclass with cardinality restrictions according to the chosen standards. For instance, Contribute is a subclass of Life Cycle and has a cardinality *max* 30.

b) Defining the Properties: Properties can be classified as Data Properties or Object Properties. Data Properties are the data itself (e.g., *has_name* String "James"). Object Properties describe the relationships between classes and individuals (e.g. *has_classes*). Object Properties are also associated with the metadata cardinality (e.g., Max 10 *has_classes*)

The cardinality restrictions can be used with Object Properties. They can be used to group individuals with specific characteristics. As an illustrative example of those relationships, refer to Figure 1.

In Figure 1, at its center, it is illustrated a sample **Learning Objects Individual** that is divided into two parts. The number one (1), shows a generic Learning Objects representation model; The number two (2) illustrates the usage of the Object Properties Contribute, in this case, named LOM:hasContribute. As can it be seen, there are three individuals represented. The higher Layer **Learning Objects Individual** and two other ontological individuals linked by the Object Properties LOM:hasContribute and each one of them with specific Data Properties.

This kind of relationship allows, for instance, the reuse of the individuals **LO + LOM:hasContribute + ID1** and/or **LO + LOM:hasContribute + ID1** in different versions of Learning Objects.

This example was prepared to exemplify the description of Learning Objects with such ontology engineering method; the next section will present the characteristics of the Layer Two Ontologies.

B. Describing Layer Two Ontologies

The Layer Two ontologies have the role in describing User Profiles, Learning Objects and their relationships during their life-cycle in an application domain. These ontologies import the properties of the *n* Layer One ontologies allowing the standardized description of individuals.

These ontologies can be stored in some formal repository, e.g., a Triple-Store, or even just defining a URI for its access. This alternative gives flexibility to content designers that can only build and publish their contents on the Web.

As a plus, it is possible to apply reasoning algorithms to verify the consistency of an individual trough some Layer One ontology. For instance, if we describe a Learning Object as an ontological individual of the LOM Layer One ontology, we can verify if the cardinality, range, and value space were correctly used. Also, if some description is incorrect we can apply an *explanation* algorithm to understand what was described wrong.

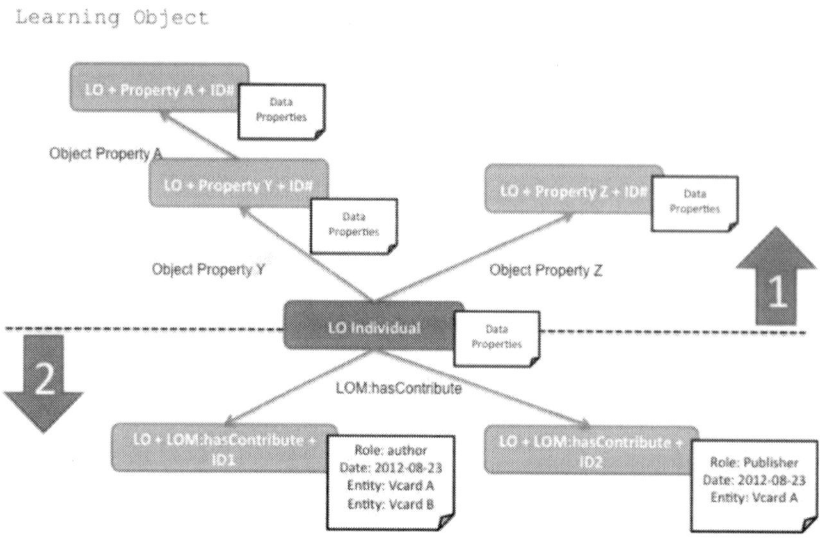

Figure 1. Sample Learning Objects with Life Cycle information

Layer Two ontologies are appropriate to describe: User Profiles; Learning Objects; application contexts; and relationships. Each one of them can be described in one or several ontologies. There is a hurdle to consider when dealing with granularity matters. Higher granularities allow by on side to delimit the processing unities and reduce computer processing, but, by the other hand, the human cost to break the information in several ontologies are elevated. We need to take this into consideration when describing an application domain with this method

For example, the description of a Learning Object as instance of the LOM ontology is performed within the following steps: convert or create a Learning Object; create an OWL file to represent the information of the Learning Objects; import the LOM OWL ontology; describe the individuals to represent information of the Learning Objects; create Object Properties and Data Properties relationships as necessary.

To illustrate this scenario, we present the *Ramis* Learning Object. *Ramis* uses two metadata standards, IEEE-LOM and OBAA. The underlying purpose for its creation was to simulate the description of an interoperable Learning Object compatible with three hardware platforms: Internet, Digital Television, and Mobile Devices. We started our conversion by analyzing that meta-information and illustrate its complexity with Figure 2.

Figure 2, has the indication **1** that emphasizes the higher layer individual; the indication **2** the Object Properties *hasRequirement*; the indication **3** the Object Properties *hasPlatformSpecificFeatures*; the indication **4** emphasizes the Object Properties hasSpecificRequirement; The indication **5** the Object Properties hasSpecificOrComposite and finally the indication **6** the Object Properties hasOrComposite. Each individual has its own set of Data Properties.

C. Describing Layer Three Ontologies

Layer Three ontologies are mainly developed to represent Application Profiles. [23] defines an Application Profile as compositions of metadata elements from one or more metadata schemas. They are used to describe an application domain.

This work adds to the application profiles computations means to reason knowledge and verify the consistency of Layer Two individuals. This process can be used to derive, for example, the users that have specific pedagogical characteristics, which Learning Objects can be used in a particular domain. Those inferences are made exploring the deduction rules of OWL ontologies.

An Application Profile ontology will be composed, at least, of a class with an axiom that will infer the individuals that match the axiom description. For example, we can create a class *UsersWithSpecialNeeds* with an axiom that describes that ontological individual with the property *hasVisual* is inferred as an instance of the class *UsersWithSpecialNeeds*. To create Layer Three ontologies we can use as many classes with domain axioms as necessary.

The Layer Three ontology is in charge of the reasoning over the Layer Two ontologies. To this proposal, we classify this type of ontology as Application Profile. Application Profile is an ontology composed of a class or a set of classes that describes specific domain knowledge and has at least one axiom for reasoning.

The reasoning is useful to verify if a Learning Object is adequately described according to some standard; to provide inferences according to specific domain characteristics; infer new relationships between Learning Objects; to support some analytical processes; among others.

To describe the Application Profile OWL ontology, we must consider: What is the knowledge to be derived from the Layer Two ontologies? Is it possible to retrieve by an SPARQL query? Reasoners are not extremely powerful; one axiom is enough? How many classes are necessary?

As an example, we shall describe an Application Profile that will infer Learning Objects, only if this Learning Object has a particular set of metadata. Considering this, we present the OBAA Lite Application Profile. This Application Profile was developed by [24]. The current research used OBAA and LOM standards to define the minimum set of metadata

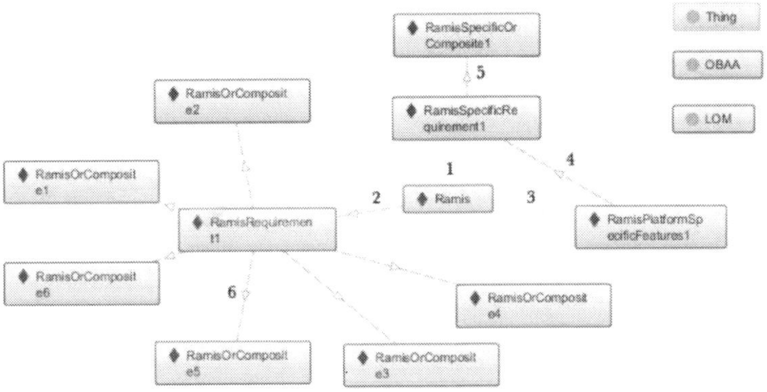

Figure 2. The representation of individuals for the *Ramis* OWL file

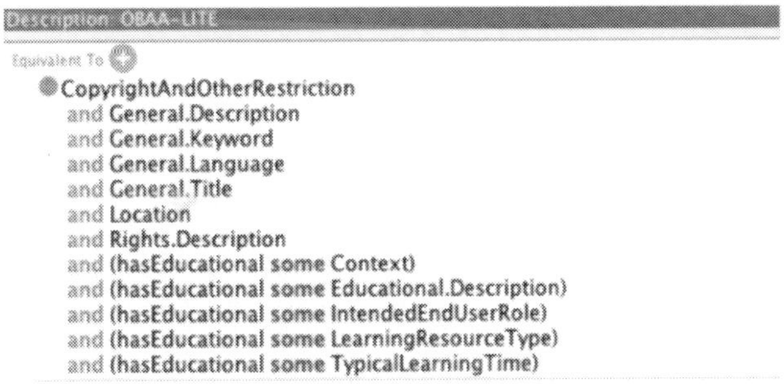

Figure 3. OBAA Lite Ontology Axiom

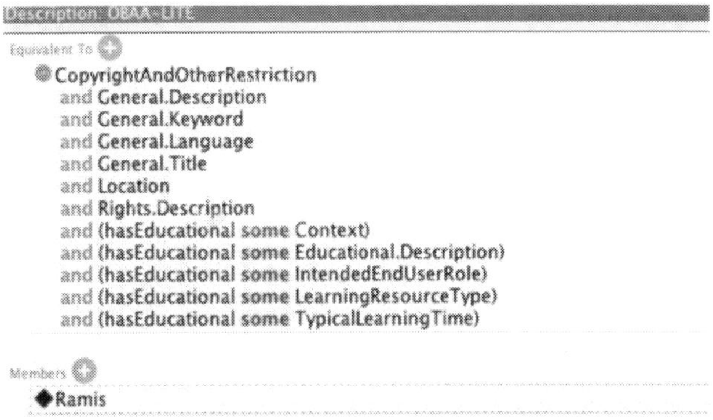

Figure 4. The *Ramis* Higher Layer individual as member of the class OBAA Lite

information that is necessary to describe domain specific Learning Objects. Figure 3 presents the class and the axiom built to infer which Learning Objects are compliant with the OBAA Lite Application Profile.

The current version of *Ramis* ontology does not get inferred by the OBAA Lite application profile because it does not comply with its axiom. To have it correctly inferred, we had to add the missing Data Properties and Object Properties to cope with the OBAA Lite Application Profile. The modification has resulted in the classification of *Ramis* as a member of the OBAA Lite Application Profile class, as can be seen in Figure 4.

III. Discussion

There are several application development alternatives for the educational domain. We can explore the authorship of Learning Objects, development of Agents for Personalized student courses, the suggestion of educational materials among others. The present work had shown an alternative to represent User Profiles and Learning Objects by ontologies to allow a reasoning alternative for educational applications based on Semantic Web. We classify this research as part of a broader overview of an integrated ecosystem for digital education.

The use of computer technologies complements formal or informal education. Educational system designers must think about the teaching and learning process before building digital education platforms. The pedagogical plans, educational contents, assessment and learning feedback, should be integrated to allow the support of Artificial Intelligence (AI) algorithms, learning analytics or statistical measures.

Those algorithms were intended to analyze the students learning performance according to the teacher's pedagogical behavior, learning style and inference of students behavior to provide warnings and suggestions that can improve the learning performance and support the teacher educational activities. To accomplish this, we must think about an ecosystem for digital education.

Teaching with the support of educational technologies should improve traditional non-digital methods and support the three stages of learning (exposure, process, and feedback). Usually, a teacher of mathematics preparing a class about trigonometry, will search for concepts such as sine, cosine or tangent at a school library, ask for word-of-mouth suggestions, on-line websites, or even reuse previous classes materials. We classify this as the Step A: Content Gathering.

After the selection of educational contents, the teacher, based on experience gathered by years of student observation, will organize the materials considering the average educational performance of students. We classify this as the Step B: Class organization.

Once the teacher organized the class, it is time to provide the contents to the students and teach. We classify this as the Step C: Class execution. Finally, the teacher will go home, or to another class, the analysis of the success of the class will be measured by assessment feedback, emotional responses, or, in the next student's essay. We classify this as Step D: Signals Processing. Those steps, are the core scenarios of a class, before the Execution Phase.

The Execution Phase is the holy grail of teachers. It can use different kinds of educational contents, various personalization features, pedagogical practices and methods of evaluation. The essence remains the same. The role of educational technology regards the design and adaptation of Components to support each Phase of this process, allowing a Feedback and Personalization Phase to support the teacher activities.

Let us repeat the exercise of imagining the mathematics teacher preparing a trigonometry class from a different perspective, the AI of an Integrated Ecosystem for Digital Education. For that, we start backward, from the Step D: Signals Processing will be the beginning. At this point, we can analyze the student's interactions with the educational contents from the Step C. The time spent on each question, their number of tentatives for solving puzzles, comments, among an infinite set of signal capture possibilities. AI algorithms can cope with the Step B and use the Learning Objects from Step A, by processing and reasoning over the learning signals; identification of usage patterns; measuring the students learning performance; identifying competencies to be developed; measuring the engagement within a class and consequently suggesting content compositions based on a measurable class learning profile.

The challenges to accomplish such ecosystem reside in open architectures, metadata standards, communication protocols and policies regarding data privacy and security of students and teachers. Also, we need to consider a standard knowledge representation alternative to cope with information interoperability.

The benefits are far from being explored. For example, the detailed usage logs for in-classroom data collection and analysis can be used to analyze and infer pedagogically relevant data streams. Those data streams can be used to measure the student engagement in Real-time or After-class.

The real-time analysis supports the teachers during their classes. Those real-time analyses are challenging since they have to establish a time-frame of signal analysis, e.g., last 30 seconds of data, which variables to choose such as students eye tracking, page navigation, open content, the type of material, students emotional inferences, among others. Mainly, the research focus resides in the analysis of context similarities between what is being thought and what are the reactions of the students to it.

After-class measures support the teacher after and before the class. They compute the percentage of students that were engaged at each time-stamp, supports the teacher by presenting a timeline of the course. The research at this stage can be extended by deep-learning algorithms to infer the model of learning from students or groups, recommender algorithms, understand the behavior of students based on past actions, and other big data statistics to support class preparation.

When dealing with this kind of data, it is an open ground for research to identify what type of students and teachers events may be necessary to build richer models of student learning.

One of the challenges resides in assessing how well a student learns the subject matter, without explicitly testing for that in an exam. Thus, it is necessary to incorporate the metrics into a greater model of student learning.

For instance a knowledge map, based upon which new content could be suggested following what the student already knows, how engaged he or she is, the learning style, and other extracted metrics to personalize each students learning experience. Alternatively, the parameters may be used to design targeted interventions in the teachers activities, for instance, alerting him/her that the class engagement level is dropping. Nevertheless, such interventions must be designed together with educators to augment the teachers experience, and not disrupt his/her day-to-day work.

The work of [25] divides the Semantic Web educational applications into three columns. This article was able to contribute with the two first columns. To cope with the first column, an alternative to reduce computational costs related to exploring SPARQL queries for simple application profiles. e.g., search Learning Objects with a particular property value. Our primary challenge will be to reuse the educational ontologies that are already available and are not compliant with Semantic Web. Also, privacy is a delicate matter, especially in this case when dealing with private and personal information.

The proposed method was built to consider a three layer proposal for ontology engineering. It is important to mention that the LOM ontology is considered complex due to its specifications and restrictions. This fact, in some cases, caused the reasoner to be overwhelmed with ontologies of the Layer Two that were composed of many individuals. An alternative could be to separate each group of the LOM metadata in a single ontology. In the best case scenario, the reasoner would only have to cope with a limited set of properties.

IV. Conclusion and Future Work

There can be several application development alternatives for the educational domain. We can explore the authorship of Learning Objects, development of Agents for Personalized student courses, the suggestion of teaching materials among others. The present work had shown an alternative to represent User Profiles and Learning Objects by ontologies to allow a reasoning alternative for educational applications.

The given ontologies made use of the three layer proposal to describe the knowledge domain. In each one, we described and presented an example of them. The LOM ontology is considered complex due to its specifications and characteristics. This fact, in some cases, caused the reasoner to be overwhelmed with ontologies of the Layer Two that were composed of many individuals. An alternative could be to separate each group of the LOM metadata in a single ontology. In the best case scenario, the reasoner would only have to cope with a limited set of properties.

Layer Two ontologies deal with a complex set of Data Properties and Object Properties. Although it can be considered a complex ontology, in an automatic process we could obtain several exciting benefits such as Easy update, for instance, an individual that is updated can be linked through an Object Properties.

The reuse of some ontological individuals by other Learning Objects, for example, a technical individual that is common to several other Learning Objects.

The described individuals can be validated according to a Layer One ontology making it possible to build relationships between Learning Objects ontologies by properties and compatible with the current Semantic Web stack.

The method to build a Layer Two ontology can be used to describe the user profile ontologies, educational domain ontologies, relationship ontologies, or any other that might describe an educational activity. Such amount of relationships can lead to performance issues, in particular by the reasoner.

There is a lot of work that still needs to be done, especially when considering students privacy matters, content usage rights, security policies over such information and, not most important, public policies that stimulate and popularize the principals of open knowledge leading to a large-scale evaluation that can measure the effectiveness of this approach for the current learning system.

As future work, we will explore a Triple-Store alternative to index and store Layer Two Ontologies such as Learning Objects (LOs), User Profiles and Relationships between them.

A Service Oriented alternative to integrating this proposal with some current educational application and describe new application profiles, to evaluate if the use of OWL-DL is the adequate solution to represent such kind of knowledge and explore the automatic conversion of Legacy Learning Objects Repositories according to this proposal.

REFERENCES

[1] M. d. Rosario, ICT in Education Policies and National Development. New York: Palgrave Macmillan US, 2012, pp. 17–38.

[2] B. Bruns, D. Evans, and J. Luque, Achieving world-class education in Brazil: The next agenda. World Bank, 2012.

[3] A. Kirkwood and L. Price, "Technology-enhanced learning and teaching in higher education: What is "enhanced" and how do we know? A critical literature review," Learning, Media and Technology, vol. 39, no. 1, 2014, pp. 6–36.

[4] H. Coelho and T. T. Primo, "Exploratory apprenticeship in the digital age with ai tools," Progress in Artificial Intelligence, vol. 1, 2016, pp. 1–9.

[5] T. Primo, J. Silva, A. Ribeiro, E. Boff, and R. Vicari, "Towards ontological profiles in communities of practice," IEEE Multidisciplinary Engineering Education Magazine, vol. 7, 2012, p. 13.

[6] T. Primo, A. Behr, and R. Vicari, "A semantic web approach to recommend learning objects," Communications in Computer and Information Science, vol. 365, 2013.

[7] A. Koster, T. Primo, A. Oliveira, and F. Koch, "Toward measuring student engagement: A data-driven approach," in Proceedings of the Thirteenth International Conference on Intelligent Tutoring Systems (ITS), Zagreb, Croatia, 2016.

[8] A. Koster, T. Primo, F. Koch, . Oliveira, and H. Chung, "Towards an educator-centred digital teaching platform: The ground conditions for a data-driven approach," in 2015 IEEE 15th International Conference on Advanced Learning Technologies, July 2015, pp. 74–75.

[9] R. Zilse, T. Primo, F. Koch, and A. Koster, An Analysis of Applying the Short Bridge Method to Digital Education. Cham: Springer International Publishing, 2016, pp. 94–102.

[10] N. Shadbolt, T. Berners-Lee, and W. Hall, "The semantic web revisited," IEEE Intelligent Systems, vol. 21, no. 3, May 2006, pp. 96–101.

[11] R. Brachman and H. Levesque, Knowledge Representation and Reasoning. San Francisco, CA, USA: Morgan Kaufmann Publishers Inc., 2004.

[12] T. Anderson and D. Whitelock, "The educational semantic web: Visioning and practicing the future of education," Journal of Interactive Media in Education, vol. 2004, no. 1, 2004.

[13] F. Ricci, L. Rokach, B. Shapira, and P. B. Kantor, Recommender Systems Handbook, 1st ed. New York, NY, USA: Springer-Verlag New York, Inc., 2010.

[14] D. Dicheva, "Ontologies and semantic web for e-learning," Handbook on Information Technologies for Education and Training, 2008, pp. 47–65.

[15] A. Ruiz-Calleja, G. Vega-Gorgojo, J. I. Asensio-Pérez, M. L. Bote-Lorenzo, E. Gómez-Sánchez, and C. Alario-Hoyos, "A Linked Data approach for the discovery of educational ICT tools in the Web of Data," Comput. Educ., vol. 59, no. 3, Nov. 2012, pp. 952–962.

[16] M. d'Aquin, "Linked data for open and distance learning," Tech. Rep., 2012.

[17] G. Adorni, S. Battigelli, D. Brondo, N. Capuano, M. Coccoli, S. Miranda, F. Orciuoli, L. Stanganelli, A. M. Sugliano, and G. Vivanet, "Caddie and iwt: two different ontology-based approaches to anytime, anywhere and anybody learning," Journal of e-Learning and Knowledge Society, vol. 6, no. 2, 2010.

[18] A. Klašnja-Milićević, B. Vesin, M. Ivanovic, and Z. Budimac, "E-learning personalization based on hybrid recommendation strategy and learning style identification," Computers & Education, vol. 56, no. 3, Apr. 2011.

[19] I. Standards, "IEEE LOM final standard metadata," 2002.

[20] R. Vicari, A. Ribeiro, J. Silva, and E. Santos, "Brazilian Proposal for Agent-Based Learning Objects Metadata Standard-OBAA," Metadata and Semantics, vol. 108, 2010, pp. 300–311.

[21] V. Devedzic, J. Jovanovic, and D. Gasevic, "The Pragmatics of Current E-Learning Standards," Internet Computing, IEEE, vol. 11, no. 3, 2007, pp. 19–27.

[22] LOM ontology accessed in february of 2017. [Online]. Available: http://gia.inf.ufrgs.br/ontologies/LOM.owl

[23] N. Manouselis and K. Kastrantas, "An IEEE LOM application profile to describe training resources for agricultural & rural smes," Proceedings of Metadata and Semanctis Research Conference, 2007.

[24] J. M. C. d. Silva, "Análise técnica e pedagógica de metadados para objetos de aprendizagem," 2011.

[25] T. Anderson and D. M. Whitelock, "The educational semantic web: Visioning and practicing the future of education (special issue)," Journal of interactive Media in Education, vol. 1, 2004.

Estimating Student's Viewpoint to Learning from Lecture/Self-Evaluation Texts

Toshiro Minami
KIIS
Dazaifu, Fukuoka, Japan
Email: minamitoshiro@gmail.com

Yoko Ohura
KIIS
Dazaifu, Fukuoka Japan
Email: ohura@kiis.ac.jp

Kensuke Baba
Fujitsu Laboratories
Kawasaki, Kanagawa Japan
Email: baba.kensuke@jp.fujitsu.com

***Abstract*—Our eventual goal is to help students learn more effectively. Toward this goal, we have asked the students to retrospectively evaluate themselves and the class by looking back at what they have learned, and we analyzed the answer-texts in order to capture them objectively. We found that their viewpoints affect their performances. Students with wider viewpoints get better performances than those with narrow viewpoints. In this paper, we analyze the answer texts for two contrasting targets; lecture (L) vs. student (S), and good point (G) vs. bad point (B). We propose an index for measuring the term usage and analyze the answer texts using this index. We find that most terms are exclusively used in either one of the contrasting questions. For the numbers of exclusively-used terms, L and G respectively outperform S and B. Thus, students pay more attentions to lectures than themselves and to good points than bad points, as they evaluate. Further, the terms exclusively used in the combination of L-S and G-B, i.e., LG, LB, SG, and SB, show the points of evaluation view of students more specifically.**

Keywords–Text Mining; Text Analysis; Term-usage; Educational Data Mining; Lecture Data Analytics.

I. INTRODUCTION

The aim of our series of studies is to know our students in order to help them succeed to their full potential in their university studies. As a part of such studies, we have been analyzing the answer texts to a retrospective evaluation questionnaire about lectures and the students themselves [4]–[10]. For example, we have been investigating the students' attitudes to the lectures/learning by analyzing the free texts obtained as the answer to the question related to what they have learned in class. The results show that the students with high examination scores incline to use the terms that indicate the students' wide viewpoints and wide interests. By contrast, those with low grades often respond the terms directly related to the lecture's main topic [8]–[10].

Such studies of educational data analysis and analytics are conducted as Educational Data Mining (EDM) [12]. For example, Romero et al. [13] gave a comparative study of data mining algorithms for classifying students using e-learning system data. Its major interest is on predicting the student's performance outcome. Our focus is on the student's psychological tendency in learning, such as eagerness, diligence, seriousness. Many studies in EDM use the target data which are obtained from learning management systems. Different from them, our target data can be obtained in everyday lectures.

The study by Ames et al. [1] has a similar motivation to ours. They investigated the students' attitudes to the class, learning, and others, on the basis of the answers to questionnaire items. However, their underlying data were obtained by asking the students to choose the rate from 1 to 5 for each question item. In our case, even though 2 of our question items are asking to rate from 0 to 100, other questions are asking for an answer in a free-text format.

Our data analysis style is different from the major studies in EDM. Most of them somehow intend to analyze the big data, and the data obtained automatically as log data. By contrast, we would rather take the approach of dealing with small data, because our target data themselves may be very small [5] [7]. Also, the data we deal with are representing students, who we have to educate and take care of them all. Thus, we have to pay attention to all the data, even the data locate as outliers, separated from the central area.

The aim of this paper is to perform an answer text analysis in order to know more about students' attitudes to learning and their points of view while taking a class. We also aim to develop new methods of analysis through case studies.

The rest of the paper is organized as follows: In Section II, we describe the data we use for analysis. In Section III, we present our interesting findings in our previous studies. In Section IV, we conduct the analysis by focusing attention on the terms used by the students in the answer texts from questions about good/bad points of the lectures and students themselves. We analyze what types of terms are used in what contexts and try to find their points of view during learning in the class. Finally in Section V, we conclude the discussions and findings in this paper.

II. TARGET DATA

The data used in this paper came from a class in 2009 named "Information Retrieval Exercise" in a two-year women's university [4]–[10]. The students were in their second year, and thus, were going to graduate. The number of registered students was 35. The class was a compulsory course for librarian certificate. Thus, the students of this course were more motivated than students in other courses. The major aim of the course for the students was to become expert information searchers so that they have enough knowledge about information retrieval, and enough skills in finding appropriate search engine sites and search keywords on the basis of understanding the aim of the retrieval. One course consists of 15 lectures. A lecture started with a five-minute quiz every time, and the answer sheets were used for recording attendance of students.

Also, homework was assigned every week. Its aim was to make the students review what they had learned in the class and to study preliminary knowledge for the next class. At the same time, the students were requested to write a lecture note every week, which was also aiming to make the students review what they had learned. The homework score reflected the frequency and quality of the submitted homework.

The term-end examination of the course consisted of 3

questions. The first question was to find the search engine sites, and to summarize their characteristic features, together with discussing the methods for information retrieval. The second question was to find the Web sites about e-books and on-line material services. The third question was to find and argue about the information crimes in the Internet environment. The aim of these questions was to evaluate the skills for information retrieval, including the skills for planning and summarizing. These skills were supposed to have been acquired during the course through in classes exercises and by doing homework. We used the score of term-end examination as the measure for the student's performance.

We also asked the students to answer some questions related to their overall evaluation of the course. These questions are [10]:

(Q1) What did you learn in this class? Did it help you?
(Q2) What are the good points of the lectures?
(Q3) What are the bad points that need to be improved?
(Q4) What score you give to the lectures as a whole? (With the numbers from 0 to 100, where the pass level is 60 as in the same way to the examination score.)
(Q5) Write comments on the course, on the lectures and the lecturer, if any,
(Q6) What are your good points in learning attitudes and efforts for the course?
(Q7) What are your bad points that should have to be improved?
(Q8) How do you evaluate your diligence and eagerness to study? Choose one of "excellent", "good", "fair", "rather poor", and "poor".
(Q9) Have you asked the lecturer any questions? Choose one of "asked questions more than once", "asked question once", "had not asked questions", "could not ask questions that came up with", and "no questions came up at all". Describe in detail about the question(s) you asked, and whether the lecturer answered appropriately,
(Q10) Have you done some research or information retrieval in order to find the answers of some questions after school hours? Choose one of "retrieved often", "retrieved sometimes", "had not retrieved for solving questions", and "no questions came up with at all". Describe in detail about what you have done,
(Q11) What score you give to yourself as the evaluation of your own efforts and attitude toward the course. (With the numbers from 0 to 100 as in the same way as in Q4), and finally,
(Q12) Write other comments, if any.

For an example of answer texts, we take a student. Her answers to the first half of the questionnaire were as follows: (Q1) I think I can learn the elementary methods of information retrieval, how to choose appropriate keywords, and others, for getting the information I am looking for. What I have learned is helpful when I do assignments of other lectures. (Q2) I got to know what I did not know before, and about foreign libraries. (Q3) Presumably, the lecturer has quite a lot of things to teach, and thus, the lecture time was often too short to cover all the contents planned in advance. I felt sorry about that. I have no idea how to solve this problem. How about ensure to finish the contents to be dealt with next time? Alternatively, how about reducing the time spent to comment on students homework? (Q4) 87. (Q5) I would like to take this lectures in the first semester, before having the practical training at a library. Then, it might be more effective in various situations; especially at the practical referencing training.

For the remaining questions about herself, she answered as follows: (Q6) The good point for me was I tried as hard as possible to tackle the homework, even though I thought I was not good at operating machines and dealing with information. Also, in order to submit better homework, I completed the homework by trying to reflect on what the lecturer had talked about. (Q7) I have been misunderstanding about homework, without thinking about the lecturer's intention. I should have recognized it earlier. Further, it was wrong to complain to the lecturer about homework assignment. Now, I know I made a mistake about it, so I will not fail again. I agree that it is my own responsibility what I learn from what are given to me in a class. Here after, I will try to recognize other person's intention first, and behave accordingly. (Q8) Fair. (Q9) No questions to ask. (Q10) No investigation for questions. (Q11) 79. (Q12) Although I was not very skilled in dealing with machines and thus, was worried whether I could follow before the lectures, it was nice that I got enough time to operate a PC and got used to it through doing the homeworks and others. From now on, I will try hard to make use of what I have learned in the lectures.

III. Findings in our Previous Studies

In this section, we illustrate a couple of findings in our previous studies. The study in Section IV is carried out on the basis of these findings.

A. Analytics of Numerical Items [4]–[7]

We started with investigating the correlation between the self-evaluation scores (which is obtained from (Q11)) and the examination scores. The result shows that the students who have high examination scores evaluate themselves from a very low scores up to a very high scores, which means that those students who evaluate low would have the self-image that "I am the person who can do better than what I have been doing". These students have a good desire of self-improvement.

By contrast, the students who have poor performance seem to believe in themselves without evidence, and evaluate themselves something like, "I do fairly well in my study". Another possibility is that they actually recognize very well about their poor efforts and poor performance. Still, or maybe because of it, they wanted to believe that they have put in good effort, instead of admitting to their lack of effort. In this way, they could avoid facing what they really were, and keep their pride. As a result of such a phenomenon, the correlation coefficient between the self-evaluation scores and the examination scores becomes a negative value of −0.1.

B. Analytics of Word Usage [8]–[10]

Table I shows the words (translated into English) that appear in the texts more than 5 times and their number of occurrences in the answer texts to (Q1), in the decreasing order of the number. We can see that the words related to the lectures appear in high frequencies. For example, the word "Search" appears 88 times in the answers for (Q1), which is the most frequently used one among all words. Also, the words "Information", "Library" and others appear in the list. The lecture-related words are 6 (20%) among 30 words, whereas 4 (29%) among 14 words with frequencies more than 10.

TABLE I. EXTRACTED WORDS AND THEIR OCCURRENCES (FREQ.> 5)

Word	Freq.	Word	Freq.	Word	Freq.
Search	88	Way	16	Think	8
Class	37	Examine	16	Do	8
Information	37	Keyword	13	Get	8
I think	34	Are various	11	Various	7
Library	33	Use *	10	Feel	7
Learn	32	Help	10	Function	7
Know	30	Necessary	9	Result	7
Myself	21	Use *	9	Important	7
How	21	Internet	8	Opportunity	6
Now	17	Personal Computer	8	This time	6

* Different words in Japanese

In a corresponding analysis between the students and the terms they used, we divided the students into 5 groups. The member of the group with the highest average examination score characteristically used the technical terms and the terms from broader points of view, in comparing Japan and the world, such as "Foreign", "National", and "Japan". It is interesting to see that the terms which are relating to the homework assignments do not appear in this group. Thus, we can say that the students in this group attended the lectures with the attitude of learning in a broad perspective.

In contrast, the students in the group with the lowest average examination score used quite a lot of frequently-used general terms, and did not use technical terms at all. It is interesting to see that many students used a lot of terms they have learned during the lectures, e.g., "Learn", "Master", "Study", "Useful", and "Use". So, we can guess, they payed a lot of attention to the terms which are directly relating to the main topics of the course, whereas they did not pay much attention to such things like, their background, their relation to the related concepts, their values in our society.

IV. ANALYSIS OF LECTURE/SELF AND GOOD/BAD POINTS OF STUDENTS

In this section, we analyze and discuss how terms are used in evaluating the lectures and the students themselves as well as whether they are used for positive points or negative ones on the basis of the results described in the previous section. Firstly in Subsection IV-A, we describe the outline of the process for data analytics, which consists of two parts; term/word extraction from the texts and investigation of their usage. The first part is described in Subsection IV-B, and the second part in Subsections IV-C and IV-D.

A. Outline of the Analytics

As we have shown in Section II, (Q2) and (Q3) asked the students to point out the good and to be improved points, respectively. Similarly, (Q6) and (Q7) respectively asked the good and to be improved points of the student herself. Thus, we call these questions LG (meaning Lecture-Good) for (Q2), LB (meaning Lecture-Bad) for (Q3), SG (meaning Self/Student-Good) for (Q6), and SB (meaning Self/Student-Bad) for (Q6) in order to recognize them with ease.

The aim of this paper is to investigate what kinds of terms are used in which evaluations for lecture, self/student, good point, bad point, and try to find the students' points of view in evaluation. First, we extract terms from the texts that are supposed to somehow represent the views for evaluations. Then, we characterize the terms using indexes for measuring the weights between lecture and self, good and bad points.

B. Term Extraction

We start with extracting the terms used in the answer texts of students for the questions (Q2), (Q3), (Q6), and (Q7), or LG, LB, SG, and SB, respectively.

Let n be the number of students, $n = 35$ in our case, and let $\mathcal{S} = \{s_1, s_2, \ldots, s_n\}$ be the set of students. Each student s_i $(i = 1, 2, \ldots, n)$ is supposed to answer the questions (Q2), (Q3), (Q6), and (Q7). Let $\mathcal{Q} = \{LG, LB, SG, SB\}$ be the set of questions, and let $Ans_{i,q}$ be the answer text, or string of characters, of the students $s_i \in \mathcal{S}$ for the question $q \in \mathcal{Q}$. Note that $Ans_{i,q} =$"" (empty string) means that the student s_i did not answer to the question q.

By applying the morphological analyzer, i.e., KH coder [2] and MeCab [3], to the text $Ans_{i,q}$, we are able to create the set of "terms" $\mathcal{T}_{i,q} = \{t_1, t_2, \ldots, t_{m_{i,q}}\}$, where each term $t_k (\in \mathcal{T}_{i,q})$ is of the form $w:p$, where w is a word and p is its part of speech (PoS). We will sometimes identify the term $w:p$ with the word w in this paper; especially when it is not important which part of speech p the word w has.

Let $\#_{i,q}t$ be the number of occurrences, or frequencies, of the term t in the text $Ans_{i,q}$. Note that $\#_{i,q}t$ represents the number of the occurrences of the term t in the bag of words of $Ans_{i,q}$, and thus, $\#_{i,q}t = 0$ if $t \notin \mathcal{T}_{i,q}$. We also define $\mathcal{T}_i = \bigcup_{q\in\mathcal{Q}} \mathcal{T}_{i,q}$, $\#_i t = \sum_{q\in\mathcal{Q}} \#_{i,q}t$, $\mathcal{T}_q = \bigcup_{s_i\in\mathcal{S}} \mathcal{T}_{i,q}$, and $\#_q t = \sum_{s_i\in\mathcal{S}} \#_{i,q}t$. Then, let $\mathcal{T} = \bigcup_{q\in\mathcal{Q}} \mathcal{T}_q (= \bigcup_{s_i\in\mathcal{S}} \mathcal{T}_i)$.

Now, we extend the set $\mathcal{Q} = \{LG, LB, SG, SB\}$ to the set $\mathcal{Q} = \{LG, LB, SG, SB, L, S, G, B, All\}$, so that $\mathcal{T}_L = \mathcal{T}_{LG} \cup \mathcal{T}_{LB}$ and $\#_L t = \#_{LG}t + \#_{LB}t$. We also define $\mathcal{T}_S$, $\mathcal{T}_G$, and $\mathcal{T}_B$ in the same way. Further, $\mathcal{T}_{All} = \mathcal{T}_L \cup \mathcal{T}_S$ and $\#_{All}t = \#_L t + \#_S t$. We may omit the suffix ALL for brevity.

In our case, $\#\mathcal{T} = 605$, $\sum_{t\in\mathcal{T}} \#t = 1322$, and thus, a term appears about 2.2 times in average. The term that appears maximum times is the verb "do" with 72 times, and 361 (about 60%) terms appear only once.

TABLE II. TERM OF FREQUENCY ≥ 9 WITH ITS TYPE

No.	Word:PoS	Frq.	Type	No.	Word:PoS	Frq.	Type
1	Do(する):v	72	L'G'	21	Say(いう):v	12	L'B'
2	Think(思う):v	46	L'B'	22	Investigate(調べる):v	11	L'G'
3	Homework(宿題):n	45	S'B'	23	No(ない):adj	11	L'G'
4	Not(ない):o	45	L'B'	24	Do(やる):v	11	L'G'
5	Can(できる):v	38	L'G'	25	See(見る):v	10	L'G'
6	Lecture(授業):n	35	L'G'	26	Good(良い):adj	10	L'G'
7	Exist(ある):v	35	L'B'	27	Other(他):n	10	L'G'
8	Become(なる):v	31	L'B'	28	Interest(気):n	10	S'B'
9	ToIntroduce(紹介):n	25	L'G'	29	NotMuch(あまり):adv	9	L'G'
10	Time(時間):o	23	L'B'	30	Good(よい):adj	9	L'G'
11	Lecturer(先生):n	20	S'N	31	Person(人):n	9	L'G'
12	ToSearch(検索):n	19	L'G'	32	Understand(わかる):v	9	L'B'
13	Me(自分):n	19	L'G'	33	Many(多い):adj	9	S'B'
14	Library(図書館):n	19	LG'	34	Easy(やすい):adj	9	S'B'
15	Know(知る):v	17	L'G'	35	Aquire(つける):v	9	S'B'
16	Assignment(課題):n	14	S'B'	36	Not(ぬ):o	9	L'G'
17	Listen(聞く):v	13	L'B'				
18	Everytime(毎回):o	13	S'B'				
19	Talk(話):n	13	S'B'				
20	DoSubmit(提出):n	13	L'G'				

Table II shows the list of most frequently used terms t with $\#t \geq 9$, which are 36 in number and the rate of their total frequencies is about 54%. Note that the noun having "To+verb" form in English shows that it is a "sahen-noun", which allows to add the verb "suru (Do)" and turns into its verb-form. For example, the 9th term "紹介 (pronounced show-kai)" is a noun, meaning "introduction", or "to introduce". By adding "する (suru)" it becomes a verb "紹介する (show-kai-suru, introduction-do)", meaning "do introduce" or the verb "introduce". In the table, such nouns are translated into English in the form of "To+Verb". As a sahen-noun and its verb form are so close to each other, they could be dealt with identically, as they are the same in the intention of those who use them.

Many terms in the table were popular for (Q1), which asked the students what they had learned in the class. For example, the most frequently used term "ToSearch(検索):n" appears as the 12th term in the table. The second one appears as the 6th. These terms might be those the students remembered most when they looked back at the lectures and at themselves.

By contrast, the terms that do not appear many in (Q1) include the very first term "Do(する):v", the 11th, and those from 17th to 22nd of Table II. The use of the term "Do", however, might not be very important because it is used so often that its usages might not mean much. The use of terms from "listen" (17th) to "investigate" (22nd) are probably related to the 16th term "investigate", and it means that it remains in their mind about what their homework assignments were like, and what they did, or did not.

C. Term Usage Analysis using LS- and GB-indexes

In order to investigate further about how terms are used in evaluation texts, we introduce a new index, which quantifies how much is a term used in contrasting evaluation context. Let t be a term ($\in T$). The LS-index of t is defined as follows:

$$\iota_{LS}(t) = \frac{\#_L t - \#_S t}{\#_L t + \#_S t}$$

By definition, $-1 \leq \iota_{LS}(t) \leq 1$, and $\iota_{LS}(t) = 1$ iff t appears only in L, i.e., t appears in either one of LG or LB and it does not appear in SG nor SB. Also, $\iota_{LS}(t) = -1$ iff t appears only in S, and $\iota_{LS}(t) = 0$ iff t appears in the same number in L as in S, or $\#_L t = \#_S t$. We define $\iota_{GB}(t)$ in the same way:

$$\iota_{GB}(t) = \frac{\#_G t - \#_B t}{\#_G t + \#_B t}$$

Figure 1 shows how terms are located with the indexes LS and GB. We divide the terms into 25 groups by combining 5 groups both for LS (x) and for GB (y) axes, namely, S, S', N, L', and L for LS axis, and G, G', N, B', and B for GB axis. Precisely, we define the groups as follows: $S = \{t \in \mathcal{T} \mid \iota_{LS}(t) = -1\}$, $S' = \{t \in \mathcal{T} \mid -1 < \iota_{LS}(t) < 0\}$, $N = \{t \in \mathcal{T} \mid \iota_{LS}(t) = 0\}$, $L' = \{t \in \mathcal{T} \mid 0 < \iota_{LS}(t) < 1\}$, and $L = \{t \in \mathcal{T} \mid \iota_{LS}(t) = 1\}$. We define G to B in a similar way, and finally, we define from SG to LB by combining the two group types. For example, $S'G' = \{t \in \mathcal{T} \mid -1 < \iota_{LS}(t) < 0, 0 < \iota_{GB}(t) < 1\}$.

From the figure, we have an impression that the first quadrant ($\iota_{LS}, \iota_{GB} > 0$) contains the most terms, followed by the fourth quadrant ($\iota_{LS} > 0, \iota_{GB} < 0$), the third quadrant ($\iota_{LS} < 0, \iota_{GB} < 0$), and the second quadrant ($\iota_{LS} < 0, \iota_{GB} > 0$) is the one with the least terms. Thus, students used more terms to evaluate lectures than themselves, and they used more terms to evaluate good points about lectures than bad points. Further,

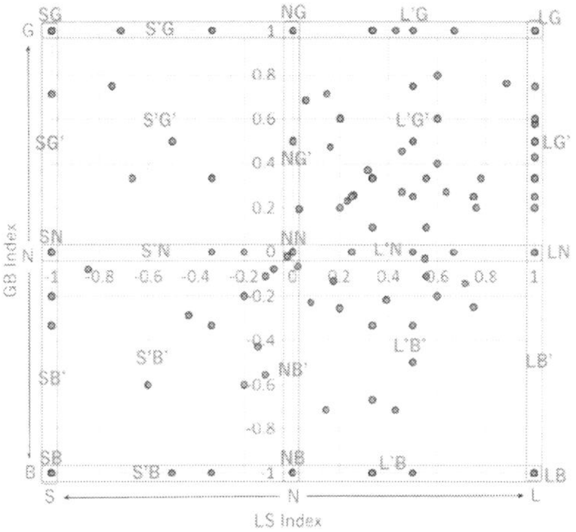

Figure 1. Distribution of Terms with LS (x-axis) and GB (y-axis) Indexes

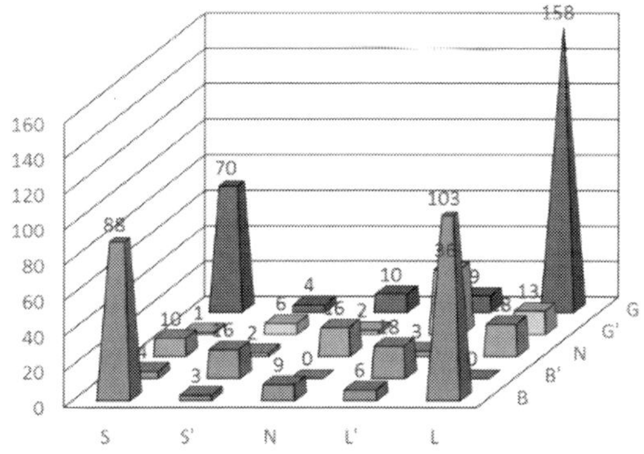

Figure 2. Term-Distribution by LS (x-axis) and GB (y-axis) Index Types

we recognize that they used more terms in evaluating bad points about themselves than good points.

Figure 2 shows how the terms are distributed to the 5×5 groups, and Table III shows the actual numbers. From the table and the figure, we can see most (nearly 70%) terms are located at the 4 corners (namely LG, SG, SB, and LB types), and #LG> #LB> #SB> #SG in their numbers of terms. This result exactly matches with the observation we had in Figure 1, where we observed that #L'G'> #L'B'> #S'B'> #S'G'.

These results say that students use more terms regarding (probably, pay more attention to) lectures than students themselves. Further, they use more terms, or pay more attention to

TABLE III. FREQUENCIES FOR COMBINED TYPES OF LS AND GB

	S	S'	N	L'	L	Sum
G	70	4	10	9	158	251
G'	1	6	2	36	13	58
N	10	2	16	3	18	49
B'	4	16	0	18	0	38
B	88	3	9	6	103	209
Sum	173	31	37	72	292	605

TABLE IV. TERMS FOR LG/LB/SG/SB TYPES

No.	SG (Self-Good) (70)	Frq.	LG (Lecture-Good) (158)	Frq.
1	ToMakeEffort(努力):n	5	Usually(普段):adv	5
2	Before(以前):adv	2	Oversees(海外):n	5
3	MakeEffort(頑張る):v	2	ForeignCountry(外国):n	4
4	Important(重要):adj	1	Fun(楽しい):adj	3
5	Yahoo(yahoo):o	1	Attmosphere(様子):n	3
6	Opportunity(きっかけ):n	1	Various(様々):adj	3
7	NotYet(まだまだ):adv	1	Japan(日本):n	3
8	Google(グーグル):o	1	Photo(写真):n	3
9	Hear(開く):v	1	IC(IC):o	3
10	ToFunction(機能):n	1	Tag(タグ):n	3
11	ToGrow(成長):n	1	Many(たくさん):adv	2
12	Immature(未熟):adj	1	Ages(時代):n	2
13	Part-TimeJob(バイト):n	1	Knowledge(知識):n	2
14	Somehow(なんとか):adv	1	Ties(縁):n	2
15	Vacancy(空き):n	1	ToPractice(実習):n	2
16	Interval(合間):n	1	Like(好き):adj	2
17	FindSpareTime(縫う):v	1	University(大学):n	2
18	All(すべて):adv	1	Engine(エンジン):n	2
19	GoodAt(得意):adj	1	Usage(使い方):n	2
20	NumbeOfTimes(回):n	1	CanGo(行ける):v	2
No.	SB (Self-Bad) (88)	Frq.	LB (Lecture-Bad) (103)	Frq.
1	ToReflect(反省):n	7	Want(ほしい):adj	5
2	FromNowOn(今後):adv	4	ToDivide(配分):n	4
3	Keep(守る):v	3	Reduce(減らす):v	3
4	When(いつ):adv	2	So(そう):adv	3
5	ToRegret(後悔):n	2	ToExplain(説明):n	3
6	OtherParty(相手):n	2	Short(短い):adj	2
7	Regret(悔しい):adj	2	One(１つ):n	2
8	ToManage(管理):n	2	Plan(予定):n	2
9	Continue(続く):v	2	Teach(教える):v	2
10	BeInterupted(途切れる):v	1	Answer(答え):n	2
11	Margine(余裕):n	1	ThisTime(今回):adv	2
12	CanGo(いける):v	1	PreviousTime(前回):n	2
13	BarelyInTime(ぎりぎり):adv	1	Painful(辛い):adj	2
14	Immediately(すぐ):adv	1	Hear(聞き取る):v	2
15	QuiteALot(たっぷり):adv	1	Wide(広い):adj	1
16	BarelyInTime(ギリギリ):adj	1	Enjoyable(うれしい):adj	1
17	Everything(何事):n	1	Lonely(さみしい):adj	1
18	Repeat(繰り返す):v	1	Sorry(すいません):o	1
19	Review(見直し):n	1	ToCut(カット):n	1
20	ToBeSatisfactory(充実):n	1	Dormitory(寮):n	1

good points than bad points for lectures, and they pay more attention to bad points than good points for themselves.

A possible interpretation of such results is that the students are generally generous to others and they try harder to find good points than bad points as they evaluate the lectures and the lecturer, and at the same time, they try hard to find something to be improved as they evaluate themselves. We need to investigate further on this issue.

D. Term-Usage Analysis for Self/Lecture-Good/Bad

In this subsection, we investigate what specific terms are used in the types at the 4 corners SG, SB, LG, and LB. Table IV shows the 20 terms belonging to each of them. As these index values are either 1 or −1, they are used exclusively in the corresponding evaluations. Note that some terms with frequency 1 may not appear in the table.

The SG (i.e., Self/Student-Good) type is the one having the least number of terms among the 4 types. As we have a look at the terms in this type, we can see that the terms relating to their efforts are conspicuous. For example, the first term "ToMakeEffort(努力):n", which occurs 5 times and the third term "MakeEffort(頑張る):v", which occurs twice are a noun and a verb expression, respectively, which admire their efforts. Another term, which occurs twice is "Before(以前):adv". It appears in the st03's answer text to (Q6) in the sentence "It made me use the PC more often than before". This sentence does not admire her effort directly. However, it is a kind of outcome of the lectures and her efforts, and it can be considered as a sort of indirect admiration of her efforts in learning.

As we have a look at the terms in the SB (i.e., Self/Student-Bad) type, we can see that a lot of terms appearing in this type are those that express regret. For example, the terms "ToReflect(反省):n", "ToRegret(後悔):n", and "Regret(悔しい):adj" directly express the student's regret.

The most frequently specified points of regret is about submitting homeworks, especially that they did not submit some of them, or they submitted late. The terms "Keep(守る):v", "ToManage(管理):n", "BarelyInTime(ぎりぎり):adv", and "BarelyInTime(ギリギリ):adj" are relating with submission of homeworks. Further, 4 out of 7 appearances of the term "ToReflect(反省):n" relate to homework submissions.

Among the remaining 3 appearances, 2 cases are relating to private talks and lack of concentration to the lectures. The rest one mentioned misunderstanding of the lecture's aim, which most other students might not be able to recognize at all.

For the LG (i.e., Lecture-Good) type, we can see that many terms relating to the introductory talks of libraries where the lecturer had visited appear in the list. All the terms "Oversees(海外):n", "ForeignCountry(外国):n", "Japan(日本):n", and "Photo(写真):n" appear in the context of introductions to the libraries, especially the ones overseas, where the students could not visit. Further, some appearances of the first term "Usually(普段):adv" are relating to this issue something like in the context "As we could not visit overseas library usually, I always admired when a foreign library was talked about".

The 9th term "IC(IC):o" and the 10th one "Tag(タグ):n" refer the talk about IC tags, or RFID tags, installed to libraries, which is a research topic of the lecturer. This is another topic which does not belong to the major topics of the lecture at all.

Even with these topics are digressed ones from the major topics of the lectures, they attracted the students so strongly, and thus, they might also arouse the students' interest to the lectures and the major topics themselves. Actually, according to our previous studies, the students who admire such talks have better outcome (examination scores) than those who do not [8]–[10]. This result inspires the importance of arousing students' interest in the lectures.

As we have a look at the terms in the LB type, we recognize that a lot of terms are related to the time scheduling problem. A lecture often started with showing one or two assignment reports of students for the previous lecture, and gave additional lecture together with some commentaries to the reports. Often it took a lot of time for such commentaries and just little time remained for the teaching of new material. Some students pointed out this problem. More specifically, the terms "ToDivide(配分):n", "Reduce(減らす):v", "ToExplain(説明):n", and "Short(短い):adj" are all related with this problem; some are just pointing out, some are suggesting solutions. Further, one case for "Want(ほしい):adj" is a requirement on this problem.

The first term "Want(ほしい):adj" shows student's requirement in general, and thus, it was used for a variety of requirements. A student asked for decreasing the amount of homeworks. Another one asked for additional explanations.

To summarize our observations in this subsection, students paid a lot of attention to their efforts mostly as they praised themselves (SG) and regretted their insufficiency of efforts and diligence (SB). For lectures, they praised the subsidiary talks because what they heard was new to them and helped them with widening their eyes to what they had never experienced before (LG), and they pointed out the problem of time management (LB).

The specific points we have from the analysis of this subsection are very specific to the data we used, and thus, it is quite hard to generalize. However, at least, we are able to demonstrate the usefulness of the methodology of taking contrasting concepts, which consists of introducing indexes for measuring usage, classifying and extracting characteristic terms, and analyzing how they are used, and why.

V. Concluding Remarks

We have been studying the student's attitudes toward the lectures. Our eventual goal in the research topic of this study is two-fold: The first one is to find new facts and tips for helping our students with more effective learning, and the other is to develop new concepts and measuring methods which can be used for the first goal. Thus, understandability is very important in our study. This is the reason why we rather choose naive methods of analysis than to use more sophisticated, but less humanly understandable methods.

In this paper, we took the questions (Q2), (Q3), (Q6), and (Q7) of a retrospective evaluation questionnaire as the target data in an answer text analytics. They asked for good/bad points of lectures and the students themselves. Different from our previous studies, we focused on the terms instead of dealing with students directly. We introduced a new index which measures the weight of usage between two contrasting concepts. By using the indexes for L vs. S and G vs. B, we divided the terms appeared in the answer texts into 5×5 groups. We found that most of them locate at the 4 corners only, which means they are used specifically to evaluate either LG, LB, SG, or SB. By investigating the terms in the 4 corners, we found that the students evaluated themselves from the viewpoint of their efforts, and they evaluated the lectures from various viewpoints; introductory talks of libraries for good points and time-scheduling problem for bad point.

In comparison with the relation to their outcome, i.e., examination scores, we found that the usage of terms did not correlate very much, which is different from the analytics for the question (Q1). This difference might come from that (Q1) asked the students for evaluation in general, and thus, the answer texts correlate more closely with the students' viewpoints. The questions for the study in this paper focused on the good/bad points, and thus, the answers came from a wide standpoints, which did not relate directly to the students' ability/attitudes in learning.

Even though our current status of study is in a very beginning stage, the methods developed in our previous studies have shown high potential in our studies. It will become a necessary knowledge management tool for student development [9] in the near future, because it is a very important topic for the institutional research (IR) for universities [5].

Our future study topics include the following: (1) To develop a method for devising the new ideas further, and to perform refinement of dedication to the study of student effort, and attitudes to learning, measuring diligence(s) of students [11], together with the further analysis of the evaluation texts. Also, it is worth comparing our model with other types of models. (2) By collecting data from a different class, to analyze them, and to verify if the results of this study are also holds. Also, it is important to find out the characteristic features of each class by comparing them. It will be interesting to investigate what features are gender-specific. (3) To generalize the analysis methods and to integrate them into an automated data analysis platform.

Acknowledgment

This work was supported in part by JSPS KAKENHI Grant Number JP15K00310.

References

[1] C. Ames, and J. Archer, "Achievement Goals in the Classroom: Students' Learning Strategies and Motivation Processes," Journal of Educational Psychology, Vol.80, No.3, 1988, pp. 260-267.

[2] K. Higuchi, "KH Coder." Available from http://khc.sourceforge.net/en/ 2017.02.04

[3] T. Kudo, "MeCab: Yet Another Part-of-Speech and Morphological Analyzer" (in Japanese) Available from http://taku910.github.io/mecab/ 2017.02.04

[4] T. Minami, and Y. Ohura, "An Attempt on Effort-Achievement Analysis of Lecture Data for Effective Teaching," Database Theory and Application (DTA 2012), in T.-h. Kim et al. (Eds.): EL/DTA/UNESST 2012, CCIS 352, Springer-Verlag, Dec. 2012, pp. 50-57.

[5] T. Minami, and Y. Ohura, "Towards Development of Lecture Data Analysis Method and its Application to Improvement of Teaching," 2nd International Conference on Applied and Theoretical Information Systems Research (2ndATISR 2012), Dec. 2012, 14pp..

[6] T. Minami, and Y. Ohura, "Lecture Data Analysis towards to Know How the Students' Attitudes Affect to their Evaluations," 8th International Conference on Information Technology and Applications (ICITA 2013), July 2013, pp. 164-169.

[7] T. Minami, and Y. Ohura, "Investigation of Students' Attitudes to Lectures with Tex-Analysis of Questionnaires," 4th International Conference on E-Service and Knowledge Management (ESKM 2013), Sep. 2013, 7pp..

[8] T. Minami, and Y. Ohura, "A Correlation Analysis of Student's Attitude and Outcome of Lectures –Investigation of Keywords in Class-Evaluation Questionnaire–," Advanced Science and Technology Letters (ASTL), Vol.73 (FGCN 2014), Dec. 2014, pp. 11-16.

[9] T. Minami and Y. Ohura, "Towards Improving Students' Attitudes to Lectures and Getting Higher Grades –With Analyzing the Usage of Keywords in Class-Evaluation Questionnaire–," in Proc. The Seventh International Conference on Information, Process, and Knowledge Management (eKNOW 2015), 2015, pp. 78-83.

[10] T. Minami and Y. Ohura, "How Student's Attitude Influences on Learning Achievement? –An Analysis of Attitude-Representing Words Appearing in Looking-Back Evaluation Texts–," International Journal of Database Theory and Application (IJDTA), Science & Engineering Research Support Society (SERSC), Vol.8, No.2, 2015, pp. 129-144.

[11] T. Minami, Y. Ohura, and K. Baba, "How Can we Assess Student's Diligence from Lecture/Self-Evaluation –An Approach with Answer-Text Analysis of Looking-back Questionnaire–," Proc. International Joint Conference on Convergence (IJCC 2017), Feb. 2017, 6pp., in press.

[12] C. Romero, and S. Ventura, "Educational data mining: A survey from 1995 to 2005," Expert Systems with Applications, Vol. 33, Issue 1, July 2007, pp. 135-146.

[13] C. Romero, S. Ventura, P. Espejo, and C. Hervas, "Data mining algorithms to classify students," 1st International Conference on Educational Data Mining (EDM 2008), June 2008, pp. 8-17.

Experimentally Analyzing the Skill Acquisition Model using Task Performance and Physiological Indices

Yoshimasa Ohmoto*, Takahiro Matsuda* and Toyoaki Nishida*
*Department of Intelligence Science
and Technology
Graduate School of Informatics
Kyoto University
Kyoto, Japan
Email: ohmoto@i.kyoto-u.ac.jp, matsuda@ii.ist.i.kyoto-u.ac.jp, nishida@i.kyoto-u.ac.jp

Abstract—**There are many tasks for which people need domain-specific skills learned through long-term practice. Many skill acquisition models were already proposed including the mental states of the learners but a few studies tried to estimate the mental states using objectively measured data. The purpose of this study was to experimentally investigate the relationship between the subjective mental states and the physiological indices for development of a method to determine skill level in detail for the skill acquisition task, using task performance and the learner's mental states. For the purpose, we conducted an experiment to obtain the data of the physiological indices and a subjective report of the feeling of difficulty during the skill acquisition task. As a result of the analysis, we confirmed the relationship between them. In addition, we suggested an approach to identify task features which was useful to acquire the skill and the stage of the skill acquisition process via task performance and the measured physiological indices.**

Keywords–Skill acquisition model; mental state estimation; physiological indices.

I. Introduction

A skill is the ability to perform a task with pre-determined results, often involving a given amount of time, energy, or both. There are many tasks for which people need domain-specific skills learned through long-term practice. We call this kind of undertaking a "skilling task." To acquire the abilities for a skilling task, people usually train by carrying it out repeatedly. However, it is difficult to learn the aptitude in question alone because in many cases, people cannot objectively monitor their skill level and task performance. Experts and instructors can support learners, but the method for supporting learning a skilling task has been established in few endeavors. Some systems are proposed to support learning based on performance.

Generally, if a person has acquired a skill (i.e., proficiency or expertise), this means that person can efficiently carry out a specific task. To assess skill level, the skilling task is divided into some sub-tasks, and sub-task performance is rated. However, to competently perform a job, many skilling tasks require various sub-skills corresponding to the sub-tasks. In this case, even when the learner acquires some sub-skills, a situation may arise where he/she cannot synthetically use them. In addition, it is often difficult to rate skilling task performance itself. In our previous study [1], we analyzed the process for learning ballroom dancing. We found that the participants became proficient at making overall body motions in parallel with each part of the dance and the motions of each body part. In this situation, we could not segment the proficiency of whole body motions, phases of the dance, and the motions of each body part along with the time series; thus, we could not define skill level in detail at a certain point in time. Under such circumstances, human instructors focus on the learner's responses to unknown situations (such as questions and answers), giving a new challenge and deliberately making mistakes. In other words, they evaluate the skilling task model that the learner has.

The important point is that we can use the learner's recognition of the skilling task to determine skill level. The Dreyfus model of skill acquisition [2] shows how students acquire abilities through formal instruction, in addition to practicing. This model identifies skill level based on four binary qualities: (1) recollection (non-situational or situational); (2) recognition (decomposed or holistic); (3) decisions (analytical or intuitive); and (4) awareness (monitoring or being absorbed). The model is intuitive, but no one knows how to evaluate the four factors concretely. We considered an approach to estimate the learner's recognition (i.e., the learner's mental state) from objectively measured data during the skill acquisition process. For this assessment, we used physiological indices that could gauge the responses of the learner's autonomic nervous system related to his/her mental states. The physiological indices are usually employed to ascertain mental stress.

The final goal of this study was to develop a method to determine skill level in detail for the skilling task, using task performance and the learner's mental states. For this purpose, we experimentally investigated the relationship between the subjective mental states and the physiological indices, as well as the method, to estimate skill level based on the physiological indices and task performance. We conducted an experiment to obtain the data of the physiological indices and a subjective report of the learner's mental states.

Section 2 briefly introduces previous works on the skill acquisition model and assessing human stress. Section 3 explains the outline of the technique for appraising human stress and the skill acquisition model via two dimensions: (1) task performance and (2) the learner's mental states. Section 4 describes the experiment and the analysis of the data. Section 5 establishes the discussion of the analysis, and Section 6 lays out our conclusions.

II. Related works

We think the Dreyfus Model of skill acquisition [2] is one of the most famous models of how students acquire skills through formal instruction and practicing. This model is used in a broad area, such as defining an appropriate level of competence, supporting to judge when a learner is ready to teach others and so on. On the other hand, there are some criticisms of this model [3]. According to these authors, there is no empirical evidence for the presence of stages in the development of expertise.

Kraiger et al. [4] attempted to move toward a training evaluation model by developing a classification scheme for evaluating learning outcomes. They integrated theory and research from a number of diverse disciplines and provided a multidimensional perspective to learning outcomes. They proposed cognitive, skill-based, and affective learning outcomes (relevant to training) and recommend potential evaluation measures. The value of their construct-oriented approach is that it provides a systematic framework for conducting training evaluation research. They provided a classification scheme for learning outcomes for training evaluation but they could not propose the method to identify the outcomes objectively.

Mitchell et al. [5] assessed that participants' self-efficacy goals, expected performance, and the degree to which certain judgments required more or less cognitive processing throughout the simulated job of an air traffic controller. The results showed that the participants during skill acquisition reported reductions in their cognitive processing for working on the task and for making self-efficacy judgments. The self-efficacy was a better predictor of performance than were expected score or goals on early trials, whereas the reverse was true for later trials. This result showed that the mental state is useful to estimate the skill level because the responses changed along with the skill acquisition.

Langan-Fox et al. [6] summarized traditional models (Fitts and Posner, 1967; Anderson, 1982; Schneide and Shiffrin, 1977). They pointed out that models of skill acquisition largely ignore the experiences and dynamic internal processes of a person while learning a skill. They attempt to highlight the importance of a dynamic description of skill acquisition in their research. Process-oriented factors such as motivation, memory, interruptions, emotion, and metacognition are investigated in relation to skilled performance. However, their discussions were conceptual and they did not experimentally investigate.

Baumeister et al. [7] conducted a series of experiments which explored the possibility that praise can impair subsequent performance. Three models were proposed: praise leads to reduced effort, it implies a pressured demand for good performance (which impairs performance), and it generates self-attention, which impairs the automaticity of skilled execution. As a result, the performance-demand model received partial support, but it had difficulty accounting for the finding that task-irrelevant praise impaired performance. This suggested that we have to carefully think about the learners' mental state and the learning method when they acquire skills.

III. The Skill Acquisition Model, Including Mental States

Some previous studies have proposed the skill acquisition model, which considers learner's mental states [2], [6]. There are also some studies focusing on the leaning process named "learning curve" [8], [9], [10]. However, the mental states were evaluated by human observation. In other words, previous studies have not focused on how to measure, evaluate, and use mental states via objective approaches to the skill acquisition model. In addition, they have centered on mental states through the lens of a specific skill level, but have not concentrated on the dynamics of people going through a learning process. This study aimed to develop a technique for assessing a learner's skill level based on his/her performance and mental states. To do so, we first confirmed the relationship between subjective reports on mental states and the measured physiological indices. We then interpreted the data and performance for estimating skill level and the process of learning. In this section, we explain the physiological indices, which were used to appraise mental states, and propose the skill acquisition model, which has two dimensions that define skill level.

A. *Physiological indices for assessing mental states*

In this study, we propose the skill acquisition model using task performance and mental states. We especially focus on how to gauge and use mental states in the skill acquisition model. It is hard to use a learner's behavior to evaluate mental states because the learner's behavior depends on the task and skill level. However, when a learner feels that an activity is difficult, he/she feels mental stress due to his/her line of thinking and stimuli from the endeavor. Therefore, we consider stress useful for appraising a typical mental state in the learning process.

Many previous investigations have reported on physiological indices for estimating mental stress. However, in ongoing daily interactions, we can often find physiological responses that are not related to the event happening at the time. One reason is that people involved in continuous interactions often plan their actions, such as what to tell and how to move. Therefore, to assess human mental states, we had to consider the context of an interaction and the response characteristics of the physiological indices.

Physiological indices are biological reactions caused by the autonomic nervous system; for example: brain waves, potential differences in cardiographs, variations in blood pressure, pulse waves, respiration, body temperature, muscle potential, and skin conductance. In continuous interactions, some of these are susceptible to noise from body motions. We used skin conductance responses (SCR) and electrocardiograms (LF/HF values) because these are relatively resistant to noise.

Since the underlying mechanisms of SCR and electrocardiograms are different, we expected that they could be used to distinguish between different responses from various sources of stress. Sweating is controlled by the sympathetic nervous system [11] and can be elicited by emotional stimuli, intellectual strain, or painful cutaneous stimulation. The underlying mechanisms of SCRs are more related to anticipation, expectation, and attention concentration [12]. We thus anticipated that SCRs could be used to tell when someone is dealing with an unexpected situation.

For electrocardiograms, the LF/HF value is calculated using instantaneous heart rate. It shows heart rate variability (HRV), which is controlled by the sympathetic and parasympathetic nervous systems and humoral factors. The underlying mechanisms of HRV are complex. Lacey and Lacey [13] suggested

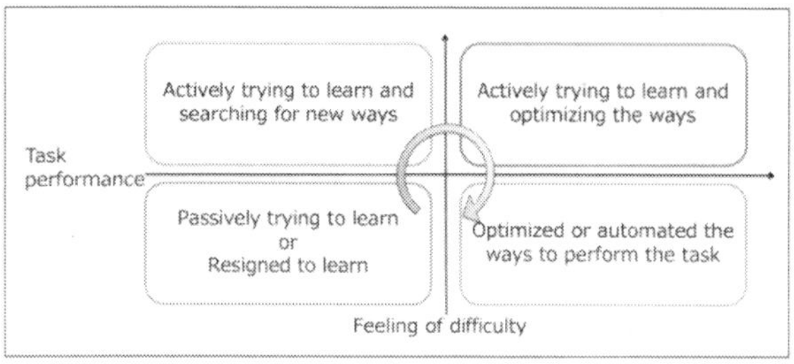

Figure 1. The outline of the skill acquisition model via two dimensions.

that it is caused by sensory intake and sensory rejection. In addition, the parasympathetic nervous system responds quickly (< 1 s) to stimuli. We thus thought that the LF/HF (HRV) would show reactive responses based on external stimuli.

B. The skill acquisition model via two dimensions

We propose the skill acquisition model via two dimensions - task performance and mental state - when a person feels that a task is challenging (we call this a "feeling of difficulty"). Fig. 1 shows the model and the two dimensions. In the traditional three phase model, Phase 1 corresponds to the lower left part, Phase 2 corresponds to the upper part, and Phase 3 corresponds to the lower right part. The "task performance" of the horizontal axis is the task result, which was quantified objectively. The "feeling of difficulty" of the vertical axis is a mental state, which was assessed based on the measured physiological indices. The traditional skill acquisition model assumes that task performance is (weakly) rising along with an increase in skill levels. When a skill can be segmented into small sub-skills, which are independent from each other, this assumption may be true in the process of acquiring sub-skills. However, attaining sub-skills does not contribute to gaining overall aptitudes at more than a certain level for many skilling tasks, such as ballroom dancing. In this case, the synthetic use of sub-skills is often important, and the synthetic use itself is a target of skill acquisition. When the learner practices synthetic use through trial and error, task performance often decreases. In our model, the trial and error process is included in the lower part. When the task performance decreases but the difficulty feeling is low, the model interprets that the process is trial and error. We expected that the learner would circulate this model through the skill acquisition process.

We assume that the skill acquisition process unfolds in the following manner. The initial state of the learner is in the upper or lower left part (i.e., performance is low). The learner usually needs trial and error to learn the skilling task, so the state of the learner is maintained or transitions to the upper part. Through the learning process, task performance increases and the learner's state moves to the upper right part. In this state, the learner can perform the task at hand more efficiently than before, but he/she is not accustomed or does not understand how to carry out the activity. Through practice at this stage, the learner can synthetically and automatically perform the task, and his/her state moves to the lower right part. In a common case, the learner continuously performs trial and error to find better ways, so task performance sometimes falls. In this case, the learner's state is ready for the next stage of the skill acquisition process. If the learner can find clues for better ways to perform the task, the skill acquisition process advances to the next phase. If the learner cannot find better ways, the skill acquisition process terminates in the lower right part of the stage.

IV. Experiment

The purpose of this experiment was to investigate whether the physiological indices were related to the subjective reports about the feeling of difficulty toward the task, and whether we could evaluate the state of transition in the proposed skill acquisition model based on task performance and physiological indices. We adopted a shooter game as a skilling task. Some previous studies (e.g., [14]) have adopted a kind of shooter game. The shooter game that we developed has features of the skilling task. The advantages of the shooter game being the skilling task include the following: (1) The learner needs to obtain game playing skills (which is hard to verbalize); (2) We can control the difficulty of a task; and (3) We can easily analyze the skill acquisition process because we can independently divide the time series of the game events, which is the target of the skill acquisition. In addition, learners can repeatedly play the game with high motivation. We conducted an experiment in which the participants played the shooter game repeatedly and we obtained the game scores and physiological indices during game play. After the experiment, we analyzed the data to confirm the relationship between the physiological indices and the subjective reports about the feeling of difficulty. Furthermore, we examined the relationship in the skill acquisition process.

A. Task

To achieve the best performance in the shooter game, the player must cultivate some skills and gain some knowledge such as operation procedures, scoring rules, the way to defeat one's enemies, the features of game stages, basic survival patterns, and specific techniques to obtain a high score. Some of them cannot be verbalized and the best method varies among the players. To obtain game playing skills, the players must practice repeatedly.

In this game, player uses two different method of attack; gatling gun and homing missile. The gatling gun is quick and out-range attack method. When the player uses the gatling gun to destroy the enemies, the game score is minimum. The homing missile is powerful but needs lock-on procedure near the enemies. When the player uses the homing missile to destroy the enemies, the game score increases exponentially with increasing the number of lock-on target at the same time. The player tries to obtain the game score as high as possible by selectively using the two different attack. Of course, the enemies attack the player so the player cannot always use the homing missile to survive in the game.

In this experiment, the participants were only trained for the first stage of the shooter game, which was segmented into eight parts. The patterns of combinations and the movements of enemies were different in each part of the stage. When the player used a suitable approach in each part of the stage, his/her score was several times higher than that obtained using an inappropriate procedure. There was a relaxation period between each part of the stage. The average clear time was designed to be about 150 seconds. The participants used a joystick with two buttons. When the enemies hit the player

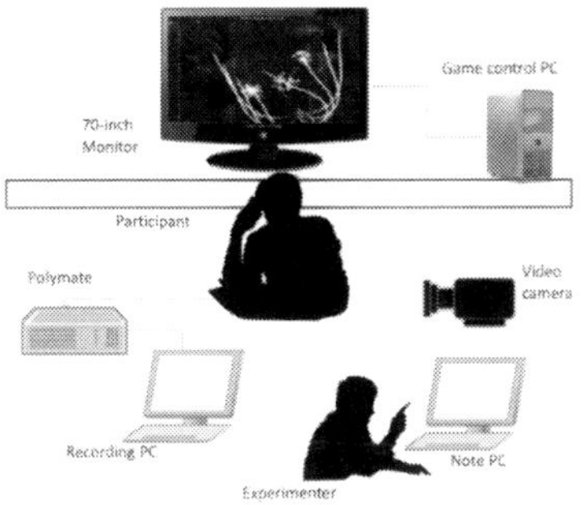

Figure 2. The experimental environment.

three times, the game was over. When the boss enemy was destroyed, the game was cleared. After the game was over or cleared, the participants could confirm their score. They were instructed what behavior produced a high score, but it was difficult to carry out such behavior during the game. The participants acquired game playing skills through repeated practice.

B. An experimental setting

The experimental setting is shown in Fig. 2. Each participant sat in front of a 70-inch monitor that displayed the game. A video camera was placed behind the participant to record his/her behavior and the game playing screen. The participant's voice was recorded using microphones. Polymate was used to measure SCR and the electrocardiogram. SCR was gauged by connecting the electrodes to the first and third fingers of the participant's non-dominant hand. The electrocardiogram was appraised by connecting electrodes with paste to the participant's left side, the center of the chest, and both ears for ground and reference. The experimenter sat out of view of the participant. The experimenter made notes about the participant's behavior and his/her subjective feeling of difficulty in each part of the stage.

C. Participants

The participants in the experiment were 21 male undergraduate students between the ages of 18 and 25 (with an average age of 21.7). We eliminated the data of four participants. We deemed that two did not acquire the skills because their game scores did not increase throughout the experiment. Regarding the other two participants, we failed to measure the physiological indices because the electrodes were removed. Therefore, we used the data of 17 participants for the analysis.

D. Procedure of the experiment

The participants repeatedly played the game in the experiment. The game was played a total of 50 times. The total time of the experiment was about 240 minutes. The experiment was divided into two sessions in the middle, and the participants took a long rest in between them because playing the game and acquiring the skills required a lot of concentration.

Each participant was briefly instructed on the experimental procedure. Electrodes for measuring SCR and the LF/HF electrocardiogram values were then attached to the participant's left hand and chest. The participant then played practice games twice. After a 2-minute relaxation period, the experimenter started the video cameras and recording the physiological indices. After that, the participant began an experimental session. The participant played the game until it was over or cleared. After playing the game, the participant relaxed for 30 seconds. The participant rested for 3 minutes every 10 games. In this, the experimenter scored the participant's feeling of difficulty subjectively and interviewed him/her about this sentiment at each part of the stage. In the first session of the experiment, the participants played 30 games because many games were over in the middle of the stage in the first session.

E. Procedure of the analysis

The data obtained in the experiment are explained below.

1) The game score of each game play
2) The game score of each part of the stage
3) The feeling of difficulty as scored by the experimenter
4) The feeling of difficulty as scored by the participant
5) The physiological indices during the game play

We used 2 as the task performance and 3, 4, and 5 as the feeling of difficulty in our model; 3 and 4 were replaced by 5 after we confirmed the relationship between the subjective reports and the physiological indices. In the analysis, we used data of the simple moving average (calculated from data for the previous 10 games and shifted by 5 games). For example, the first data point was calculated from the data for 1 to 10 games, the second data point was calculated from the data for 5 to 15 games, and so on. The task performance took the value, which was the product of the obtained game score at each part of the stage, divided by the maximum game score of each part of the stage. The feeling of difficulty took on the value +1 (i.e., felt difficulty at that part of the stage) and 0 (i.e., did not feel difficulty at that part of the stage). The physiological responses took a value that was the product of the total time over the threshold (LF/HF: 3.0, SCR: 15.5) divided by the total time of the part of the stage.

We had eight parts of the stage. The eighth part was the battle with the boss enemy. We did not analyze the eighth part because we could not objectively segment the battle with the boss enemy. In this section, we analyzed the first through seventh parts of the stage.

F. Analysis of the relationship between the feeling of difficulty and the physiological indices

We calculated correlation coefficients between the values of the task performance (TP) and the physiological responses (PRs), and those between the values of the feeling of difficulty (FD) and the physiological responses (PRs). The results are shown in Table I. Between the values of the task performance and the responses of SCR, there is a weak positive correlation in one out of seven parts. Between the values of the feeling of difficulty and the responses of SCR, there are weak positive correlations in five out of seven parts, and strong correlations in two out of seven parts. We could find the correlations in all parts of the stage between the values of the feeling of difficulty and the responses of SCR. This means that we can confirm the relationship between the feeling of difficulty and SCR.

In our previous study, we reported that SCR relatively reflected intrinsic stress (concentrating on the task, considering it, and so on) and that LF/HF relatively reflected extrinsic

TABLE I. CORRELATION COEFFICIENTS BETWEEN THE VALUES OF THE TP AND THE PRS, AND THOSE BETWEEN THE VALUES OF THE FD AND THE PRS.

section	1	2	3	4	5	6	7
TP, LF/HF	0.0080	-0.11	-0.15	0.038	-0.018	0.081	-0.079
TP, SCR	-0.14	-0.066	-0.043	-0.13	0.26	-0.000	-0.067
FD, LF/HF	-0.067	0.021	0.055	-0.16	-0.096	-0.034	0.092
FD, SCR	0.33	0.22	0.29	0.34	0.38	0.52	0.44

stimuli [15]. These results support the hypothesis. We expected that SCR would respond when the participant considered how to destroy enemies and what a bad point was in prior game plays. Therefore, we could find a relationship between the feeling of difficulty and SCR. However, we expected that the LF/HF would respond when the participant encountered impressive game events such as getting a high score or making a mistake. Impressive game events occurred independently of task performance and the feeling of difficulty. Therefore, we could not find a relationship with LF/HF.

G. Analysis of the relationship between the LF/HF and SCR in sections where task performance rapidly increased

If SCR reflects intrinsic stress, there is a link between SCR responses and task performance, especially in the parts of the task where it is important to plan how to destroy enemies. On the other hand, there is no connection between them in the parts of the task where the operational technique is important. In addition, the LF/HF responses are independent of them. We thus believe that the relationship between the LF/HF and SCR in sections where task performance rapidly increased through practice is important for assessing the skill acquisition process in some parts of the stage. We refer to the section where task performance rapidly rose as a "rapid increasing section (RIS)." A rapid increasing section is defined as a section in which task performance rises past 0.1 after five games. If the task performance continuously goes beyond 0.1 after five games, it is regarded as one large section.

We compared the values of (LF/HF responses) - (SCR responses) in rapid increasing sections, and looked at other sections in each part of the stage as well. If the participant did not have rapid increasing sections, we eliminated the participant's data from the analysis. We performed the Wilcoxon signed-rank test. The results are shown in Table II. There are significant differences (SCR > LF/HF) in the fifth ($p = 0.0098$) and seventh parts ($p = 0.0024$). In the fifth and seventh parts, there is one optimized playing procedure. This means that it is important to increase task performance to identify the optimized procedure. In other words, the fifth and seventh parts are the sections where it is important to plan how to destroy one's enemies. This means that we may distinguish the task features in the skill acquisition process using the transitions of task performance and the physiological indices.

H. Analysis of the relationship between the LF/HF and SCR in sections where task performance decreased

The rapid increasing section is a good example in the skill acquisition process. However, task performance sometimes decreases because the learner continuously performs trial and error to find better solutions. We refer to the section where the task performance falls into a "plateau section (PS)." A plateau section is one where task performance decreases after five games. If task performance continues to drop after five games, it is regarded as one large section. The plateau section is important because it is the preparation phase for the skill acquisition process.

TABLE II. RESULTS OF THE WILCOXON SIGNED-RANK TEST BETWEEN DATA IN NON-RIS AND THAT IN RIS.

section	mean in not-RIS	mean in RIS	p-value
1	-0.016	0.036	0.20
2	-0.0030	0.0078	0.85
3	0.0094	-0.019	0.94
4	0.0066	-0.023	0.13
5	-0.014	0.029	0.0098*
6	-0.0038	0.014	0.31
7	-0.016	0.051	0.0024*

TABLE III. RESULTS OF THE WILCOXON SIGNED-RANK TEST BETWEEN DATA IN NON-PS AND THAT IN PS.

section	mean in not-PS	mean in PS	p-value
1	-0.036	0.023	0.011*
2	0.0070	0.0045	0.62
3	-0.00040	0.0081	0.32
4	-0.0031	0.010	0.32
5	-0.021	0.013	0.0032*
6	-0.0030	0.027	0.31
7	-0.038	0.039	0.018*

We compared the values of (LF/HF responses) - (SCR responses) in plateau sections and other sections in each part of the stage. If the participant did not have the plateau sections, we eliminated the participant's data from the analysis. We performed the Wilcoxon signed-rank test. The results are shown in Table III. There are significant differences (LF/HF > SCR) in the first part ($p = 0.011$), fifth part ($p = 0.0032$), and seventh part ($p = 0.0018$). In these parts, participants could learn the optimized procedure in a step-by-step manner. In addition, in many cases, the plateau sections appeared before the highest score was updated. This suggests that plateau sections comprise the preparation phase for the skill acquisition process.

In this study, we know the maximum game scores in each part of the stage. Therefore, we can determine that a section is a plateau or a ceiling. However, in terms of general skilling tasks, we cannot know the maximum performance of the endeavor. Hence, we propose a method to identify plateau sections using task performance and the learner's mental state.

V. DISCUSSION

This study aimed to develop a method to estimate the learner's skill level based on task performance and his/her mental states. To achieve this, we conducted an experiment to obtain data from the subjective reports of a feeling of difficulty and the physiological indices during the skill acquisition process. We then confirmed the relationship between the subjective reports of the feeling of difficulty and the physiological indices. In addition, we suggested an approach to identify task features (e.g., whether planning or operational practice is required) and the stage of the skill acquisition process (e.g., plateau section) via task performance and the measured physiological indices. These could not be identified in the traditional models because they could not be used to assess the learner's mental state using an objective technique.

We applied the results of the analyses to our proposed skill acquisition model, then illustrated the typical states of the task performance and physiological indices. The initial state of the learner is the upper or lower left part (i.e., performance is low). When the learner's state is in the lower left part, his/her state transitions to the upper part through trial and error for skill acquisition. If the learner does not try to acquire an ability, the skill acquisition process ends. In the upper left part, task performance is low and physiological indices indicate LF/HF > SCR because the learner usually pays attention to understanding the task features for efficiently learning. After understanding the task features and finding clues to improve performance, the learner's state advances to the upper right part. In this state, task performance becomes higher than before and physiological indices indicate LF/HF < SCR, especially in the parts of the task where it is important to plan how to carry it out. Through repeated practice, the learner comes to synthetically and automatically perform the undertaking and his/her state transitions to the lower right part. In this state, task performance is high and the physiological indices show no characteristic responses. When the learner is not satisfied with his/her task performance or the way the activity is carried out, he/she continuously strives to find better ways. In this state, task performance is maintained or decreases, and the physiological indices indicate LF/HF > SCR. Thus, task performance and the physiological responses suggest that the learner's state is ready to move on to the next stage of the skill acquisition process. If the learner can find clues to improved ways of carrying out a task, the skill acquisition process moves to the lower left part in the next stage. If the learner cannot do so, the skill acquisition process terminates in the lower right part in the current stage.

The most important contribution of this study is that we experimentally analyzed the effects of the learner's mental states as based on the physiological indices. In a traditional skill acquisition model, the impacts of the learner's mental states are conceptually proposed but not confirmed objectively. Of course, our study has some limitations. The most serious limitation was that we could not find significant differences; we only found them in three out of seven parts of the task. One reason is that the characteristics of each part are different from each other, such that planning or the operational technique becomes important. Especially in the part where the operational technique is critical, the participants were absorbed in practicing it, and it was difficult to assess the changes in their mental states. In this part, we had to find other relationships between the learner's behavior and mental states, such as the response time to an event between the physiological indices and the reactive operation.

VI. Conclusions

The purpose of this study was to experimentally investigate the relationship between the subjective mental states and the physiological indices for development of a method to determine skill level in detail for the skilling task, using task performance and the learner's mental states. For the purpose, we conducted an experiment to obtain the data of the physiological indices and a subjective report of the feeling of difficulty during the skill acquisition task. As a result of the analysis, we confirmed the relationship between them. In addition, we suggested an approach to identify task features, which was useful to acquire the skill and the stage of the skill acquisition process via task performance and the measured physiological indices. In the future work, we will analyze the different features of the skill acquisition task and the method to segement the task acqisition process for learning the different features.

VII. Acknowledgement

This research is supported by Grant-in-Aid for Young Scientists (B) (KAKENHI No. 16K21113), and Grant-in-Aid for Scientific Research on Innovative Areas (KAKENHI No. 26118002) from the Ministry of Education, Culture, Sports, Science and Technology of Japan.

References

[1] M. Yoshino, Y. Ohmoto, and T. Nishida, "Constructing knowledge structure of ballroom dance from teacher's instruction behavior," IEICE HCS (Japanese), vol. 114, no. 273, 2014, pp. 55–60.

[2] S. E. Dreyfus and H. L. Dreyfus, "A five-stage model of the mental activities involved in directed skill acquisition," DTIC Document, Tech. Rep., 1980.

[3] F. Gobet and P. Chassy, "Expertise and intuition: A tale of three theories," Minds and Machines, vol. 19, no. 2, 2009, pp. 151–180.

[4] K. Kraiger, J. K. Ford, and E. Salas, "Application of cognitive, skill-based, and affective theories of learning outcomes to new methods of training evaluation," Journal of applied psychology, vol. 78, no. 2, 1993, p. 311.

[5] T. R. Mitchell, H. Hopper, D. Daniels, J. George-Falvy, and L. R. James, "Predicting self-efficacy and performance during skill acquisition," Journal of Applied Psychology, vol. 79, no. 4, 1994, p. 506.

[6] J. Langan-Fox, K. Armstrong, N. Balvin, and J. Anglim, "Process in skill acquisition: Motivation, interruptions, memory, affective states, and metacognition," Australian Psychologist, vol. 37, no. 2, 2002, pp. 104–117.

[7] R. F. Baumeister, D. G. Hutton, and K. J. Cairns, "Negative effects of praise on skilled performance," Basic and applied social psychology, vol. 11, no. 2, 1990, pp. 131–148.

[8] C. Konrad, G. Schupfer, M. Wietlisbach, and H. Gerber, "Learning manual skills in anesthesiology: is there a recommended number of cases for anesthetic procedures?" Anesthesia & Analgesia, vol. 86, no. 3, 1998, pp. 635–639.

[9] F. E. Ritter and L. J. Schooler, "The learning curve," International encyclopedia of the social and behavioral sciences, vol. 13, 2001, pp. 8602–8605.

[10] T. P. Grantcharov and P. Funch-Jensen, "Can everyone achieve proficiency with the laparoscopic technique? learning curve patterns in technical skills acquisition," The American Journal of Surgery, vol. 197, no. 4, 2009, pp. 447–449.

[11] E. F. Bartholomew, F. Martini, and W. B. Ober, Essentials of anatomy & physiology. Benjamin Cummings, 2007.

[12] K. Hugdahl, Psychophysiology: The mind-body perspective. Harvard University Press, 1995.

[13] B. C. Lacey and J. I. Lacey, "Two-way communication between the heart and the brain: Significance of time within the cardiac cycle," American Psychologist, vol. 33, no. 2, 1978, p. 99.

[14] E. A. Day, W. Arthur Jr, and D. Gettman, "Knowledge structures and the acquisition of a complex skill," Journal of applied psychology, vol. 86, no. 5, 2001, p. 1022.

[15] Y. Ohmoto, S. Takeda, and T. Nishida, "Distinction of intrinsic and extrinsic stress in an exercise game by combining multiple physiological indices," in Games and Virtual Worlds for Serious Applications (VS-Games), 2015 7th International Conference on. IEEE, 2015, pp. 1–4.

Learning by Building Cognitive Models that Reflect Cognitive Information Processing:

A Preliminary Class Exercise

Kazuhisa Miwa

Graduate School of Information Science
Nagoya University
Nagoya, Japan 464-8601
Email: miwa@is.nagoya-ua.jp

Hitoshi Terai

Faculty of Human-oriented Science
Kindai University
Iizuka, Japan 820-8555
Email: terai@fuk.kindai.ac.jp

***Abstract*—It has been confirmed that it is important for students to monitor their own cognitive activities during learning. We challenge this idea based on our "learning by creating cognitive models" paradigm. Within a learning environment developed for cognitive modeling, we let students construct cognitive models that reflect their own cognitive information processing. A cryptarithmetic task was used. We conducted a cognitive science class in which participants were required to build computational models that behaved in a manner similar to how the students themselves behaved. As a result, 9 of the 22 (41%) models accurately reflected the participants' problem-solving paths.**

Keywords - Cognitive Models; Procedural Knowledge; Production System

I. OBJECTIVES

The model-based approach is a primary methodology in cognitive science. Cognitive scientists have used computational models as research tools to understand the human mind [1]. The authors have examined the functions of cognitive modeling as a learning tool and proposed the "learning by creating cognitive models" [2][3].

Previous studies have confirmed that creating cognitive models improves active construction of rule-based mental models [4]. Through such activities, participants learn to cultivate meaningful insights into the kinds of procedural knowledge that underlie the observed behaviors of problem solvers.

It appears important for students to monitor their own cognitive activities while learning [5][6][7]. This monitoring activity may correct learners' incorrect knowledge, and improve their learning processes. However, it is generally not easy for naive students to correctly understand their own mental activities. This effort relates to meta cognitive activities. Previous research indicated that performing such a meta cognitive activity is difficult for naive learners, and should be trained.

We investigated this issue based on our "learning by creating cognitive models" paradigm. Fig. 1 shows a diagram of our approach. It is difficult for students to grasp their inner mental activities, but easy to understand their problem solving behaviors that can be observed in the external world. In our approach, students first assume a set of procedural knowledge used for problem solving, and externalize the set as a cognitive model. The model runs as a computer program, and derives the behavior deducted from the assumed knowledge. The model functions as a hypothesis-deduction machine. The participants detected differences between derived behaviors deducted by the hypothesized knowledge and how their own problem solving actually behaved. These detected differences revealed significant information about their own internal thought processes. This assume-execute-observe cycle thus improved students' understandings of their own cognitive processing.

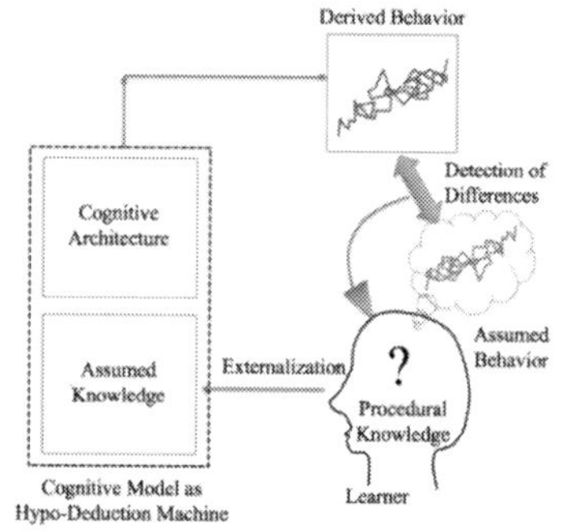

Figure 1. Conceptual diagram of our approach.

Our research question in this study is whether students can construct cognitive models that reflect their own cognitive information processing. We conducted a cognitive science class in which participants were required to build computational models that behaved in a manner similar to the students themselves. This paper provides a preliminary analysis of the model and its findings.

In Section 2, we explain an arithmetic task used in the current study. In Sections 3 and 4, we introduce our learning system, and explain an overall structure of the class practice. Finally, in Section 5, we report results of the class practice. Section 6 summarizes our conclusions.

II. TASK

We used a cryptarithmetic task [8][9] in our study. The following is an example problem used in our class practice.

```
 IGEAF    F = 6
+DBJAD
------
 CIHEGH
```

This problem is simple; however, the cognitive information processing for its solution is relatively complex. In fact, multiple types of procedural knowledge are used during the solution processes. The following discussion describes some examples.

- **Numeral processing**: If a column is x + y = z, and both x and y are known, then we can infer z by summing x and y. For example, in the rightmost column, when we know F = 6 and D = 9, we can assign H a value of 5.
- **Specific numeral processing**: If a column is x + y = x, then we can infer that y = 0 or 9. For example, in the fifth column, we can obtain D = 0 or 9 independently without any other information. In this case, we can determine that D = 9 because C should be 1, meaning that a carry is sent to the left-side column.
- **Parity processing**: If a column is x + x = y and we have a carry from the right column, then we can infer that y is an odd number. For example, in the second column, we obtained a carry by the inference from the first (i.e., rightmost) column; therefore, we conclude that G is an odd number.
- **Inequality processing**: If a column is x + x = y, and no carry is sent to the left column, then we can infer that x is less than 5. For example, in the second column, when we know there is no carry to the left column; A is less than 5.

University students easily understand such procedural knowledge sets if they are given; however, they may face challenges finding the knowledge by themselves and externalizing it while working on the problem.

III. The Learning System

We have developed a learning environment that enables students to construct rule-based cognitive models. The system consists of two modules, i.e., a knowledge editor and a problem-solving simulator.

A. Knowledge editor

First, students externalize a set of procedural knowledge (such as describing rules to solve cryptarithmetic tasks) using the knowledge editor.

Fig. 2 shows an example screenshot of the knowledge editor in which the rule of inequality processing is described, i.e., if a column is x + y = z and no carry is sent to the left column (b == 0 in the figure), then we can infer that z is greater than x.

B. Problem-solving simulator

The problem-solving simulator is mounted on the learning system. The problem solver that simulates the behavior has the potential to perform an exhaustive search for the assignment of digits to letters. Specifically, it selects one of the letters whose numeral value has not been determined and systematically assigns each digit to a letter. If a contradiction is found in the inference process, another assignment is tested. If the problem solver has no procedural knowledge, it is impossible to derive the solution because the problem space spreads exhaustively. Students must give the problem solver adequate procedural knowledge through the knowledge editor.

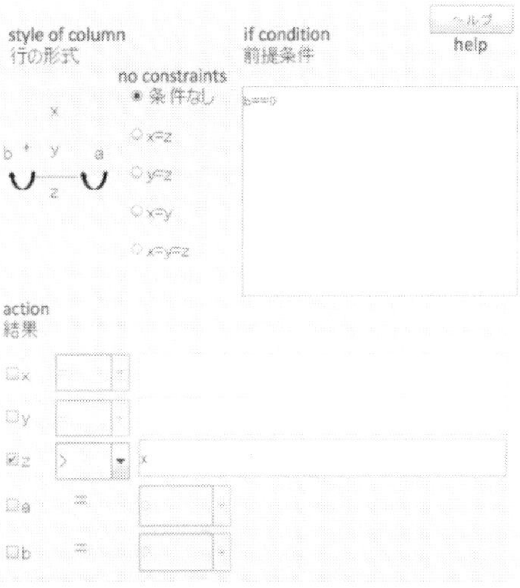

Figure 2. Example screenshots of Knowledge Editor of the learning system.

Fig. 3 shows an example screenshot of the problem-solving simulator, which presents a problem status (the assignment status of digits to letters) and an inference status (a step-by-step series for information processing). A list of rules installed for the problem solver is presented on the right-hand side of the window. Rules that can fire at a specific problem-solving step are marked by bold red lines. In this case, three rules are available. The conflict resolution mechanism is simple, and the most specific rule that provides the most specific inference result has priority for firing. Students can test any rule by forcibly firing it and confirming the resulting inferences. Moreover, students can modify the model very easily. For example, if we uncheck items in the list, students can simulate the behavior of the problem solver with that knowledge excluded.

The system also presents the problem solver's behavior, represented as a search tree of problem-solving processes. Students can confirm inference steps one at a time by clicking the inference button to apply the inference. At any point in the problem-solving process, students can install, delete, or revise knowledge using the editor and restart the inference from a given point in their problem-solving.

IV. Class Practice

Class practice was performed as part of a cognitive science class at the first author's university. Participants included 25 undergraduates from Nagoya University. In the initial week, the participants spent one hour learning how to manage the knowledge editor and operate the problem-solving simulator. Specifically, participants were given an example problem: MEST + BADE = MASER. They then installed seven pieces of procedural knowledge to solve the given problem with a tutor's guidance, and they then simulated behavior at each stage of the construction process.

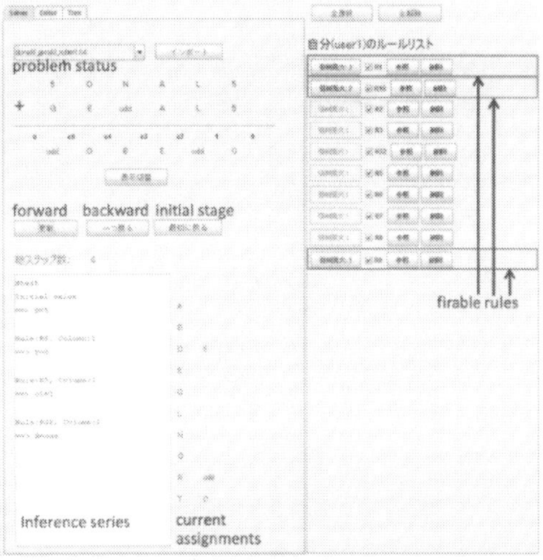

Figure 3. Example screenshots of Problem-solving simulator of the learning system.

In the second week, in a 70-minute training phase, the participants were given a training problem: DONALD + GERALD = ROBERT. They were then required to find a procedural knowledge set for the solution independently, install it in the problem solver with the knowledge editor, and then construct a model. In the third week, the participants were given the target problem: IGEAF+DBJAD = CIHEGH. They were required to construct a model for its solution. After model construction, they were required to solve the same problem by hand while writing their solution processes on an experimentation sheet. Both the model and participant solution processes were analyzed.

V. Results

One participant could not construct a complete model that reached the solution within 100 problem-solving steps. Two other participants' problem-solving paths were not clearly identified due to insufficient written descriptions on the examination sheets. We excluded these three participants from our analysis.

The average number of problem-solving steps for the other 22 participants was 20.9 steps. Fig. 4 shows the detailed result of the models' performances. The horizontal axis indicates problem-solving steps, and the vertical axis indicates the number of participants who constructed the model that reached the solution using that step.

We analyzed the participants' problem-solving paths. All participants initially processed the fifth column (I + D = I) and derived the decisive information D = 9. Then, the participants processed the other columns, coordinated multiple pieces of information obtained through the preceding problem-solving processes, and focused on a specific letter with a limited range of possible numerical values for the following trial-and-error search. Specifically, for the example in Fig. 5, first, G = odd was determined by processing the second column in which the same letters (A and A) were summed and a carry was received from the right-side column. Then, based on the information that G = odd, a limited range of possible assignments (i.e., G

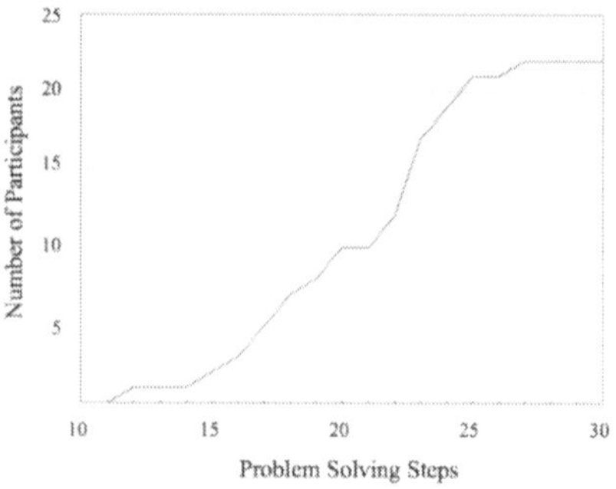

Figure 4. Number of participants who constructed successful models for problem solving.

= 3 or 7) was obtained because other odd numbers (1, 5, and 9) had already been assigned to other letters (C, H, and D, respectively). Next, the participant began to examine G = 3 in a trial-and-error search.

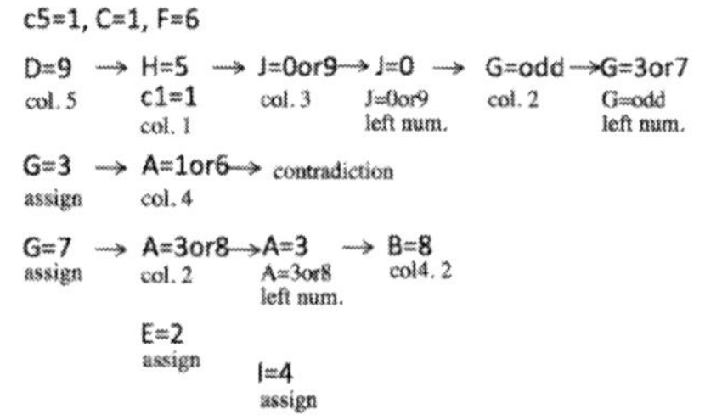

Figure 5. Human problem solving behavior; example case of similar processes.

Fig. 6 shows the problem-solving path of this participant's model. The path is similar to that of the participant shown in Fig. 5. Initially, the model drew G = 3 or 7, found that G = 3 was impossible, and reached the solution by examining another assignment, G = 7.

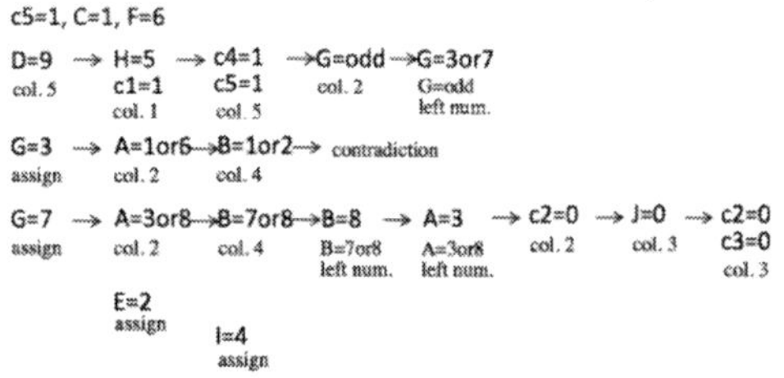

Figure 6. Model problem solving behavior; example case of similar processes.

We focused on the overall patterns of the problem-solving paths determined by trial-and-error search driven by an examined letter, such as G in Fig. 5 and Fig. 6. Table I shows the result of analysis. In 9 of the 22 cases, the patterns of the participants' behaviors were similar to those of the models; however, the 13 other cases were not similar.

Fig. 7 and Fig. 8 show an example case in which the

TABLE I. RESULTS OF REVIEW TEST

IGEAF+DBJAD		DONALD+GERALD	
Match	9 (.41)	Solved	7 (.78)
		Unsolved	2 (.22)
UnMatch	13 (.59)	Solved	3 (.23)
		Unsolved	10 (.77)

participant and model behaviors did not match. In Fig. 7, the participant inferred that A = 2, 3, or 4 by combining A < 5, which had been determined by processing the second column with the information that no carry was sent to the left-side column and the information that 1 was already assigned to C. Based on this information, the participant examined each assignment to the letter A. Fig. 8 shows the problem-solving path through which the model that the participant constructed had run. The model initially inferred that G = 3 or 7, guiding a subsequent trial-and-error search that differed from the participant's path. The model did not infer information related to the letter A and did not focus on the letter A for the initial trial-and-error search, thereby changing the problem-solving path.

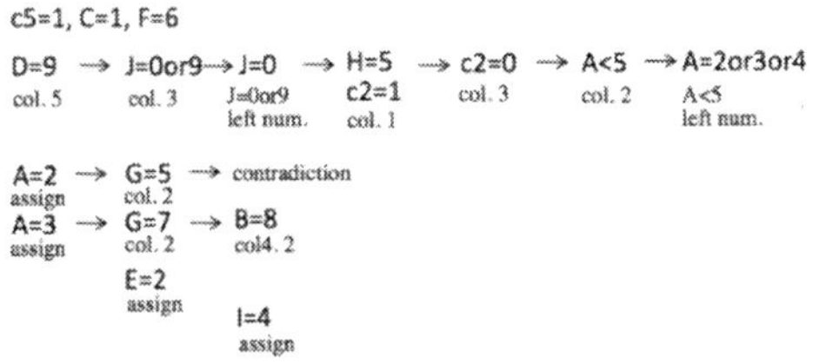

Figure 7. Human problem solving behavior; example case of different processes.

We also investigated the general capacities of the models. The participants intended to construct the models to solve the target problem: IGEAF+DBJAD=CIHEGH. However, if the models were constructed by general rules for problem solving, those could also solve other problems. We examined if each model was able to solve the training problem: DONALD + GERALD = ROBERT. Table I shows that models that successfully trace the participants' problem solving paths are more likely to solve the training problem.

VI. CONCLUSIONS

We analyzed 22 participants who successfully constructed sophisticated models that could solve the given task in approximately 21 steps. However, only 9 of the 22 (41%) models traced the participants' problem-solving paths. This implies that it was relatively difficult for the participants to construct a model that reflected their own cognitive information processing. First, this problem comes from the participants' programming abilities. Some participants appeared unable to implement appropriate rules even though they noticed their own procedural knowledge. This implies that our next step is to improve the learning environment developed in the current study. Another reason is that model construction that reflects each participant's cognitive processing was not emphasized in this class practice. Some participants attempted to construct high-performance models that solved the task as quickly as possible or general models that could perform a variety of tasks. We believe this can be improved based on instructor suggestion.

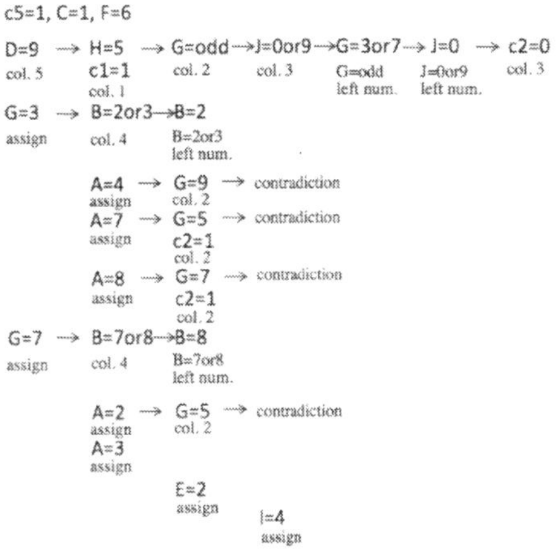

Figure 8. Model problem solving behavior; example case of different processes.

ACKNOWLEDGMENTS

This research was partially supported by HAYAO NAKAYAMA Foundation for Science & Technology and Culture, and JSPS KAKENHI Grant Numbers 15H02927, 15H02717.

REFERENCES

[1] D. Fum, F. D. Missier, and A. Stocco, "The cognitive modeling of human behavior: Why a model is (sometimes) better than 10,000 words," Cognitive Systems Research, vol. 8, 2007, pp. 135–142.

[2] K. Miwa, R. Nakaike, J. Morita, and H. Terai, "Development of production system for anywhere and class practice," in Proceedings of the 14th International Conference of Artificial Intelligence in Education, 2009, pp. 91–99.

[3] K. Miwa, J. Morita, R. Nakaike, and H. Terai, "Learning through intermediate problems in creating cognitive models," Interactive Learning Environments, vol. 22, 2014, pp. 326–350.

[4] K. Miwa, N. Kanzaki, H. Terai, K. Kojima, R. Nakaike, J. Morita, and H. Saito, "Learning mental models on human cognitive processing by creating cognitive models," Lecture Notes in Computer Science (AIED 2015), vol. 9112, 2015, pp. 287–296.

[5] C. Conati and K. Vanlehn, "Toward Computer-Based Support of Meta-Cognitive Skills: a Computational Framework to Coach Self-Explanation," International Journal of Artificial Intelligence in Education (IJAIED), vol. 11, 2000, pp. 389–415.

[6] R. Azevedo and A. F. Hadwin, "Scaffolding self-regulated learning and metacognition–implications for the design of computer-based scaffolds," Instructional Science, vol. 33, no. 5, 2005, pp. 367–379.

[7] R. K. Atkinson, A. Renkl, and M. M. Merrill, "Transitioning from studying examples to solving problems: Effects of self-explanation prompts and fading worked-out steps," Journal of Educational Psychology, vol. 95, no. 4, 2003, p. 774.

[8] A. Newell and H. A. Simon, Human problem solving. Englewood Cliffs, NJ: Prentice-Hall, 1972.

[9] K. Miwa, "A cognitive simulator for learning the nature of human problem solving," Journal of Japanese Society for Artificial Intelligence, vol. 23, 2008, pp. 374–383.

Incremental Face Recognition By Tagged Neural Cliques

Ehsan Sedgh Gooya

Institut Mines-Telecom
Telecom Bretagne
UMR CNRS 6285 Lab-STICC
Department of Electronic
Technopôle Brest Iroise-CS 83818
29238 Brest Cedex, France
Email: ehsan.sedghgooya@imt-atlantique.fr

Dominique Pastor

Institut Mines-Telecom
Telecom Bretagne
UMR CNRS 6285 Lab-STICC
Department of Signal and communication
Technopôle Brest Iroise-CS 83818
29238 Brest Cedex, France
Email: dominique.pastor@imt-atlantique.fr

***Abstract*—We present a system aimed at performing an incremental learning based on a neural network of tagged cliques for face recognition. A crucial component of the system is the network of neural tagged cliques. In its original version, cliques are a set of binary connections linking a set of fired neurons. Tagged cliques make it then possible to identify these cliques. The incremental learning is achieved through two phases: the first one is supervised by an oracle and the second one is automatic. Experimental results on the ORL (Olivetti Research Laboratory) face database pinpoint that incremental learning significantly reduces the number of features to store and yields substantial recognition rate improvement, in comparison with no incremental learning.**

Keywords–Face recognition; incremental learning; neural tagged cliques; SIFT (Scale-Invariant Feature Transform) features.

I. Introduction

Developing brain-like systems has become a cutting-edge research topic in bio-inspired computational methodologies and approaches to address complex real-world problems to which traditional approaches are ineffective or infeasible.

Facing a new situation, human beings use their past experience to remember similar situations and enrich their knowledge. The purpose of this paper is to introduce a neural network system aimed at mimicking this behavior.

Basically, our approach is inspired by advances in cognitive science, such as [1], which led to the theory of dynamic memory, according to which the cognitive processes of understanding, memorization and training are based on the same memory structure. This structure is described by the *Organization Packets* and represented via knowledge representation schemata such as conceptual graphs and scripts. This structure is adapted to cope with new situations because "In the human memory, patterns are both a way of representing the knowledge organization and a way to express how this knowledge is used to understand, remember and make inferences." [2].

On the basis of the foregoing references in cognitive science, we hereafter propose a new incremental learning system based on neural network of tagged cliques for face recognition.

Regarding face recognition, much attention has been given to feature-based methods, such as SIFT (Scale-Invariant Feature Transform) [3], due to the fact that these descriptors remain invariant under rotation, scaling and variation in lightning condition. In the conventional face recognition method using local SIFT features [4] [5], SIFT features are extracted from all the faces of the database. Then, given a query face image, each feature extracted from that face is compared to those of each face contained in the database. A query feature is considered to match one of the database according to a certain threshold-based criterion. The face in the database with the largest number of matched descriptors is considered as the nearest face.

This new architecture relies on the neural network of tagged-cliques presented in [6], as a continuation of [7]–[11]. Cliques exhibit properties that are particularly relevant for incremental learning.

In Section II, we describe the proposed clique-based incremental learning system. In Section III, an implementation of the proposed system is described. Then the system is tested on ORL face database. Finally, we conclude in section IV.

II. Clique-based incremental learning system

A. Overview

The system we propose relies on two spaces: the knowledge space and the space of tagged cliques. These two spaces form what is hereafter called the knowledge structure. The knowledge space and the space of tagged-cliques are updated during the training via several processes. These processes, associated with the knowledge structure, are organized according to three phases during incremental learning (see Figures 1 and 2). These three phases are the initialization phase, the off-line phase and the on-line phase. Thanks to the initialization phase, the knowledge space and the space of tagged-cliques are created. The processes evoked above are then used to update incrementally the knowledge space and the space of tagged-cliques. The processes involved in the off-line phase are: recall, verification, adaptation, evolution and memorization. This updating of the knowledge structure is firstly performed off-line, during which an oracle supervises the learning. During the on-line phase, the updating is carried out automatically without any supervision. In this phase, the verification process is replaced by a validation process.

Let us now specify the approach with respect to face recognition. Basically, face recognition is aimed at determining a person identity, given a face image of this person. This objective requires prior knowledge of the person identity, on the basis of one or several images of this person's face. The system acquires this prior knowledge by a training phase based on a training database of images. A test base of images is then usually employed to assess the performance of the face recognition system.

In the incremental-training system proposed in this paper, one image is randomly chosen in the training database so as to initialize the knowledge structure and store the identity of the several persons to recognize. Afterwards, during the off-line phase, the system is upgraded under the supervision of the oracle. During the on-line phase, the system estimates itself the identity of the input image before updating the knowledge structure.

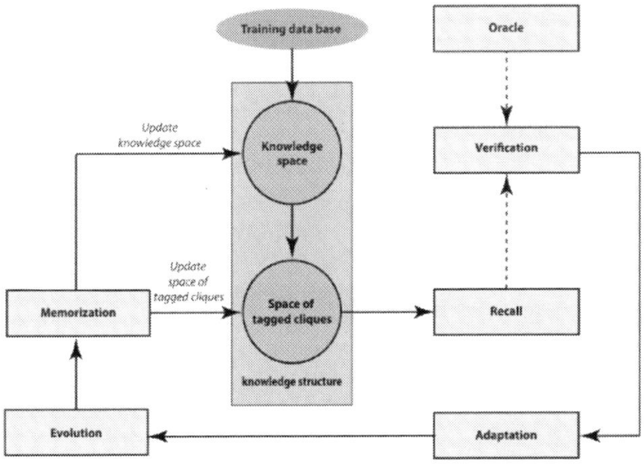

Figure 1. Off-line training

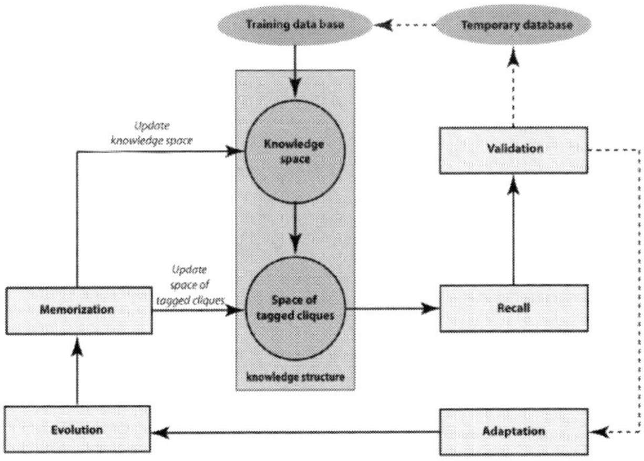

Figure 2. On-line training

III. Implementation

A. System initialization

Let us denote by $\{I_i\}_{i=1}^{L}$ the set of L images that are available in the training database. In the initialization phase, we begin by randomly selecting one single image for each person k represented in the training database. By so proceeding, we obtain c images $\{J_k\}_{k=1}^{c}$, where c is the number of persons to cope with. This set of images is used to create and initialize the knowledge structure as follows.

The space of tagged-cliques: This space is created as proposed in [6]. More specifically, we consider n neurons. This set of neurons is split into two non-intersecting clusters. Cluster #1 contains d neurons and cluster #2 involves c neurons so that: $n = d + c$. The d neurons of cluster #1 are indexed from 1 to d and the c neurons of cluster #2 are indexed from $d + 1$ to n. The space of tagged-cliques is then constructed to store the c gallery-vectors $\mathbf{g}_k$ for $k = 1, 2, \ldots, c$ corresponding to the c persons to recognize. This construction is carried out according to the several steps described below.

Initialization of the knowledge space: We calculate the set F_k of the local features of each given image J_k [3], [4], [12]. Let us suppose that $F_k = \{F_k^1, \ldots, F_k^m\}$, where the F_k^j's are the local SIFT features and m is the number of these local SIFT features extracted from the image. Note that m may differ from one image to another. To each F_k^j, we associate a neuron n_k^j in cluster #1. This choice may be random, but constrained so as to be one-to-one for person k. Let Ψ stand for this correspondence so that $\Psi(F_k^j) = n_k^j$. We then create the one-to-one correspondence that assigns to each $F_k = \{F_k^1, \ldots, F_k^m\}$ the set $N_k = \{n_k^1, \ldots, n_k^m\}$. This correspondence can be represented by the set of pairs: $\mathbf{D}_k = (F_k; N_k)$. This set $\mathfrak{S} = \{\mathbf{D}_k : k = 1, 2, \ldots, c\}$ is the initial knowledge space and our purpose is then to upgrade this knowledge space.

Initialization of the space of tagged-cliques: After determining and storing $\mathbf{D}_k$, the vector N_k of neuron indexes is stored in the space of tagged-cliques by proceeding as follows.

1) We define the binary pattern $\boldsymbol{x}_k$ with dimension d ($\boldsymbol{x}_k \in \{0; 1\}^d$) by setting:

$$(\boldsymbol{x}_k)_i = \begin{cases} 1 & \text{if } i \in N_k \\ 0 & \text{otherwise} \end{cases} \tag{1}$$

2) We associate to $\boldsymbol{x}_k$ the kth element e_k of the canonical basis of $\mathbb{R}^c$, which can be regarded as a very basic full disjunctive coding:

$$(\boldsymbol{e}_k)_i = \begin{cases} 1 & \text{if } i = k \\ 0 & \text{otherwise} \end{cases}$$

In other words, vector e_k represents the identity of person k.

3) The gallery-vector $\boldsymbol{g}_k$ is then defined by

$$\boldsymbol{g}_k = \begin{pmatrix} \boldsymbol{x}_k \\ \boldsymbol{e}_k \end{pmatrix} \tag{2}$$

4) The storage of the gallery-vectors $\boldsymbol{g}_k$ is performed by calculating the adjacency matrix:

$$\boldsymbol{W} = \bigvee_k \boldsymbol{g}_k \boldsymbol{g}_k^T \tag{3}$$

where $(\cdot)^T$ is the standard transpose operator.

B. Off-line training

After initializing the knowledge space and the space of tagged-cliques as described above for only one single image per person to recognize, the off-line phase is engaged. This off-line updating makes it possible to reduce the number of features to store in the knowledge base and the number of possibly contentious connections in the space of tagged-cliques. Only features of interest will be added in the knowledge structure during the updating.

The off-line phase is applied to the images

$$\bar{I} = \{I_i\}_{i=1}^L \setminus \{J_k\}_{k=1}^c$$

that were not selected in the initialization phase. The several processes (recall, verification, adaptation, evolution and memorization) are performed as follows.

1) Recall process: Given $\bar{I}_j \in \bar{I}$, we calculate as above the feature vector $\bar{F}_j$ by extracting the local SIFT vector features in $\bar{I}_j$. We then look for the closest feature vector $\bar{F}$ in the knowledge space via a simple L_2 minimization. This vector feature $\bar{F}$ is associated with a set of neurons $\bar{N}$. We derive the input pattern $\boldsymbol{x}$ associated with $\bar{F}$ and $\bar{N}$ via (1) with $N_k = \bar{N}$. According to [12], we then use Algorithm 1 with

$$f(\mathbf{v})_i = \begin{cases} 1 & \text{if } \mathbf{v}_i = \max_j \mathbf{v}_j \\ 0 & \text{otherwise} \end{cases} \tag{4}$$

to estimate the pattern and identity corresponding to $\bar{F}$ and its associated set $\bar{N}$ of neurons. In this algorithm, $\pi_{\mathbf{x}}(\mathbf{v})$ (resp. $\pi_{\mathbf{e}}(\mathbf{v})$) extracts the vector made of the first (resp. last) d (resp. c) coordinates of $\mathbf{v} \in \mathbb{R}^n$.

Algorithm 1: Recall algorithm by neural network of tagged cliques

---

Input: Input pattern $\boldsymbol{x}$ and adjacency matrix $\boldsymbol{W}$
Output: $\widehat{\boldsymbol{e}}_k$, the class indicator vector estimated for $\mathbf{x}$

1 $\widehat{\boldsymbol{x}} = \pi_{\boldsymbol{x}}\left(f(\boldsymbol{W}\begin{pmatrix}\boldsymbol{x}\\ \mathbf{0}^c\end{pmatrix})\right)$;

2 $\widehat{\boldsymbol{e}}_k = \pi_{\boldsymbol{e}}\left(f(\boldsymbol{W}\begin{pmatrix}\widehat{\boldsymbol{x}}\\ \mathbf{0}^c\end{pmatrix})\right)$;

---

2) Verification process: During the off-line training phase, we suppose that the identity of the face image is known. We thus propose a verification process by oracle. By thus proceeding, the identity returned by the system is verified and compared to the supervisor knowledge during the off-line training phase. This verification avoids that the system makes erroneous identifications, which is probable as long as the system has not acquired enough knowledge to allow for automatic identification.

3) Adaptation process: At the end of the recall and verification processes, the identity of the face query image is determined. For a given identity k issued from these processes and validated by the supervisor, the purpose of the adaptation process is to discriminate the knowledge already stored in the knowledge structure for person k from that brought by the new image.

During the adaptation process, the neuron indexes used to encode person k as a clique are determined from the space of tagged cliques by algorithm 2, where $\mathbf{0}^d$ is the zero vector with dimension d.

Algorithm 2: Algorithm used to retrieve pattern $\boldsymbol{x}_k$ when $\boldsymbol{e}_k$ is known.

Input: $\boldsymbol{e}_k$, the class indicator vector
Output: $\boldsymbol{x}_k$, pattern associated to $\boldsymbol{e}_k$

1 $\boldsymbol{x}_k = \pi_x\left(W\begin{pmatrix}\mathbf{0}^d\\ \boldsymbol{e}^k\end{pmatrix}\right)$

At the end of the adaptation process, we obtain pattern $\boldsymbol{x}_k$. By inverting (1), we then determine the set N_k of neurons corresponding to $\boldsymbol{x}_k$. The set N_k can be regarded as the knowledge already stored for person k in the space of tagged-cliques. The new knowledge brought by a new image of person k is collected in a set denoted N^* and determined by:

$$N^* = \bar{N} \setminus N_k \tag{5}$$

The new features that can be associated with person k are then given by $F^* = \Psi^{-1}(N^*)$, where Ψ is defined in Section III-A. In order to maintain the one-to-one correspondence between features and neurons for person k, the neurons in N^* are replaced by new randomly selected neurons in cluster #1 to form a new set of neurons. This new set is still denoted N^* in what follows and can then be associated univoquely to F^* so as to form the new pair:

$$\mathbf{D}^* = (F^*; N^*). \tag{6}$$

4) Evolution process: For person k, the adaptation process has separated new pieces of knowledge brought by a new image of k and knowledge already stored in the knowledge structure. The evolution process aims to combine these two types of information, namely the new pieces of knowledge and those already stored in the system. The combination then amounts to creating the new pattern $\boldsymbol{x}_k^* \in \{0;1\}^d$ as follows:

$$(\boldsymbol{x}_k^*)_i = \begin{cases} 1 & \text{if } i \in N_k \cup N^* \\ 0 & \text{otherwise} \end{cases}$$

In addition, the new gallery-vector $\boldsymbol{g}_k^*$ calculated according to

$$\boldsymbol{g}_k^* = \begin{pmatrix}\boldsymbol{x}_k^*\\ \boldsymbol{e}_k\end{pmatrix}$$

where $\boldsymbol{e}_k$ is the kth element of the canonical basis in $\mathbb{R}^c$.

5) Memorization process: The memorization process has the role of storing the updated pattern $\boldsymbol{g}_k^*$ in the space of tagged cliques and adding the new identified features to the knowledge space. More precisely, updating the knowledge space is simply performed by adding $\mathbf{D}^*$ to the knowledge space by making:

$$\mathfrak{S} \leftarrow \mathfrak{S} \cup \{\mathbf{D}^*\}.$$

Regarding incremental learning in the space of tagged cliques, the new gallery-vector $\boldsymbol{g}_k^*$ is stored as a tagged clique as:

$$\boldsymbol{W} \leftarrow \boldsymbol{W} \bigvee \boldsymbol{g}_k^* (\boldsymbol{g}_k^*)^T$$

During the off-line phase, the update is performed for all the face images in the training database. This update will continue automatically and without the supervision of the oracle during the on-line phase.

C. On-line training

At the end of the off-line training phase, by engaging the testing database, the system continues to update automatically the knowledge structure without any supervision of the oracle. The processes involved in the on-line training phase are *Recall*, *Validation*, *Adaptation*, *Evolution* and *Memorization*.

During the on-line training phase, the recall, adaptation, evolution and memorization processes are the same as those used by the off-line training phase described in Section III-B.

Without supervision, the system may incorporate false information to persons. To avoid this, the system must reject query images whose identification is uncertain. Deciding whether a face query image must be rejected or not is performed by the *Validation* process, which replaces the verification process of the off-line training phase.

1) Validation process: At a given time t, accepting or not new information provided by a query face image I is the task of the validation process. This process determines the score Φ assigned to the recognition of I by:

$$\Phi = \pi_e \left(W \begin{pmatrix} \boldsymbol{x} \\ \mathbf{0}^c \end{pmatrix} \right), \qquad (7)$$

where $\boldsymbol{x}$ is the input pattern calculated according to Eq. (1). The ith coordinate of Φ represents the number of connections between the ith neuron in cluster #2 and the neurons in cluster #1 that are associated with $\boldsymbol{x}$. The idea is to validate and thus incorporate the new information brought by I if only one single neuron in cluster #2 has received a significantly larger number of votes than any other neuron. The significance of the number of votes is determined by deriving the sorted values of Φ in descending order. More specifically:

- Let $\bar{\Phi} = (\Phi_{(1)}, \Phi_{(2)}, \cdots, \Phi_{(c)})$ be the sequence of the values of Φ sorted in descending order: $\Phi_{(1)} \geqslant \Phi_{(2)} \geqslant \ldots \geqslant \Phi_{(c)}$.
- Set up the test:

$$\Gamma = \begin{cases} 1 & \text{if } card(C) = 1 \\ 0 & \text{otherwise} \end{cases}$$

where $C = \{(1), (2), \cdots, \arg\max_{1 \leq i \leq c} \bar{\Phi}'\}$ and $\bar{\Phi}'$ is the derivative of $\bar{\Phi}$.

As a result, if the test decision Γ returns 1, the query face image is used to enrich the knowledge structure by the processes of the on-line training phase. At a given time t, if the test decision Γ returns 0, this image is sent to a temporary database. When the on-line training phase is completed, the images collected in the temporary database are re-injected into the system for a new re-evaluation.

D. Experimental results on the ORL database

We tested the incremental learning system described above on the Olivetti and Oracle Research Laboratory (ORL) database. There are 10 different images for each of the 40 distinct subjects. For some subjects, the images were taken at different times, varying lighting, with different facial expressions (open / closed eyes, smiling / not smiling), facial details (glasses / no glasses) and head pose (tilting and rotation up to 20 degrees). All the images were taken against a dark homogeneous background.

These experimentation make it possible to better assess the effect of the oracle's supervision. This supervision is basically parametrized by the number K of images used during the off-line training phase. More specifically, if only one image per person is used to initialize the training, $K-1$ images among the remaining ones in the database for a given person will be employed. After off-line upgrading of the knowledge structure, the on-line training is engaged on the images remaining in the database. Once the on-line training is terminated, we assess the ability of the system to recognize the identity of the persons whose images are present in the test database. For every given K, the face recognition performance measurements of the system are given in Table I by averaging the results over 10 different tests where the images during the training are randomly chosen for every test. By so proceeding, we follow standard recommendations of the literature on the topic.

TABLE I. FACE RECOGNITION RATES OBTAINED WITH AND WITHOUT INCREMENTAL TRAINING

Method	Number of training images			
	K = 5	K = 6	K = 7	K = 8
Static leaning	98.82	99.55	99.71	99.88
Incremental learning	**98.91**	**99.6**	**99.91**	**100**

According to these results, it turns out that from $K = 8$ onwards, the system commits no error to recognize the images of the test database. In any case, even when the face recognition rate is not 100%, incremental learning always yields performance improvement.

We can also consider the number of features stored in the knowledge space. We expect that incremental learning also optimizes this number. This is actually the case as shown by Figure 3. The number of features stored in the knowledge space is significantly lesser than that obtained without incremental learning.

IV. Conclusion

We have presented an approach that performs face recognition after incremental learning on the basis of

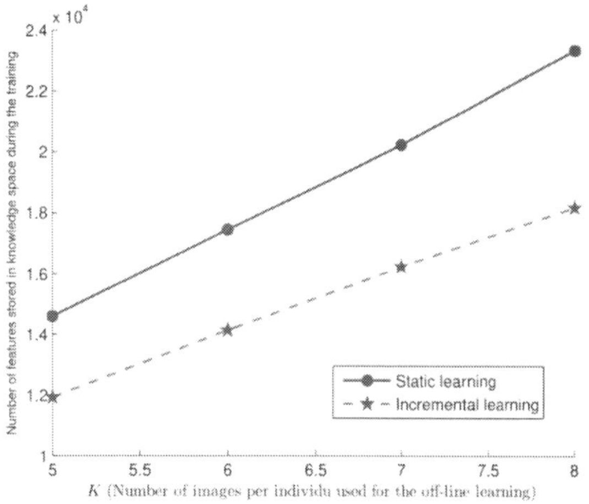

Figure 3. The number of features stored in knowledge space during the training

a neural network of tagged cliques. This system is an extension of the face recognition system introduced in [12]. Nevertheless, the reader will easily notice that the neural network of tagged cliques could certainly be replaced by other types of classification. For instance, features could be stored without any coding and exhaustive search would even be thinkable. However, networks of neural cliques present two fundamental advantages. First, the coding and decoding processes are fast and the storage of a new clique is performed independently of all the cliques previously stored.

The system proposed in this paper is then capable of updating its knowledge structure incrementally, first via a supervised phase and then automatically. Experimental results on the ORL database enhance the relevance of the incremental approach, which makes it possible to optimize the number of features stored and yield face recognition rates better than that obtained without incremental learning.

References

[1] C. Riesbeck and R. Schank, Inside case-based reasoning. Psychology Press, 2013.

[2] J. Richard, C. Bonnet, R. Ghiglione, M. Bromberg, J. Beavois, and W. Doise, "Traité de psychologie cognitive: cognition, représentation, communication," 1990.

[3] D. Lowe, "Object recognition from local scale-invariant features," in Computer vision, 1999. The proceedings of the seventh IEEE international conference on, vol. 2. Ieee, 1999, pp. 1150–1157.

[4] M. Aly, "Face recognition using sift features," CNS/Bi/EE report, vol. 186, 2006.

[5] L. Lenc and P. Král, "Novel matching methods for automatic face recognition using sift," Artificial Intelligence Applications and Innovations, 2012, pp. 254–263.

[6] S. Larroque, E. Sedgh Gooya, V. Gripon, and D. Pastor, "Using tags to improve diversity of sparse associative memories," in Proceedings of Cognitive, March 2015, pp. 1–7.

[7] V. Gripon and C. Berrou, "Sparse neural networks with large learning diversity," Neural Networks, IEEE Transactions on, vol. 22, no. 7, 2011, pp. 1087–1096.

[8] B. Kamary Aliabadi, C. Berrou, V. Gripon, and X. Jiang, "Learning sparse messages in networks of neural cliques," arXiv preprint arXiv:1208.4009, 2012.

[9] X. Jiang, V. Gripon, and C. Berrou, "Learning long sequences in binary neural networks," in COGNITIVE 2012, The Fourth International Conference on Advanced Cognitive Technologies and Applications, 2012, pp. 165–170.

[10] R. Danilo, H. N. Wouafo, C. Chavet, and P. Coussy, "Associative memory based on clustered neural networks: improved model and architecture for oriented edge detection," in Conference on Design & Architectures for Signal & Image Processing, 2016.

[11] D. Ferro, V. Gripon, and X. Jiang, "Nearest neighbour search using binary neural networks," in Proceedings of IJCNN, July 2016.

[12] E. Sedgh Gooya, D. Pastor, and V. Gripon, "Automatic face recognition using sift and networks of tagged neural cliques," in Cognitive 2015, The Seventh International Conference on Advanced Cognitive Technologies and Applications, 2015.

Finding All Matches in a Database using Binary Neural Networks

Ghouthi Boukli Hacene, Vincent Gripon, Nicolas Farrugia, Matthieu Arzel and Michel Jezequel
IMT Atlantique
Brest, France
email: name.surname@telecom-bretagne.eu

Abstract—**The most efficient architectures of associative memories are based on binary neural networks. As example, Sparse Clustered Networks (SCNs) are able to achieve almost optimal memory efficiency while providing robust indexation of pieces of information through cliques in a neural network. In the canonical formulation of the associative memory problem, the unique stored message matching a given input probe is to be retrieved. In this paper, we focus on the more general problem of finding all messages matching the given probe. We consider real datasets from which many different messages can match given probes, which cannot be done with uniformly distributed messages due to their unlikelyhood of sharing large common parts with one another. Namely, we implement a crossword dictionary containing 8-letter english words, and a chess endgame dataset using associative memories based on binary neural networks. We explain how to adapt SCNs' architecture to this challenging dataset and introduce a backtracking procedure to retrieve all completions of the given input. We stress the performance of the proposed method using different measures and discuss the importance of parameters.**

Keywords–Neural Networks, Associative Memories, Sparse Coding, Iterative Information Processing

I. Introduction

Associative memories are devices in which stored content may be addressed from part of it. Consider for instance a melody which is brought back to memory from the first music notes. Their functioning offer an alternative to classical indexed-based memories in which an absolute address is required in order to access content. For this reason, they are considered as a plausible model for human memory [1]. Associative memories are also very popular in electronics as they are key components of many systems[2]-[8]

There are basically two ways to design associative memories. In errorless applications, the content of the memory is typically indexed in such a way that it is possible to perform a fully parallel search to find a match of a given request. This is in particular the functioning of Content Addressable Memories (CAMs) [2]. When errors are tolerable, the most effective systems are based on recurrent neural networks [3]. These networks then split into two categories: binary systems and weighted ones. It is well known that weighted systems offer poorer performance than their binary counterpart [4].

Binary associative memories have been introduced in the 60s and popularized since thanks to their remarkable performance. These systems have in common that they embody pieces of information as patterns in binary graphs. For uniformly distributed messages and well scaled parameters, it has been conjectured for a long time and proven recently [5] that these systems are able to achieve very good performance asymptotically. Experiments support that performance is also very good for medium size neural networks (i.e., networks containing a few thousands of units). Because they compare favorably to other existing works [5], we decided to focus on SCNs in this paper.

A key component to obtain good performance in binary associative memories is the choice of the retrieval process. There is a vast literature on the subject [6]. However, most of the existing works focus on the scenario where there is a unique match associated with the given probe (with the noticeable exception of [7]). In this paper, we are interested in finding all stored contents that are associated with the given probe. This problem is of paramount importance when targeting applications in artificial intelligence and cognitive science [8].

In order to stress our proposed method on real datasets, we decided to focus on the implementation of a crossword dictionary able to retrieve any 8-letter english words from a partially erased input, and a chess endgame database to validate the genericity of the method. Mainly, our contributions are twofold: we show a) how to design a binary associative memory able to store then retrieve messages with almost zero error probability. For this purpose, we propose a strategy loosely based on "twin neurons" [9]. And b) we propose a backtracking solution to find all completions of the given input instead of a unique one. Our proposed solution is evaluated and parameters influence is discussed thoroughly.

The outline of the paper is as follows. In Section II, we introduce related work. In Section III, we present the proposed methodology used to store nonuniform data and to retrieve all matches associated with a given request. Mathematical analysis is performed in Section IV. Experiments results are presented in Section V. Finally, Section VI is a conclusion.

II. Related work

Solutions have been proposed in the literature in order to handle nonuniform distributions in binary associative memories. It is in particular the case in [10] for the Willshaw model. However, the lack of structure in this type of associative memories makes it difficult to propose efficient strategies.

In the context of SCNs, interesting results have been obtained using restricted models [11] inspired by the functioning of restricted Boltzmann machines. In this work, the authors propose to use a bipartite graph in which stored messages are associated with i.i.d. uniform ones. They show that this strategy allows for very efficient processing of visual signals.

A comparison of proposed approaches have been proposed in [12] and then extended and applied to real datasets in [9].

In their work, the authors show the interest of using data driven approaches in which overused parts of the network are scaled accordingly in order to counterbalance the effect of nonuniformity on performance. Our proposed solution is in the same vein.

In [13], the authors use a combination of twin neurons and a "boosting" technique in order to retrieve messages in adversarial scenarios. In [7], the authors propose for the first time to adapt retrieval procedures of neural network based associative memories in order to solve complex challenges, including finding all matches associated with a given request. In this work, the authors propose to use a simulated annealing approach to solve this specific problem, leading to very good performance at the cost of dramatically increased complexity. The solution we propose obtain exactly the same output but with reduced complexity.

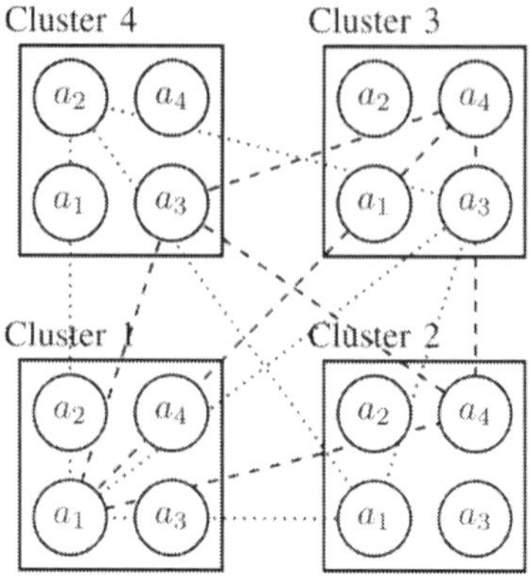

Figure 1. Illustration of the storage procedure in SCNs.

III. METHODOLOGY

Our proposed solution is based on SCNs. In the next subsections, we introduce SCNs using the notations of the initial works [14][15]. We then explain how to manage nonuniformly distributed messages. Finally, we propose a solution to obtain all stored messages that are completions of the given input (instead of only one in classical SCNs).

A. *Sparse Clustered Networks*

Consider a finite alphabet $\mathcal{A}$ made of ℓ symbols. We call message a word over $\mathcal{A}$ containing c symbols exactly. We denote by m such a message and by m_i its i-th symbol.

SCNs are binary associative memories that are able to store a set $\mathcal{M}$ of M messages and retrieve one of them with a nonzero probability when part of its symbols are missing. More precisely, it has been shown that for i.i.d. uniform messages and for some parameters (*e.g.*, $c = \log(\ell)$, $M < 2\log(\log(\ell))\ell^2$), this probability tends to one [5].

The storage procedure is as follows: a neural network made of $c \times \ell$ units is considered. Units are split into c parts (we term them "clusters") of equal size indexed from 1 to c. Inside each cluster, units are then indexed using symbols of $\mathcal{A}$, *i.e.*, each unit is associated one-to-one with a symbol in $\mathcal{A}$. As a result, each unit is uniquely determined by a couple (i, a), where $1 \leq i \leq c$ and $a \in \mathcal{A}$.

It is thus possible to associate a message with a set of c units, through the function:

$$f : m \mapsto \{(i, m_i), 1 \leq i \leq c\}.$$

To store the messages contained in $\mathcal{M}$, the procedure consists in, starting from a neural network with no connection, adding all connections between units in $f(m)$ for each message $m \in \mathcal{M}$. Let us denote by $W_{(i,a)(i',a')}$ the adjacency matrix of the neural network ($W_{(i,a)(i',a')} = 1$ iff units (i, a) and (i', a') are connected). This process is illustrated in Figure 1. In Figure 1 the alphabet is $\mathcal{A} = \{a_1, a_2, a_3, a_4\}$ and $c = 4$. The stored messages are $m_1 = [a_1, a_1, a_3, a_2]$ and $m_2 = [a_1, a_4, a_4, a_3]$. Connections added by the storage of m_1 and m_2 have been depicted differently (dashed vs. dotted lines) in order to ease reading, but connections in the network are binary and thus not labelled.

Once a set of messages has been stored, an iterative retrieval procedure is used to recall one of them from a partially erased probe.

Consider a message $m \in \mathcal{M}$, we introduce the erasure function:

$$\tilde{\cdot} : m \mapsto \tilde{m} \text{ such that } \forall i, \tilde{m}_i = m_i \vee \tilde{m}_i = \perp,$$

where $\perp \notin \mathcal{A}$ denotes an erased symbol. Consider an indicator function $v : \{1, 2, \ldots, n\} \times \mathcal{A} \to \{0, 1\}$ which associates a unit with its binary activation state (active or not).

Considering $\tilde{m}$ as an input, an optimized retrieval procedure [6] consists in repeating the following two steps, starting with v^0 the indicator function of $f(\tilde{m})$:

1) Estimate a likelihood score for each unit in the network to be activated, based on the connection they share with other units in the network. To do so, for each unit (i, a) is computed the score $s^{t+1}_{i,a} = \sum_{i'=1}^{c} \max_{a' \in \mathcal{A}} \left[W_{(i,a)(i',a')} v^t_{i',a'}\right]$. In other words, for each unit we count how many clusters of the neural network contain an activated unit which they are connected to.
2) Based on the previously computed score, select the units to activate or not. Here, we simply activate the units with the maximum score among their clusters.

It can easily be shown that this iterative procedure converges as the set of activated units is nonincreasing with iterations, starting at the second iteration [5].

The converged state v^∞ corresponds to the output of the neural network. In case a unique unit is activated in each cluster, this state can be mapped to the corresponding message m such that v^∞ is the indicator function of $f(m)$.

Obtaining mathematical proofs of performance can prove to be challenging [5]. This is why many works make the simplifying assumption that, when messages to store are i.i.d. uniform, existence of connections in the neural network can be considered independent. Numerous experimental works justify this assumption [15]. In this context, it is possible to derive probability of success in retrieving a stored message from a

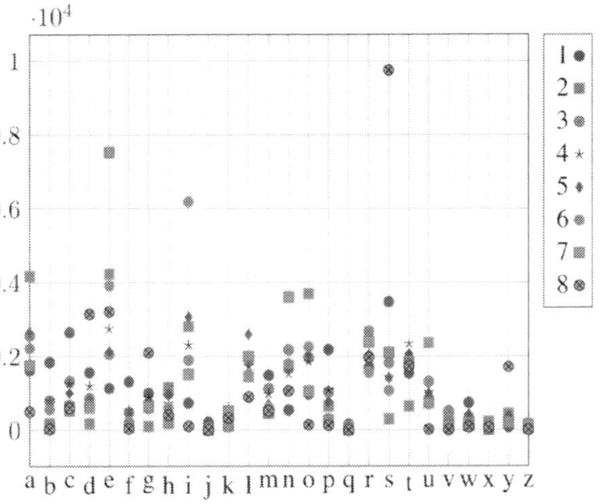

Figure 2. Histogram representing the frequency of apparition of each symbol ('A' to 'Z') for each possible position (1 to 8).

partially erased probe containing c_e erased symbols [15]:

$$P_e = 1 - \left(1 - \left(1 - (1 - \ell^{-2})^M\right)^{c-c_e}\right)^{(\ell-1)c_e}.$$

B. Nonuniformity of Stored Messages

It is well known that nonuniformity of stored messages can lead to dramatic loss in performance [10]. Many solutions have been proposed [12]. All of them consist in adding material, either units in each cluster or new clusters, in order to counterbalance the effect of nonuniformity.

The technique known to offer best performance is called "twin neurons" [9]. It consists in duplicating overconnected units in the network. The method we propose in this paper, is inspired by this mechanism.

First, let us introduce the first dataset used in this paper. We decided to use english words made of 8 letters. We use a database containing $M = 28'557$ such words [16]. Obviously this database contains a nonuniform distribution of words, such that some letters are more frequent than others. As an illustration, Figure 2 depicts the frequency of apparition of each symbol at each possible position. Using the classical method – namely we assign the same number of units with each symbol – some units are saturated with connections, leading to dramatically low performance. To avoid this, we duplicate units in the neural network corresponding to the overused symbols, such that the connections are divided accordingly. This process is depicted in Figure 3 and more precisely described in the following paragraphs.

In our proposed method, words of 8 symbols are represented using 8 clusters (one per position in the word). But contrary to classical SCNs, we use more than the required 26 units. Specifically, in order to represent a symbol at a given position, we use possibly more than a single unit. Consider symbol a at position i, and denote λ (here λ is no longer the cardinality of $\mathcal{A}$) the number of units in each cluster, $W(i,a)$ the number of eight symbol which i-th one is a, then the number of units representing a in cluster i is

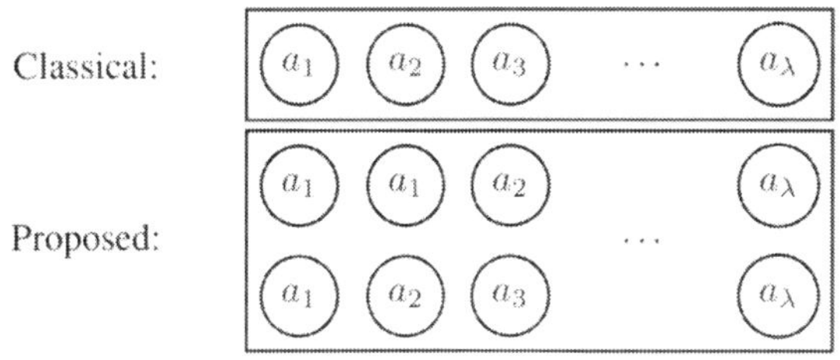

Figure 3. Illustration of the proposed solution to duplicate units corresponding to more frequent symbols.

$$N(i,a) = \frac{W(i,a)}{M}\lambda.$$

Said otherwise, units representing symbol a at position i are proportional to the frequency of 8-letter words containing symbol a at position i.

The storing process is then modified. As a matter of fact, there is now multiple choices of units to activate in each cluster. The idea is to choose one of them alternatively in order to balance the number of connections per unit. This is depicted in Figure 4. Depending on the frequency of each symbol at each position, some units have been duplicated. The first stored message is $[a_1, a_1, a_3, a_3]$, as depicted in the first step. Because there are two units representing symbol a_1 in cluster 1, an arbitrary choice has been performed. The second message to store is $[a_1, a_2, a_2, a_1]$, making use again of symbol a_1 in cluster 1. This time the other unit has been chosen to balance connections in the neural network. The first added message makes use of a unit representing symbol a_1 in cluster 1 and the next message makes use of another unit representing a_1 in cluster 1.

C. Finding all Matches of a Given Request

Crosswords players are familiar with configurations where a few characters erased can lead to many different combinations. This is typically not expected with uniformly distributed messages, as the probability λ^{-c_0} two words share c_0 common given symbols vanishes exponentially fast to zero with c_0.

When multiple stored messages are completions of the input probe, the retrieval process is expected to converge to a state where active units contain at least the union of the units corresponding to the different possible outputs. Finding which unit is associated with each other is a combinatorial problem that may prove challenging in practice.

To illustrate the problem, consider that at the end of the retrieval process, 10 units are activated in the 4 initially erased clusters. A possible explanation is that there are 10 completions of the initial probe, corresponding to the activation of its own unit in each cluster. But, in terms of combinatorial possibilities, there are $10'000$ possibilities.

In practice, having to check every single possibility would lead to considerable increase in complexity. This is why we introduce a backtracking alternative solution.

Suppose we have a set of activated units s_i in the i-th cluster. We propose to select one of them arbitrarily, unactivate all others, and pursue the retrieval process. Once

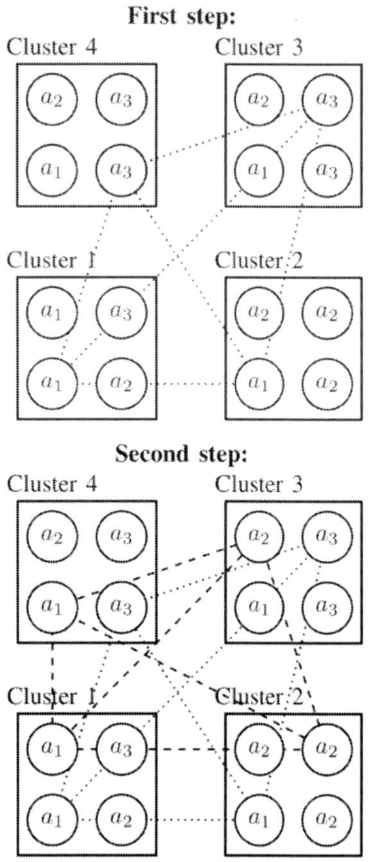

Figure 4. Illustration of the updated storage procedure. Here the alphabet is $\mathcal{A} = \{a_1, a_2, a_3\}$ and $c = 4$.

it is completed, we unactivate the previously selected unit and remove it from s_i, and select another unit arbitrarily in s_i to start the process again. Once all units have been activated once in s_i, the process is over. Such strategy is commonly known as backtracking in computer science literature.

In ideal conditions, that is to say when solutions are nonoverlapping over the initially erased clusters, this procedure reaches a complexity that is linear with the number of solutions. This is why it is expected to perform well in practice. On the other hand, the complexity is upper bounded by the product of cardinalities of s_i, which correspond to the combinatorial factor previously introduced.

This backtracking solution offers another advantage when combined with the twin neurons strategy described in the previous subsection. As a matter of fact, selecting arbitrarily a unit in each cluster when storing a message is a good strategy to balance connections, but as a result this association is lost and when a probe is given to the network, all units corresponding to the given symbols should be activated. Said otherwise, a lot of spurious units are likely to be activated at the beginning of the retrieval process, due to the duplication of some units in the neural network.

In order to avoid this added difficulty, we propose to use the same backtracking solution previously described at the beginning of the process also, in order to erase most of spurious units at the beginning of the retrieval process.

We can illustrate this by a good example from the database. For $\lambda = 512$, consider the words aardvark and aardwolf, that could be addressed from the request aard****, where '*' denotes an erased symbol. For this scenario, we obtain 29 units corresponding to the letter 'a' in the first cluster, 75 to the letter 'a' in the second cluster, 48 to the letter 'r' in the third cluster and 21 to the letter 'd' in the fourth cluster. Thus, there are $2'192'400$ possible combinations. Using the backtracking algorithm to reduce this number, we obtain only 2 units active in each of these clusters. Actually, these two active units in each cluster are those corresponding to the two words aardvark and aardwolf exactly.

IV. Mathematical Analysis

The overall procedure corresponding to the retrieval of the messages matching a given input probe is summarized in Algorithm 1.

1. Activate all units corresponding to the nonerased symbols of $\tilde{m}$
2. Use the backtracking algorithm to remove some of the spurious units
3. Perform the decoding procedure
4. Use the backtracking algorithm to obtain guesses

Algorithm 1: Algorithm used to retrieve the stored messages corresponding to an initially partially erased probe $\tilde{m}$.

A first result is that Algorithm 1 will output all of the messages in $\mathcal{M}$ that match the probe $\tilde{m}$:

Proposition 1. *Consider a binary associative memory in which the messages in $\mathcal{M}$ have been stored. For any message $m \in \mathcal{M}$, the output of Algorithm 1 given $\tilde{m}$ as input contains all the messages in $\mathcal{M}$ that are completions of $\tilde{m}$.*

Proof: The proof is a straightforward adaptation of the proof for the classical SCNs in [5]. It is mainly based on the fact a stored message which is a completion of the input will always achieve the maximum scores in the retrieval process, and therefore the corresponding units will remain activated. ■

Note that this result does not imply that the output messages given by Algorithm 1 is exactly the correct answer, but only that it contains the correct answers. In practice, it is expected that for some queries the output contains more messages than it should.

Another interesting result is that, for large enough values of λ, the obtained associative memory has vanishing error probability:

Proposition 2. *Consider a set of messages $\mathcal{M}$. Then, the probability the output messages given by Algorithm 1 for some query $\tilde{m}$ with $m \in \mathcal{M}$ is exactly the set of messages in $\mathcal{M}$ that are completions of $\tilde{m}$ tends to one as λ tends to infinity.*

Proof: Indeed, consider the extreme case where messages in $\mathcal{M}$ are stored in the binary neural network using completely disjoint sets of units. Using very simple arguments of binomials, this happens with probability that tends to one as λ

tends to infinity. In such situation, step 2 of Algorithm 1 will keep active only the units that correspond to the targeted set of messages. Indeed, a unit can only remain active if sharing connections with all initially active units, which happens by definition only if part of a targeted message. For similar reasons, a message retrieved after step 4 of Algorithm 1 is such that all its units are interconnected, so it must correspond to a stored message. Because it is in particular connected with all the initially activated units, it is a targeted message. ■

Obviously, in practical applications, it is of paramount importance to find a good tradeoff between precision and complexity of the method, varying the value of λ. This will be discussed in the next section.

V. Experiments

In this section, we present an analysis of complexity and error rates of the proposed method, in comparison with the one described in [7]. We refer to complexity as the average number of elementary operations, which are arithmetical operations or memory accesses.

First, we examine the influence of cluster size λ on complexity using the 8-letter words dataset. The number of elementaru operations is 409 millions for $\lambda = 256$, 64 millions for $\lambda = 384$ and 8.1 millions for $\lambda = 512$.

Interestingly, larger networks have dramatically lower complexity than small networks. This phenomenon can be easily explained by examining the influence of network size on error rates results; as error decreases with increasing network size, the size of the search space decreases because fewer units are interconnected. As a consequence, the proposed backtracking algorithm eliminates more cases, resulting in a reduction of complexity.

We then compute the error rate of the proposed method. We note N the number of examples in the dataset. The add result error rate (ARER) is defined using the number P of undesirable cases obtained (cases which do not figure on the dataset). The forget result error rate (FRER) is defined using the number F of cases which figure in the dataset, but are not obtained by the method. These two error rates can be expressed in the following way:

$$ARER = \frac{P}{P+N} \qquad FRER = \frac{F}{N}$$

As stated in Proposition 1, the proposed method will always output at least the actual matches in the dataset, so FRER is equal to zero. Unless stated otherwise, we will refer to the ARER when using the term "error rate".

We examine error rate as a function of a) the number of stored messages and b) the size of the network, expressed as the number of units λ in each cluster. To do so, we randomly select a message $m \in \mathcal{M}$, and then erase randomly 4 symbols, getting a partially erased probe $\tilde{m}$ as an input of Algorithm 1. We repeat this procedure to compute the average error over the testset. Figure 5 shows simulation results for the 8-letter words. A network containing 256 units cannot memorise more than 7100 Messages, otherwise it retrieves them when they are half erased with a low probability (Figure 5), so it cannot handle the entire testset. A network with 384 units obtains a 3% error rate, while a network with 512 units retrieves half

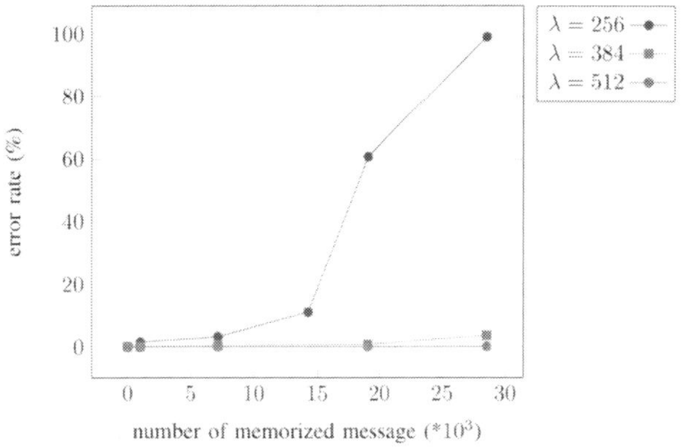

Figure 5. Error rate as a function of the number of stored messages and network size λ for the 8-letter words dataset. In these experiments, the retrieval procedure performs 4 iterations.

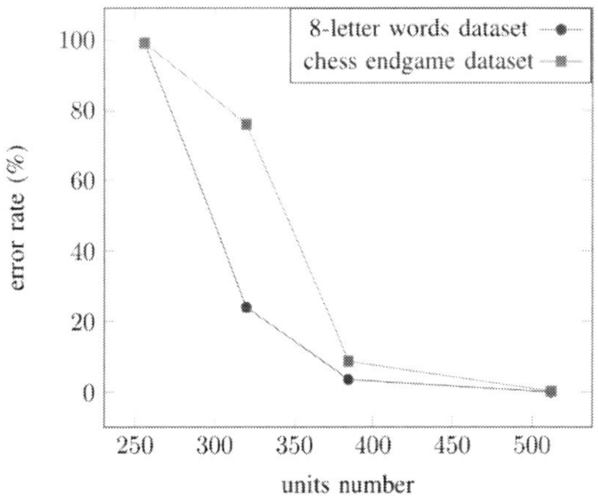

Figure 6. Error rate as a function of network size λ in two different datasets. Retrieval using 4 iterations.

erased messages with an error rate approaching the zero (blue line in Figure 6).

We use a second dataset to validate the genericity of the method. The chess endgame database [17] contains 7 attributes which represent white King position (2 attributes), white Rook position (2 attributes), black King position (2 attributes) and the optimal depth-of-win for white (1 attribute). The test protocol is the same as for the 8-letter words dataset, except that we randomly erase 3 symbols instead of 4. Figure 6 depicts for both datasets a decrease in error rate when increasing the number of units in the cluster.

Importantly, we observe that a network with 512 units leads to an optimal solution, in the sense that it minimizes both error and complexity. We choose this network to perform a comparison with the work in [7] which featured a network with 8 clusters of 512 units. Table I compares the two methods in terms of complexity and the two types of error rates.

The complexity of the proposed method is largely reduced. The ARER is almost the same for both methods, while FRER is 43% for [7] and 0% for the proposed method. This demonstrates that the proposed method leads to substantial enhancements both in terms of complexity and error rates

TABLE I. Comparing the complexity and the errors of our method and the method described in [14]

	Elementary operations	ARER	FRER
Proposed solution ($\lambda = 512$)	8.1 millions	0.045%	0%
Method described in [14]	878 millions	0.05%	43%

demonstrates that the proposed method leads to substantial enhancements both in terms of complexity and error rates compared to previous work.

VI. Conclusion and Future Work

We introduced a method to store nonuniform messages in networks of neural cliques and a method to find all matches associated with a given query. The proposed method involves the use of additional computational resources, but offers asymptotically ideal precision.

We stressed the efficiency of our method on two challenging datasets, an 8-letters english words dataset and a chess endgame dataset. We demonstrated the ability of our solution to obtain very good precision while keeping computational complexity largely reduced compared to previous work.

In future work, we will leverage the full potential of this method by developing parallel hardware architectures derived from the proposed algorithm. In addition, we plan to develop methods to automatically select hyperparameters (in particular the value of λ).

References

[1] J. R. Anderson and G. H. Bower, Human associative memory. Psychology press, 2014.

[2] T. Manhas and M. Wang, "Scalable packet classification using associative memory." Google Patents, 2012.

[3] H. Jarollahi, N. Onizawa, T. Hanyu, and W. J. Gross, "Associative memories based on multiple-valued sparse clustered networks," in 2014 IEEE 44th International Symposium on Multiple-Valued Logic. IEEE, 2014, pp. 208–213.

[4] S. Di Carlo, P. Prinetto, and A. Savino, "Software-based self-test of set-associative cache memories," vol. 60, no. 7. IEEE, 2011, pp. 1030–1044.

[5] A. Papadogiannakis, M. Polychronakis, and E. P. Markatos, "Improving the accuracy of network intrusion detection systems under load using selective packet discarding," in Proceedings of the Third European Workshop on System Security, ser. EUROSEC '10, 2010, pp. 15–21.

[6] E. Lehtonen, J. H. Poikonen, M. Laiho, and P. Kanerva, "Large-scale memristive associative memories," IEEE Transactions on Very Large Scale Integration (VLSI) Systems, vol. 22, no. 3, 2014, pp. 562–574.

[7] R. S. Indeck, R. K. Cytron, and M. A. Franklin, "Associative database scanning and information retrieval," May 31 2011, uS Patent 7,953,743.

[8] H. J. et al, "A non-volatile associative memory-based context-driven search engine using 90 nm CMOS MTJ-Hybrid logic-in-memory architecture," Journal on Emerging and Selected Topics in Circuits and Systems, vol. 4, 2014, pp. 460–474.

[9] K. Pagiamtzis and A. Sheikholeslami, "Content-addressable memory (CAM) circuits and architectures: A tutorial and survey," IEEE Journal of Solid-State Circuits, vol. 41, no. 3, 2006, pp. 712–727.

[10] V. Gripon and M. Rabbat, "Maximum likelihood associative memories," in Proceedings of Information Theory Workshop, 2013, pp. 1–5.

[11] G. Palm, "Neural associative memories and sparse coding," Neural Networks, vol. 37, 2013, pp. 165–171.

[12] V. Gripon, J. Heusel, M. Lwe, and F. Vermet, "A comparative study of sparse associative memories," Journal of Statistical Physics, vol. 164, 2016, pp. 105–129.

[13] A. Aboudib, V. Gripon, and X. Jiang, "A study of retrieval algorithms of sparse messages in networks of neural cliques," in Proceedings of Cognitive 2014, 2014, pp. 140–146.

[14] A. Aboudib, V. Gripon, and B. Tessiau, "Implementing relational-algebraic operators for improving cognitive abilities in networks of neural cliques," in Proceedings of Cognitive, 2015, pp. 36–41.

[15] T. Kohonen, Self-organization and associative memory. Springer Science & Business Media, 2012, vol. 8.

[16] B. Boguslawski, V. Gripon, F. Seguin, and F. Heitzmann, "Twin neurons for efficient real-world data distribution in networks of neural cliques. applications in power management in electronic circuits," IEEE Transactions on Neural Networks and Learning Systems, vol. 27, no. 2, 2016, pp. 375–387.

[17] A. Knoblauch, G. Palm, and F. T. Sommer, "Memory capacities for synaptic and structural plasticity," Neural Computation, vol. 22, no. 2, 2010, pp. 289–341.

[18] R. Danilo, V. Gripon, P. Coussy, L. Conde-Canencia, and W. J. Gross, "Restricted clustered neural network for storing real data," in proceedings of GLSVLSI conference, 2015, pp. 205–210.

[19] B. Boguslawski, V. Gripon, F. Seguin, and F. Heitzmann, "Huffman coding for storing non-uniformly distributed messages in networks of neural cliques," in proceedings of the Twenty-Eighth AAAI Conference on Artificial Intelligence, volume 1, 2014, pp. 262–268.

[20] X. Jiang, M. R. S. Marques, P.-J. Kirsch, and C. Berrou, "Improved retrieval for challenging scenarios in clique-based neural networks," in International Work-Conference on Artificial Neural Networks. Springer, 2015, pp. 400–414.

[21] V. Gripon and C. Berrou, "A simple and efficient way to store many messages using neural cliques," in Proceedings of IEEE Symposium on Computational Intelligence, Cognitive Algorithms, Mind, and Brain, 2011, pp. 54–58.

[22] ——, "Sparse neural networks with large learning diversity," IEEE transactions on neural networks, vol. 22, no. 7, 2011, pp. 1087–1096.

[23] "Eight letters words database," http://www.morewords.com/wordsbylength, accessed: 2016-10-03.

[24] "Chess database," http://archive.ics.uci.edu/ml/datasets/Chess+%28King-Rook+vs.+King%29, accessed: 2016-10-03.

A Study of Deep Learning Robustness Against Computation Failures

Jean-Charles Vialatte[1,2] and François Leduc-Primeau[1]
[1]Electronics Dept., IMT Atlantique, Brest, France
[2]Cityzen Data, Guipavas, France
emails: {jc.vialatte, francois.leduc-primeau}@imt-atlantique.fr

***Abstract*—For many types of integrated circuits, accepting larger failure rates in computations can be used to improve energy efficiency. We study the performance of faulty implementations of certain deep neural networks based on pessimistic and optimistic models of the effect of hardware faults. After identifying the impact of hyperparameters such as the number of layers on robustness, we study the ability of the network to compensate for computational failures through an increase of the network size. We show that some networks can achieve equivalent performance under faulty implementations, and quantify the required increase in computational complexity.**

***Index Terms*—Deep learning; quasi-synchronous circuits; energy-efficient computing.**

I. Introduction

Deep neural networks achieve excellent performance at various artificial intelligence tasks, such as speech recognition [1] and computer vision [2]. Clearly, the usefulness of these algorithms would be increased significantly if state-of-the-art accuracy could also be obtained when implemented on embedded systems operating with reduced energy budgets. In this context, the energy efficiency of the inference phase is the most important, since the learning phase can be performed offline.

To achieve the best energy efficiency, it is desirable to design specialized hardware for deep learning inference. However, whereas in the past the energy consumption of integrated circuits was decreasing steadily with each new integrated circuit technology, the energy improvements that can be expected from further shrinking of CMOS circuits is small [3]. A possible approach to continue improving the energy efficiency of CMOS circuits is to operate them in the near-threshold regime, which unfortunately drastically increases the amount of delay variations in the circuit, which can lead to functional failures [4]. There is therefore a conflict between the desire to obtain circuits that operate reliably and that are energy efficient. In other words, tolerating circuit faults without degrading performance translates into energy gains. Neural networks are interesting algorithms to study in this context, because their ability to process noisy data could also be useful to compensate for hardware failures. It is interesting to draw a parallel with another important class of algorithms that process noisy data: decoders of error-correction codes. For the case of low-density parity-check codes, it was indeed shown that a decoder can save energy by operating unreliably while preserving equivalent performance [5].

Of course, a perhaps more straightforward way to decrease the energy consumption is to reduce the computational complexity. For example, [6] proposes an approach to decrease the number of parameters in a deep convolutional neural network (CNN) while preserving prediction accuracy, and [7] proposes an approach to replace floating-point operations with much simpler binary operations while also preserving accuracy. The approach of this paper is the opposite. We consider increasing the number of parameters in the model to provide robustness that can then be traded for energy efficiency. The two aims are most likely complementary, and the situation is in fact similar in essence to the problem of data transmission, where it is in many practical cases asymptotically (in the size of the transmission) optimal to first compress the data to be transmitted, and then to add back some redundancy using an error-correction code.

In this preliminary study, we consider the ability of simple neural network models to increase their robustness to computation failures through an increase of the number of parameters. It was shown previously for an implementation of a multilayer perceptron (MLP) based on stochastic computing that it is possible to compensate for a reduced precision by increasing the size of the network [8]. The impact of hardware faults on CNNs is also considered in [9] using a different approach that consists in adding compensation mechanisms in hardware while keeping the same network size. The deviation models that we consider in this paper attempt to represent the case in which computation circuits are not protected by any compensation mechanism. We consider a pessimistic model and a more optimistic deviation model, but in both cases the error is only bounded by the finite codomain of the computations. We show that despite this, increasing the size of the network can sometimes compensate for faulty computations. The results provide an idea of the reduction in energy that must be obtained by a faulty circuit in order to reduce the overall energy consumption of the system.

The remainder of this paper is organized as follows. Section II provides a quick summary of the neural network models used in this paper, and Section III presents the methodology used for selecting hyperparameters of the models and for training. Section IV then describes the modeling of deviations, that is of the impact of circuit faults on the computations. Section V discusses the robustness of the inference based on simulation results. Finally, Section VI concludes the paper.

II. Background and Naming Conventions

A neural network is a neural representation of a function f that is a composition of *layer* functions f_i. Each layer function is usually composed of a linear operation followed by a non-linear one. A *dense layer* is such that its inputs and outputs are vectors. Its linear part can be written as a matrix multiplication between an input x and a *weight matrix* W: $x \mapsto Wx$. The *number of neurons* of a dense layer refers to the number of rows of W. A *n-dimensional convolutional layer* is such that its inputs and outputs are tensors of rank n. Its linear part can be written as a n-dimensional convolution between an input x and a *weight tensor* W of rank $n+2$: $x \mapsto (\sum_p W_{pq} *_n x_p)_{\forall q}$, where p and q index slices at the last ranks and $*_n$ denotes the n-dimensional convolution. The tensor slices indexed by p and q are called *feature maps*. A pooling operation is often added to convolutional layers to scale them down.

An MLP [10] is composed only of dense layers. A CNN [11] is mainly composed of convolutional layers. For both network types, to perform supervised classification, a dense output layer with as many neurons as classes is usually added. Then, the weights are trained according to an optimization algorithm based on gradient descent.

III. Neural Network Models

We consider two types of deep learning models and train them in the usual way, assuming reliable computations. To simplify model selection, we place some mild restrictions on the hyperparameter space, since we are more interested in the general robustness of the models, rather than in finding models with the very best accuracy. As described below, we restrict most layers to have the same number of neurons, and the same activation function. We also try only one optimisation algorithm, and consider only one type of weight initialization.

The first model type that we consider is an MLP network composed of L dense layers, each containing N neurons, that we denote as MLP-L-N. The activation function used in all the layers is chosen as the rectified linear unit (reLU) [12]. In fact, since a circuit implementation (and particularly, a fixed-point circuit implementation) can only represent values over a finite range, we take this into account in the training by using a clipped-reLU activation, which adds a saturation operation on positive outputs. We note that such an activation function has been used before in a different context, in order to avoid the problem of diverging gradients in the training of recurrent networks [13]. The use of the $\tanh$ activation was also considered, but reLU was observed to yield better accuracy.

The second model type is a CNN network composed of L convolutional $C \times C$ layers with $P \times P$ pooling of type *pool*, ultimately followed by a dense layer of 200 neurons [11]. This class is denoted as CNN-L-C-P-F-*pool*, where F is the number of feature maps used in each convolutional layer. Clipped-reLU activations are used throughout. The type of pooling *pool* can be either "max" pooling or no pooling.

For simplicity, we opted to train the networks on the task of digit classification using the MNIST dataset [14]. In addition to the layers defined above, each model is terminated by a dense "softmax" layer used for classification, and containing one neuron per class. Initialization was done as suggested in [15]. To prevent overfitting during training, a dropout [16] of 25% and 50% of the neurons have been applied on convolutional and dense layers, respectively, except on the first layer. We used categorical crossentropy as the loss function and the "adadelta" optimizer [17]. The batch size was 128 and we trained for 15 epochs. The saturation value of the clipped-reLU activation is chosen as 1 as this provides a good balance between performance and implementation complexity. Note that as the range is increased, more bits must be used to maintain the same precision, leading to larger circuits.

IV. Deviation Models

We consider that all the computations performed in the inference phase are unreliable, either because they are performed by unreliable circuits, or because the matrix or tensor W is stored in an unreliable memory. We do, however, assume that the softmax operation performed at the end of the classification layer (i.e. the output layer) is performed reliably. We assume that each layer is affected by deviations independently, and that deviations occur independently for each scalar element of a layer output.

We are interested in circuits with a reasonably low amount of unreliability, and therefore it is useful to partition the outcome of a computation in terms of the occurrence or non-occurrence of a deviation event. We say that a deviation event occurs if the output of a circuit is different from the output that would be generated by a fully reliable circuit. The probability of a deviation event is denoted by p.

Obtaining a precise characterization of the output of a circuit when timing violations or other circuit faults are possible requires knowledge of the specific circuit architecture and of various implementation parameters. We will rely here on two simplified deviation models. We assume that the circuits operate on fixed-point values defined over a certain range, which is motivated by the fact that fixed-point computations are much simpler than floating-point ones, and reducing circuit complexity is the obvious first step in trying to improve energy efficiency. The first deviation model is a pessimistic model that assumes that when a deviation occurs, the output is sampled uniformly at random from the finite output domain of that circuit. We call this deviation model *conditionally uniform*. The second model is more optimistic, and assumes that the occurrence of a deviation can be detected. Therefore, when a deviation occurs, we replace the output by a "neutral" value, in this case 0. We call this deviation model the *erasure* model.

In a synchronous circuit, the deviations can be observed in the memory elements (registers) that separate the logic circuits. By changing the placement of these registers, we can in effect select the point where deviations will be taken into account. Note however that register placement cannot be arbitrary, as we also seek to have similar logic depth separating all registers. When considering the effect of the deviations on the inference, we noticed that robustness can be increased if deviations are sampled before the activation function of each layer. This is not surprising, since these activation functions act as denoising operations. All simulation results presented in this paper therefore consider that deviations are sampled before

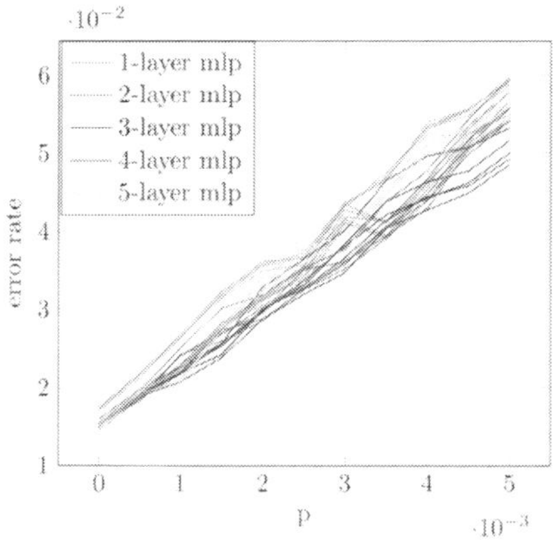

Fig. 1. Error rate of MLP under conditionally uniform deviations with prob. p. (Best viewed in color.)

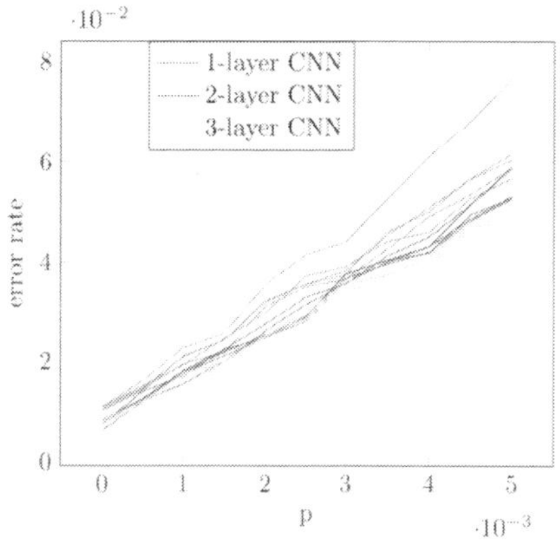

Fig. 2. Error rate of CNN under conditionally uniform deviations with prob. p. (Best viewed in color.)

the activation function. In the case of convolutional layers, the pooling operation is also performed after the sampling of deviations.

V. Results

A. *Effect of some hyperparameters on robustness*

Robustness refers to the ability to maintain good classification accuracy in the presence of deviations. A model has better robustness if it achieves a lower classification error at a given p. We investigated the impact of several hyperparameters on the robustness of the inference. We evaluated the performance using the clipped-reLU and $\tanh$ activation functions, and found robustness to be similar in both cases. For CNN models, we also evaluated the impact of the choice of pooling function. In this case, we found that using no pooling, rather than max pooling, provided a slight improvement in robustness. Finally, we considered the impact of the number of layers L. The effect of L on classification error is shown in Figure 1 for an MLP-L-N network and in Figure 2 for a CNN-L-C-P-F-*pool* for the case where the inference is affected by conditionally uniform deviations. For each value of L, we select the 5 best models based on their deviation-free performance to show the variability of the model optimization. In the case of MLP models, the number of layers does not have a clear impact on robustness. However, while the 2-layer models minimize error under reliable inference, we see that models with more layers sometimes minimize error when the deviation probability increases. However, in the case of CNN models, we can see that increasing the number of layers usually improves robustness.

B. *Fault tolerance*

Since neural networks are designed to reject noise in their input, we might expect them to also be able to reject the "noise" introduced by faulty computations. We investigate this ability for networks trained with standard procedures, in order to provide a baseline for future targeted approaches.

We first choose an error rate target that we want the network to achieve. We then consider various deviation probability values, and for each, look for a model with the smallest number of parameters that can achieve or outperform the performance target under the deviation constraint. For MLP networks, the results are shown in Figure 3 for the case of conditionally uniform deviations, and in Figure 4 for the case of erasure deviations. Similarly, Figures 5 and 6 show the results for CNN networks, respectively for conditionally uniform and erasure deviations.

We consider deviation probabilities on the order of 10^{-3}, which are already considered quite large for digital circuit design. We can see that in all cases, there are indeed many performance targets at which it is possible to compensate computation failures by increasing the number of parameters in the model. However, if one wishes to obtain the best performance achievable by deviation-free inference under conditionally uniform deviations, there is no parameter increase that can compensate for $p \geq 10^{-3}$ within the model sizes that were considered. On the other hand, all performance targets can be achieved under erasure deviations.

Finally, we can note that the CNN models are much more robust than MLP models. For instance, under conditionally uniform deviations and with an error rate target of 0.024, an MLP requires a 318% increase in the number of parameters to tolerate a deviation probability $p = 10^{-3}$, while a CNN can achieve an error rate target of 0.023 at $p = 10^{-3}$ with only a 0.2% increase in the number of parameters.

VI. Conclusion

In this paper, we have considered the effect of faulty computations on the performance of MLP and CNN inference, using a pessimistic and an optimistic deviation model. We showed that using standard training procedures, it is in many cases possible to find models that will compensate for computation failures, when the deviation probability is on the order of 10^{-3} and at the cost of an increase in the number of parameters. This increase is generally small for CNNs or when modeling deviations as erasures, but quite large for the case of MLP models under conditionally uniform deviations. These

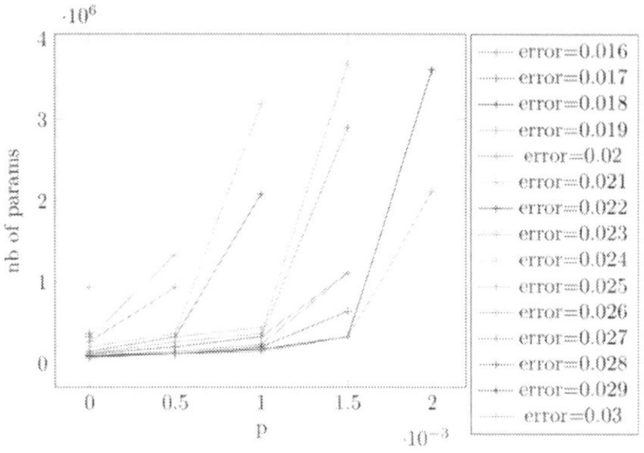

Fig. 3. Number of model parameters needed to achieve error rate target using MLP under conditionally uniform deviations.

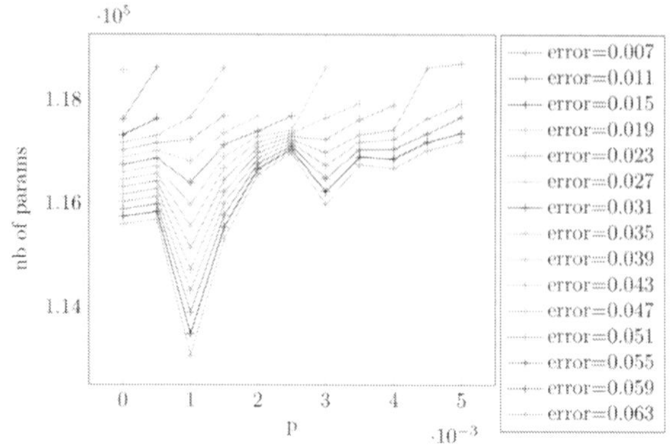

Fig. 5. Number of model parameters needed to achieve error rate target using CNN under conditionally uniform deviations.

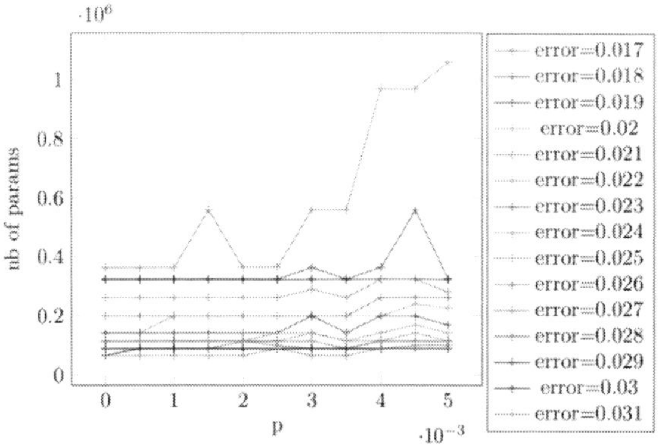

Fig. 4. Number of model parameters needed to achieve error rate target using MLP under erasure deviations.

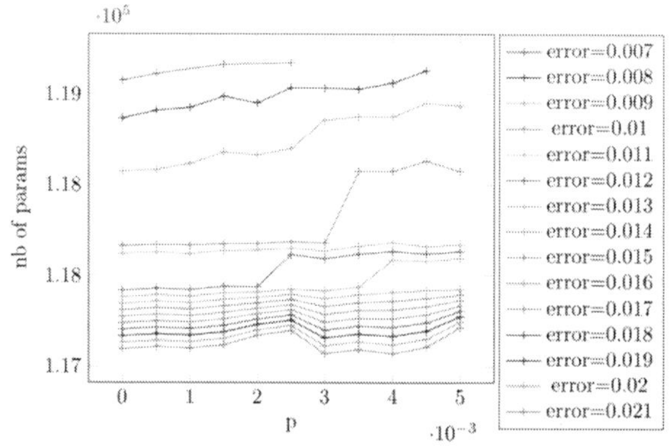

Fig. 6. Number of model parameters needed to achieve error rate target using CNN under erasure deviations.

results provide a baseline for future work seeking to identify systematic ways of designing robust deep neural networks.

References

[1] D. Amodei *et al.*, "Deep speech 2: End-to-end speech recognition in english and mandarin," *CoRR*, vol. abs/1512.02595, 2015. [Online]. Available: http://arxiv.org/abs/1512.02595

[2] A. Krizhevsky, I. Sutskever, and G. E. Hinton, "Imagenet classification with deep convolutional neural networks," in *Advances in Neural Information Processing Systems*, 2012, pp. 1097–1105.

[3] R. Dreslinski, M. Wieckowski, D. Blaauw, D. Sylvester, and T. Mudge, "Near-threshold computing: Reclaiming Moore's law through energy efficient integrated circuits," *Proc. of the IEEE*, vol. 98, no. 2, pp. 253–266, Feb. 2010.

[4] M. Alioto, "Ultra-low power VLSI circuit design demystified and explained: A tutorial," *Circuits and Systems I: Regular Papers, IEEE Transactions on*, vol. 59, no. 1, pp. 3–29, 2012.

[5] F. Leduc-Primeau, F. R. Kschischang, and W. J. Gross, "Modeling and energy optimization of LDPC decoder circuits with timing violations," *CoRR*, vol. abs/1503.03880, 2015. [Online]. Available: http://arxiv.org/abs/1503.03880

[6] F. N. Iandola, M. W. Moskewicz, K. Ashraf, S. Han, W. J. Dally, and K. Keutzer, "SqueezeNet: AlexNet-level accuracy with 50x fewer parameters and <1mb model size," *CoRR*, vol. abs/1602.07360, 2016. [Online]. Available: http://arxiv.org/abs/1602.07360

[7] M. Rastegari, V. Ordonez, J. Redmon, and A. Farhadi, "XNOR-Net: ImageNet classification using binary convolutional neural networks," *CoRR*, vol. abs/1603.05279, 2016. [Online]. Available: http://arxiv.org/abs/1603.05279

[8] A. Ardakani, F. Leduc-Primeau, N. Onizawa, T. Hanyu, and W. J. Gross, "VLSI implementation of deep neural network using integral stochastic computing," *IEEE Trans. on VLSI Systems*, 2017, to appear.

[9] Y. Lin, S. Zhang, and N. R. Shanbhag, "Variation-tolerant architectures for convolutional neural networks in the near threshold voltage regime," in *2016 IEEE International Workshop on Signal Processing Systems (SiPS)*, Oct 2016, pp. 17–22.

[10] K. Hornik, M. Stinchcombe, and H. White, "Multilayer feedforward networks are universal approximators," *Neural networks*, vol. 2, no. 5, pp. 359–366, 1989.

[11] Y. LeCun, L. Bottou, Y. Bengio, and P. Haffner, "Gradient-based learning applied to document recognition," *Proceedings of the IEEE*, vol. 86, no. 11, pp. 2278–2324, 1998.

[12] X. Glorot, A. Bordes, and Y. Bengio, "Deep sparse rectifier neural networks," in *International Conference on Artificial Intelligence and Statistics*, 2011, pp. 315–323.

[13] A. Y. Hannun *et al.*, "Deep speech: Scaling up end-to-end speech recognition," *CoRR*, vol. abs/1412.5567, 2014. [Online]. Available: http://arxiv.org/abs/1412.5567

[14] Y. LeCun, C. Cortes, and C. J. Burges, "The MNIST database of handwritten digits," 1998.

[15] X. Glorot and Y. Bengio, "Understanding the difficulty of training deep feedforward neural networks," in *International conference on artificial intelligence and statistics*, 2010, pp. 249–256.

[16] N. Srivastava, G. Hinton, A. Krizhevsky, I. Sutskever, and R. Salakhutdinov, "Dropout: A simple way to prevent neural networks from overfitting," *The Journal of Machine Learning Research*, vol. 15, no. 1, pp. 1929–1958, 2014.

[17] M. D. Zeiler, "ADADELTA: an adaptive learning rate method," *CoRR*, vol. abs/1212.5701, 2012. [Online]. Available: http://arxiv.org/abs/1212.5701

Sparse Clustered Neural Networks for the Assignment Problem

Saïd Medjkouh, Bowen Xue, Ghouthi Boukli Hacene
IMT Atlantique, Brest, France
{said.medjkouh,bowen.xue,ghouthi.bouklihacene}@telecom-bretagne.eu

Abstract—**The linear assignment problem is a fundamental combinatorial problem and a classical linear programming problem. It consists of assigning agents to tasks on a one-to-one basis, while minimizing the total assignment cost. The assignment problem appears recurrently in major applications involving optimal decision-making. However, the use of classical solving methods for large size problems is increasingly prohibitive, as it requires high computation and processing cost. In this paper, a biologically inspired algorithm using an artificial neural network (ANN) is proposed. The artificial neural network model involved in this contribution is a sparse clustered neural network (SCN), which is a generalization of the Palm-Wilshaw neural network. The presented algorithm provides a lower complexity compared to the classically used Hungarian algorithm and allows parallel computation at the cost of a fair approximation of the optimal assignment. Illustrative applications through practical examples are given for analysis and evaluation purpose.**

Keywords–assignment problem, artificial neural network, hungarian algorithm.

I. INTRODUCTION

Assignment problems are essential among problems involving linear optimization as they are needed in various fields and applications that involve assigning machines to tasks, students to groups, jobs to workers, and so on. The aim is to find the optimum assignment that minimizes the total cost or maximizes the global benefit. Moreover, many seemingly different linear optimization problems can be solved as assignment problems by an accurate transformation [1]. In addition, the linear assignment problem occurs usually as a subproblem of more complex problems, such as the traveling salesman problem [2].

In addition to its theoretical importance, the assignment problem is applied in many areas ranging from military applications, such as the well-known weapon to target assignment (WTA) aiming to maximize the total expected damage done to the opponent, to economic-industry applications such as finding the optimal shipping schedule minimizing the shipment cost. Over the last few years, the linear assignment problem has received a particular attention in robotics and control theory due to applications involving task or target allocation [3].

Many algorithms have been proposed to solve this problem, most of them are based on an iterative improvement of a given global cost function [4] while the so-called Kunh Hungarian algorithm [5] was the first algorithm especially designed to solve the assignment problem given a polynomial complexity.

However, high-performance processing is needed for many of its applications, in addition to an increasing need of parallel computing. Recently, contributions have been made to accelerate the Hungarian algorithm with an efficient parallelization using the GPUs [6]. Thus, it is worth to explore more efficient methods, targeting a reduced complexity and distributed computation.

In this paper, a biologically inspired algorithm using an artificial neural network is proposed. The artificial neural network model involved in this contribution is adapted from the SCN designed by Gripon and Berrou in [7], which is a generalization of the Palm-Wilshaw neural network [8]. This algorithm has been explored for the similar Feature Correspondence problem in [9], which can be viewed, just as the assignment problem, as a graph matching problem.

The proposed algorithm provides a lower computation complexity compared to the classical Hungarian algorithm and allows parallel computation at the cost of a fair approximation of the optimal assignment. However, we do not pretend providing a complete solving algorithm. We hope that our approach will be a step forward for further research seeking biologically inspired algorithms.

This paper is organized as follows. Section II gives a brief description of the assignment problem and its combinational and mathematical formulation. Then, the Hungarian algorithm is described. Section III presents and analyses the proposed SCN algorithm. Section IV provides three examples of application of the assignment problem using both algorithms. Section V concludes the paper.

II. ASSIGNMENT PROBLEMS AND THE HUNGARIAN ALGORITHM

A. Assignment problems

Assignment problems describe situations where we have to find an optimal way to assign n agents to n tasks. They consist of two components: the assignment as an underlying combinatorial structure and an objective function modeling the "optimal way".

Assume for example that we have n tasks ($j = 1, 2, ..., n$) that need to be executed by n machines ($i = 1, 2, ..., n$). The ith machine has a different performance regarding the jth task, for instance, the time required to perform a task depends on the machine which is assigned to it. Thus, a rating (or cost c_{ij}) is given to each machine-task assignment.

An optimal assignment is one which makes the sum of the costs (e.g., execution time) a minimum. There are $n!$ possible assignments. This corresponds to a permutation ϕ of a set $N = \{1, 2, ..., n\}$. So, a straightforward method to solve the assignment problem is to consider all the permutations with their corresponding cost. But as the computation complexity increases terribly with n, it is not worth to consider it as a solving method.

There are different ways to model assignment problems depending on the targeted application. In the following, we give a mathematical model which represents the assignment problem by a matrix that we will call *the cost matrix*.

The following mathematical description is adopted from [10]. Mathematically an assignment is a bijective mapping of a finite set into itself, i.e., a *permutation*. Assignments can be modeled and visualized in different ways: every permutation ϕ of the set $N \in \{1, ..., n\}$ corresponds in a unique way to a permutation matrix $X_\phi = (x_{ij})$ with $x_{ij} = 1$ for $j = \phi(i)$ and $x_{ij} = 0$ for $j \neq \phi(i)$. We can view this matrix X_ϕ as adjacency matrix of a bipartite graph $G_\phi = (V, V'; E)$, where the node sets V and V' have n nodes, i.e., $|V| = |V'| = n$, and there is an edge $(i, j) \in E$ if $j = \phi(i)$. Thus, the assignment problem can be formulated as a graph matching problem, as shown in Figure 1, in this case $n = 4$.

$$\phi = \begin{pmatrix} 1 & 2 & 3 & 4 \\ 3 & 2 & 4 & 1 \end{pmatrix}$$

$$X_\phi = \begin{pmatrix} 0 & 0 & 1 & 0 \\ 0 & 1 & 0 & 0 \\ 0 & 0 & 0 & 1 \\ 1 & 0 & 0 & 0 \end{pmatrix}$$

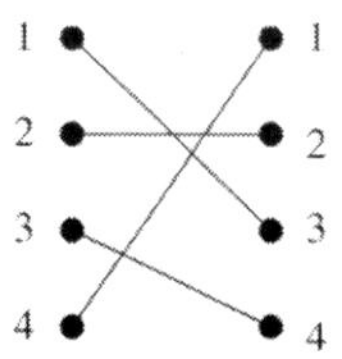

Figure 1. Different representations of assignments.

Thus, we can model the problem as follows: let c_{ij} be the cost (performance rating). A set of elements of a matrix are said to be independent if no two of them lie in the same line (the word "line" applies both to the rows and to the columns of a matrix). The goal is to choose a set of n independent elements of the *cost matrix* $C = (c_{ij})$ so that the sum for these elements is maximum or minimum depending on whether it's a maximization or minimization problem. We assume, for this, model that the elements of C are integers. The sum of the assigned elements of C in the final assignment is its *cost*. So, the assignment permutation matrix X_ϕ is constituted by 1 in the independent assigned elements (in C) and zeros elsewhere.

The assignment problem can be expressed as the minimization of an objective function $z(\mathbf{X})$:

$$\text{minimize } z(\mathbf{X}) = \sum_{i=1}^{N} \sum_{j=1}^{N} c_{ij} x_{ij} \tag{1}$$

This minimization is subject to the *assignment constraints*:

$$\begin{aligned} &\sum_{i=1}^{n} x_{ij} = 1 \text{ for } j = 1, ..., n \\ &\sum_{j=1}^{n} x_{ij} = 1 \text{ for } i = 1, ..., n \\ &x_{ij} \in \{0, 1\} \text{ for all } i, j = 1, ..., n \end{aligned} \tag{2}$$

If the cost matrix is not a square matrix, which means that the two graphs to match don't have the same number of nodes, we can simply wrap the matrix with the needed number rows or columns of its maximum value (minimization problem) or minimum value (maximization problem). This is equivalent to assigning a worker to a fictive job for which we suppose a performance that doesn't influence the global cost. Typical problems of this type are treated in Section IV.

B. The Hungarian algorithm

The Hungarian algorithm was developed and published in 1955 by Harold Kuhn [11], who gave the name "Hungarian method" because the algorithm was largely based on the earlier works of two Hungarian mathematicians: Dnes Knig and Jen Egervry. James Munkres reviewed the algorithm in 1957 [12] and observed that it is (strongly) polynomial [3].

The Hungarian method is an algorithm which finds an optimal assignment for a given cost matrix C. In our case, we consider the Hungarian algorithm for a minimization problem where the goal is to find the assignment which minimizes the cost.

It is worth to mention some of the mathematical foundations on which the Hungarian algorithm is based.

Theorem 1 [13]: *If a number is added to or subtracted from all of the elements of any row or column of a cost matrix C, then on optimal assignment for the resulting cost matrix is also an optimal assignment for the original cost matrix.*

Theorem 2 [14]: *If m is the maximum number of independent zero elements merits of a matrix C, then there are m lines (each line covering a column or a row) which contain all the zero elements of C.*

The algorithm consists of the six steps below. The first two steps are executed once at the beginning, while Steps 3, 4 and 5 and are repeated until an optimal assignment is found. Then, step 6 is executed to find this assignment. The input of the algorithm is an n by n cost matrix C with only positive elements.

Step 1: Subtract row minimum.

Subtract the lowest element in each row from all the elements of its row.

Step 2: Subtract column minimum.

Similarly, for each column, subtract the lowest element of each column from all the elements in that column.

Step 3: Cover all zeros with a minimum number of lines.

Cover all zeros in the resulting matrix using a minimum number of lines, each line covers one row or one column.

Step 4: Check the number of lines.

If n lines are required, an optimal assignment exist among the zeros. Go to step 6. If less than n lines are required, return to Step 3.

Step 5: Create additional zeros.

Find the smallest element that is not covered by a line in Step 3. Subtract it from all uncovered elements, and add it to all elements that are covered twice and return to step 3.

Step 6: Find the independent zeros.

Find the n independent zeros in the resulting matrix. The positions of these independent zeros correspond to the optimal assignment in the cost matrix.

III. Sparse Clustered Neural Network algorithm

In this section, we describe our ANN model and specify the details of the assignment problem-solving algorithm it implements. We also study its complexity and accuracy compared to the classical Hungarian algorithm.

A. Algorithm description

The neural network we propose for solving assignment problems is constructed, initially, on the cost matrix C. The architecture of this network is adapted from the SCN in [7], which was proposed as a generalization of Palm-Wilshaw networks [8].

The network grid structure corresponds to the 2D configuration of the cost matrix C, this means that each neuron is initialized to its corresponding value in the cost matrix C. Neuron values are represented in a matrix Y, as shown in Figure 2. As in SCNs, we impose a grouping configuration on the network neurons in the form of clusters; neurons of the same row are grouped into one cluster, and the same holds for neurons of the same column. Thus, each neuron belongs to two clusters as shown in Figure 2. Within each cluster, a winner-takes-all (WTA) activation constraint is imposed; only one neuron per cluster can be active at the end of the network activity with a binary activation level (0 or 1), which corresponds to the assignment matrix X_ϕ. However, during the network activity, and before the network matrix Y reaches its final state, this constraint is relaxed into a relaxed-winners-take-all (rWTA) constraint, this constraint is relaxed into a soft winner-takes-all where the highest value is maintained and the others are decreased. Thus, we allow the network to temporarily contain real values. Each neuron is connected to all the other neurons despite those in the same cluster, no connections exists between neurons of the same cluster as in SCNs.

The WTA and rWTA constraints we impose within clusters are meant to encourage the bijective matching constraint between the two graphs V and W.

It is worth to mention that the below description of the algorithm is for a maximization assignment problem. We can use the exact same method by, for example, multiplying the starting cost matrix by -1.

The network activity starts by assigning to each neuron its unary affinity value ($y_{ij} \leftarrow c_{ij}$). Then, within each row cluster, every neuron receives the max-pooled propagated activity of all other neurons to which it connects as shown in Figure 2.

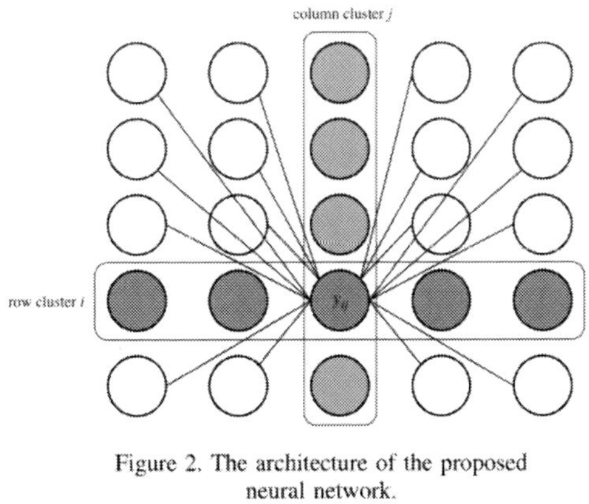

Figure 2. The architecture of the proposed neural network.

This means that each neuron receives the sum of the maximum values of each row (assuming we are processing the row clusters) of the sub-matrix constituted by all the elements of the network matrix despite those containing the processed value. It is worth noting that the max-pooled activity is received in parallel for all neurons, as shown in (3).

$$y_{ij}^{t+1} \leftarrow \sum_{k \in A} \max_{m \in B}(y_{km}^t) \quad \text{with } A = \{1, ..., n\} \backslash i \text{ and } B = \{1, ..., n\} \backslash j \tag{3}$$

Where the superscript t denotes the current iteration. The activity values within this cluster are then normalized to their maximum. Then, an rWTA operation is applied. This means that the neurons of the same cluster, despite the maximum value of the cluster (of index (i_{Cmax}, j_{Cmax})), are penalized using a certain activation function that we note $h(.)$. Thus this penalization function doesn't apply to the normalized maximum, which means that $h(1) = 1$. The aim of this penalization is to converge to a certain assignment.

$$y_{ij}^{t+1} \leftarrow h(y_{ij}^t) \quad \text{for } (i, j) \in \{1, ..., n\}^2 \backslash (i_{Cmax}, j_{Cmax}) \tag{4}$$

An iteration is finished when both row clusters and column clusters are alternatively processed once as up-described. Notice that for row clusters, max-pooling and rWTA are applied row-wise, while they are applied column-wise for column clusters.

Figure 3. Proposed Sparse Neural Network Algorithm.

Input : Cost matrix C
Output: Assigned matrix Y
$Y \leftarrow C$
repeat
  foreach $i \in \{1, ..., N_{rows}\}$ **do**
    foreach $j \in \{1, ..., N_{col}\}$ **do**
      $y_{ij}^{t+1} \leftarrow \sum_{k \in A} \max_{m \in B}(y_{km}^t)$
    end
  end
  foreach $i \in \{1, ..., N_{rows}\}$ **do**
    foreach $j \in \{1, ..., N_{col}\}$ **do**
      $y_{ij}^{t+1} \leftarrow y_{ij}^{t+1} / max(y_{ik}^{t+1})_{k \in \{1, ..., N_{col}\}}$
      $y_{ij}^{t+1} \leftarrow h(y_{ij}^{t+1})$
    end
  end
  foreach $j \in \{1, ..., N_{col}\}$ **do**
    foreach $i \in \{1, ..., N_{rows}\}$ **do**
      $y_{ij}^{t+1} \leftarrow \sum_{m \in B} \max_{k \in A}(y_{km}^t)$
    end
  end
  foreach $j \in \{1, ..., N_{col}\}$ **do**
    foreach $i \in \{1, ..., N_{rows}\}$ **do**
      $y_{ij}^{t+1} \leftarrow y_{ij}^{t+1} / max(y_{kj}^{t+1})_{k \in \{1, ..., N_{rows}\}}$
      $y_{ij}^{t+1} \leftarrow h(y_{ij}^{t+1})$
    end
  end
until *Y converges OR last iteration attained*;

Finally, we obtain a processed matrix with final values of y_{ij}. An activation threshold is applied, where only neurons with a maximal activation value are kept active ($y_{ij} \leftarrow 1$)

while others are deactivated ($y_{ij} \leftarrow 0$). A WTA operation is then applied within every row and column cluster; if more than one neuron is active in a given cluster, we choose randomly one neuron to activate while we deactivate the others in order to give (at least) a partial assignment, meaning that the assignment is not complete and some tasks may have not been assigned to some machines. The obtained partial-assignment is part of a fair approximation assignment.

B. Algorithm analysis

The main advantage of the proposed method is its lower complexity compared to the classical Hungarian approach. Another advantage is that our approach implements a cooperative algorithm, meaning at each neuron needs only to know about the activity of few neighboring neurons, which allows the algorithm to run in a parallel fashion.

As Munkres has shown in [12], the Hungarian algorithm solves the assignment problem in $\mathcal{O}(n^3)$ time and demonstrated that the final maximum on the number of operations needed is $(11n^3 + 12n^2 + 31n)/6$.

The proposed artificial neural network algorithm attains its final solution either by converging or after N_{iter} iterations in $\mathcal{O}(n^2)$ time. This can be done by implementing it in a slightly different way from the proposed version. In fact, in order to avoid the three nested loops when carrying the max-pooling step, we can first calculate the two maximums of each row (resp. column) keeping their index, and then process the max-pooled propagated activity. Considering an operation as one iteration in the loop, we need n^2 operations to calculate the maximums with their respective index. Then, n^2 operations to process the max-pooled propagated activity. Finally, n^2 operations to carry out the penalization. Thus, processing the rows costs $3n^2$ and $3n^2$ for the columns. All this is executed N_{iter} times. The overall number of operations is

Figure 4 shows the worst-case complexity curves of each method referenced to the total number of operations.

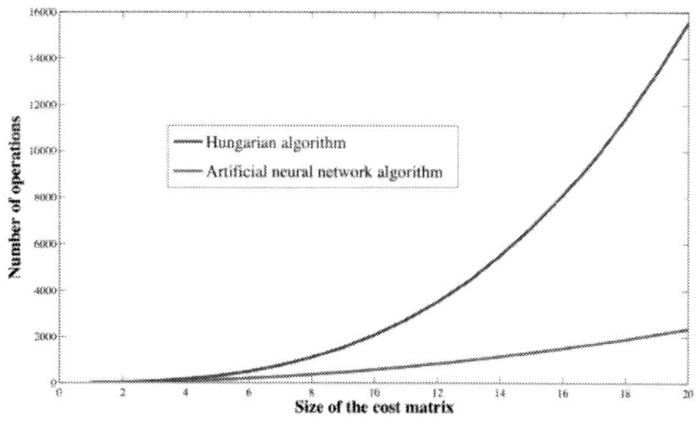

Figure 4. Worst-case complexity of the Hungarian and the proposed algorithms.

However, even though the proposed algorithm enjoys a $\mathcal{O}(n^2)$ complexity and a high parallelism level, it gives only a partial assignment of the overall approximate assignment.

In some cases, the artificial neural network algorithm gives an exact solution. For example, if the final optimal assignment corresponds to the maximum value of each row (or column), respecting the independence constraint, we can easily notice that the solution is attained by the neural networks algorithm in one iteration. This because the activity of the most active neuron increases with the max-pool propagation while decreasing the activity of the other neurons by penalizing them. As in this case, every most active neuron is in an independent cluster, the result is directly obtained.

In a more general case, an interesting way to use the proposed algorithm is to implement it as a preprocessing before the Hungarian algorithm. This combined "ANN-Hungarian" approach, is worth to be considered. In fact, the preprocessing with the neural network algorithm of a given cost matrix C_n outputs a partially assigned matrix. This means that we can remove the assigned rows and columns and process the resulting partial sub-matrix C_p of size $p < n$ to find the rest of assignments. The overall resulting assignment X_n is a fair approximation of the optimal assignment. This approach is illustrated in Figure 5.

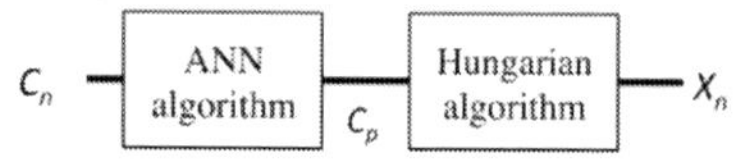

Figure 5. The proposed Artificial Neural Network used as a preprocessing for the Hungarian algorithm.

An experimental study of the accuracy of this combined method is shown in Figure 6. It has been made on a normally distributed matrix of size $n = 4$ for increasing standard deviation values, in the context of a maximization assignment problem. The accuracy is calculated as the ratio between the optimal cost and the approximate cost given by this combined approach. The used penalization function $h()$ for the ANN algorithm is a simple multiplication by a penalization factor $h(x) = 0.5x$. In this experiment, we used only one iteration.

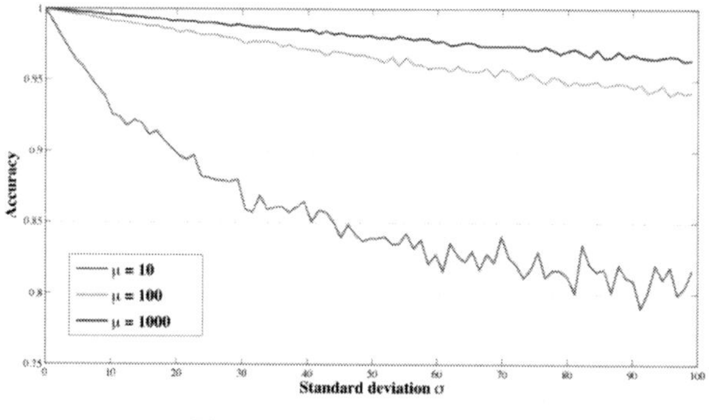

Figure 6. Experimental study of the proposed model's accuracy for randomly generated cost matrix of size $n = 4$.

From these experimental results, we can confirm that the approximation of the combined method is worth to be considered. Especially, for high values matrix because the gap between values due to the penalization function is more significant for high values. Thus, the approximation is more fairly made and the approximate assignment provides a cost close to the optimal one.

IV. APPLICATIONS

In this section, three major applications of the assignment problem are illustrated through practical examples. A comparison is made in each case between the Hungarian algorithm's optimal cost and the result obtained by the proposed neural network approach combined to the Hungarian algorithm.

A. *Military application*

In military operations, problems in planning and scheduling often require feasible and close to optimal solutions with limited computing resources and within very short time periods [15]. Especially the weapons developed in contemporary technology give very less chance to defend friendly assets as enemy forces execute complex saturated attacks. Therefore, quick and efficient reactions to subsidize these attacks become very vital to survive in the combat arena. Thus, assigning the limited resources (own weapons) to the hostile targets to achieve certain tactical goals [15] becomes an important issue called as Weapon Target Assignment (WTA) problem.

Nowadays, there are more and more algorithms being applied in military affairs to design those advanced equipments. The Hungarian algorithm is also attractive enough to solve the problems of how to assign tasks to one's own limited number of weapons and obtain a maximum gain. For example, the Hungarian algorithm has already been used for distributing missions to an array of radars. Each radar in one's own array can emit interference signal to interfere each radar in enemy's array, but the coefficients of these effects of interference for different enemy radars are different. So, that it needs to find the best combination to finish this interfere mission to get a maximum effect of interference. Thus, this radar assignment problem is modeled by a graph matching problem and solved with the Hungarian algorithm. In this case, as quick decisions have to be made, it can be interesting to consider using the neural networks proposed algorithm as a more time-efficient alternative as it allows a lower time complexity and a better level of parallelism.

$$\begin{pmatrix}
0.0384 & 0.3818 & 0.0165 & 0.1033 & 0.2596 & 0.2281 & 0.0229 & 0.0227 \\
0.0181 & 0.2689 & 0.0117 & 0.0497 & 0.2818 & 0.0179 & 0.1084 & 0.1450 \\
0.0692 & 0.2526 & 0.1153 & 0.2433 & 0.1697 & 0.1013 & 0.0705 & 0.0967 \\
0.0261 & 0.4215 & 0.1693 & 0.0953 & 0.0316 & 0.0244 & 0.2169 & 0.0917 \\
0.0146 & 0.1314 & 0.2029 & 0.1619 & 0.0863 & 0.2202 & 0.1170 & 0.0242 \\
0.0187 & 0.3480 & 0.0282 & 0.0507 & 0.3440 & 0.0011 & 0.2469 & 0.1423 \\
0.0459 & 0.3464 & 0.1236 & 0.1844 & 0.0574 & 0.1774 & 0.0493 & 0.1037 \\
0.0352 & 0.1748 & 0.1020 & 0.0806 & 0.3111 & 0.1871 & 0.0715 & 0.0585 \\
0.0262 & 0.2309 & 0.0026 & 0.2004 & 0.2028 & 0.1989 & 0.0394 & 0.0856
\end{pmatrix} \quad (5)$$

In one case, there are 9 radars in our own side when there are 8 in enemy's side to interfere. According to the properties of each radar, a jamming effective matrix can be built as the matrix (5). The Hungarian algorithm aims to obtain the minimum result of the best combination. In our case, we want to obtain from this jamming effective matrix is the maximum effect of interference. Thus, the matrix can not be treated by the Hungarian algorithm directly because the matrix is not a square matrix and is not adapted for minimization version of the Hungarian algorithm previously described.

To build the final matrix, the first step is to use the maximum value 0.4215 and subtract it from all the elements of the matrix in order to build a new matrix whose size is 9×8. The matrix needed for a minimization problem is built, with respect to Theorem 1 in Section II. The second step is to add a new column whose values are all 0.4215 so that the in-existent radar won't change the final result in order to have a 9×9 square matrix. The final built cost matrix is:

$$\begin{pmatrix}
0.3831 & 0.0397 & 0.4050 & 0.3182 & 0.1619 & 0.1934 & 0.3986 & 0.3988 & 0.4215 \\
0.4034 & 0.1526 & 0.4098 & 0.3718 & 0.1397 & 0.4036 & 0.3131 & 0.2765 & 0.4215 \\
0.3523 & 0.1689 & 0.3062 & 0.1782 & 0.2518 & 0.3202 & 0.3510 & 0.3248 & 0.4215 \\
0.3954 & 0.0000 & 0.2522 & 0.3262 & 0.3899 & 0.3971 & 0.2046 & 0.3298 & 0.4215 \\
0.4069 & 0.2901 & 0.2186 & 0.2596 & 0.3352 & 0.2013 & 0.3045 & 0.3973 & 0.4215 \\
0.4028 & 0.0735 & 0.3933 & 0.3708 & 0.0775 & 0.4204 & 0.1746 & 0.2792 & 0.4215 \\
0.3756 & 0.0751 & 0.2979 & 0.2371 & 0.3641 & 0.2441 & 0.3722 & 0.3178 & 0.4215 \\
0.3863 & 0.2467 & 0.3195 & 0.3409 & 0.1104 & 0.2344 & 0.3500 & 0.3630 & 0.4215 \\
0.3953 & 0.1606 & 0.4189 & 0.2211 & 0.2187 & 0.2226 & 0.3821 & 0.3359 & 0.4215
\end{pmatrix} \quad (6)$$

Finally, all of the essential requirements have been met and the assignment matrix (7) is obtained using the Hungarian algorithm. From this matrix, it can be found that the 9th radar in our side is assigned to interfere the additional in-existent radar. So, that the 9th radar will not participate in this mission.

$$\begin{pmatrix}
0 & 0 & 0 & 0 & 0 & 1 & 0 & 0 & 0 \\
0 & 0 & 0 & 0 & 0 & 0 & 0 & 1 & 0 \\
0 & 0 & 0 & 1 & 0 & 0 & 0 & 0 & 0 \\
0 & 1 & 0 & 0 & 0 & 0 & 0 & 0 & 0 \\
0 & 0 & 1 & 0 & 0 & 0 & 0 & 0 & 0 \\
0 & 0 & 0 & 0 & 0 & 0 & 1 & 0 & 0 \\
1 & 0 & 0 & 0 & 0 & 0 & 0 & 0 & 0 \\
0 & 0 & 0 & 0 & 1 & 0 & 0 & 0 & 0 \\
0 & 0 & 0 & 0 & 0 & 0 & 0 & 0 & 1
\end{pmatrix} \quad (7)$$

In this example, the optimal cost obtained by the Hungarian algorithm is 1.8446 and the one obtained by the ANN-Hungarian combined approach is 1.087, which corresponds to an accuracy of 59%. This result can be explained by Figure 6. In this case, the mean of the matrix (6) is too low so that the combined method gives an average accuracy.

B. *Express company application*

Assignment problems have various economic-industry applications such as finding the optimal shipping schedule minimizing the shipment cost.

The assignment problem is a particular case of the well known transportation problem which deals with problems involving several product sources and several destinations of products. The assignment problem that we consider in this case is a balanced transportation problem where all supplies and demands are equal to 1. The cost considered between sources and destinations is for example the shipment time and the problem is to assign each source to one destination.

In the following example, we consider an express company in France which aims to send fast mail to capitals of other European countries every day through shipment points in different cities in France. The problem is to assign each shipment point to a destination in Europe. So, the cost of the assignment is the time of time of travel between each 2 cities. The objective is to find the assignment that minimizes this global cost. A matrix of the transport time between different cities is built as the cost matrix C as shown in the matrix (8). Where c_{ij} = time from i to j. These values have been estimated using Google map for illustrative purpose.

$$\begin{pmatrix}
70 & 95 & 105 & 70 & 195 & 110 & 120 & 190 & 95 & 135 & 205 & 130 \\
90 & 110 & 135 & 100 & 345 & 90 & 115 & 160 & 100 & 245 & 220 & 200 \\
95 & 200 & 255 & 115 & 360 & 75 & 100 & 160 & 120 & 265 & 330 & 235 \\
75 & 130 & 220 & 95 & 235 & 130 & 95 & 200 & 125 & 270 & 330 & 265 \\
90 & 145 & 240 & 105 & 320 & 110 & 75 & 190 & 140 & 285 & 355 & 275 \\
110 & 135 & 235 & 110 & 300 & 105 & 80 & 180 & 130 & 280 & 325 & 235 \\
105 & 235 & 135 & 120 & 350 & 85 & 245 & 280 & 235 & 270 & 380 & 275 \\
215 & 210 & 240 & 95 & 260 & 140 & 105 & 355 & 215 & 280 & 330 & 290 \\
190 & 175 & 195 & 75 & 155 & 230 & 140 & 315 & 85 & 235 & 295 & 210 \\
100 & 395 & 375 & 235 & 400 & 330 & 305 & 355 & 340 & 410 & 490 & 380 \\
90 & 335 & 420 & 255 & 520 & 355 & 350 & 440 & 305 & 455 & 515 & 405 \\
115 & 120 & 135 & 120 & 305 & 70 & 115 & 150 & 100 & 175 & 215 & 140
\end{pmatrix} \quad (8)$$

The matrix shows how many minutes are needed to get to different destinations from different cities. For each column, the table describe the time for getting to "London","Berlin", "Copenhagen", "Amsterdam", "Bern", "Roma","Madrid","Athens", "Prague", "Stockholm","Moscow","Warsaw". And for each rows, the table shows those principal French cities "Paris", "Lyon", "Marseille", "Nantes", "Bordeaux", "Toulouse", "Montpellier", "Rennes", "Strasbourg", "Limoges", "La Rochelle" and "Nice". It can be found that when we need to send a mail to Bern, the capital of Switzerland, there is no through-flight so in such a situation, it will be faster to transport by car. The resulting optimal assignment provided by the Hungarian algorithm is shown in the following Table:

TABLE I. Optimal assignment

Paris	to	Stockholm	Lyon	to	Moscow
Marseille	to	Roma	Nantes	to	Prague
Bordeaux	to	Amsterdam	Toulouse	to	Berlin
Rennes	to	Madrid	Montpellier	to	Copenhagen
Strasbourg	to	Bern	La Rochelle	to	London
Limoges	to	Athens	Nice	to	Warsaw

The optimal cost obtained for this assignment is 1422. The cost resulting from the ANN-Hungarian combination is 1582.This corresponds to an accuracy of 90%. In this case, the combined method offers an acceptable result as the mean of the matrix (8), which represents the average time of traveling in minute, is high enough to ensure a fine accuracy.

C. *Students to projects assignment*

A classical problem in various areas is to assign tasks to agents. We provide the following example using a real case situation to illustrate the solving process.

The students of a university, namely Telecom Bretagne, are asked to make their semester projects preference. Each student chooses 5 projects from a range of 25 and rank them from 1 to 5 depending on his preference. There are 108 students and no more than 5 students are assigned to each project. The goal is to find a combination of students-project that maximizes the global satisfaction. This means that every student may not have its first choice, but globally all the students get a fair project assigned based on their preference. This situation is modeled by table II where **Stu** stands for student and **P** for project. The data used in this section has been provided by Telecom Bretagnes project committee.

TABLE II. Choices of students

	P1	P2	P3	P4	P5	P6	...	P19	P20	21	22	...	24	25
Stu 1		...	4	3				...				5	...	2
Stu 2	4	...			5	2		...		3			...	1
Stu 3	5	...			4	2	1	...	3				...	
...	...	...	...	...	...	...	...	...	...	...	...	...	...	...
Stu 108	4	...				3		...	1	5	2		...	

This is a typical asymmetric assignment problem, meaning that the graphs to match are not of the same size and the cost matrix not a square matrix. We have 108 students to match with 25 projects. A couple of transformations are needed to model it as an assignment problem.

A matrix of 108×25 is built from Table II to show these 108 students different preferences. For the other projects that a student did not choose, the matrix needs to be filled with an integer of a bigger value than 5 in order not to compromise the preferences and to represent this students unwillingness. In our experiment, we choose the integer 100. Then, to embody that each project will be filled with 5 students, the columns of this matrix needs to be extended. We do this by repeating each column 5 times building 125 columns. This means that each project corresponds to 5 students. The size of the matrix is then 108×125, but as we need a square cost matrix, another 17 inexistent students are added with all preferences set to 100. Their affectation to a project is considered empty and will not affect the global assignment. Thus this final 125×125 cost matrix, as shown in the matrix (9) is processed by the solving algorithms.

$$\begin{pmatrix} 100 & 100 & 100 & 100 & 100 & \dots & 2 & 2 & 2 & 2 & 2 & 1 & 1 & 1 & 1 & 1 \\ 100 & 100 & 100 & 100 & 100 & \dots & 1 & 1 & 1 & 1 & 1 & 100 & 100 & 100 & 100 & 100 \\ 100 & 100 & 100 & 100 & 100 & \dots & 100 & 100 & 100 & 100 & 100 & 100 & 100 & 100 & 100 & 100 \\ \dots & \dots & \dots & \dots & \dots & \dots & \dots & \dots & \dots & \dots & \dots & \dots & \dots & \dots & \dots & \dots \\ 100 & 100 & 100 & 100 & 100 & \dots & 100 & 100 & 100 & 100 & 100 & 100 & 100 & 100 & 100 & 100 \end{pmatrix} \quad (9)$$

The real assignment made by the university has a cost of 181, which means that the unsatisfactoriness rate is 181 - 108 = 73. The Hungarian algorithm gives a final optimal assignment with a cost of 146, which means that the unsatisfactoriness rate is 38. The artificial neural network algorithm combined with the Hungarian algorithm gives a fair cost of 151 with an unsatisfactoriness rate of 43. The obtained results correspond to an accuracy of 96.7%. The ANN-Hungarian works better in this case because for row 109 to row 125, choices of students will all be filled with the high value 100 as for row 1 to row 108, only 25 columns represent student's real choices of each row will not be 100. So, the mean of the matrix (9) is high (≈ 814) while the variance (≈ 75) is enough to ensure a high accuracy. Therefore, ANN-Hungarian method is a good choice to solve this problem.

V. Conclusion and Future Work

In this paper, we proposed a new approach for treating assignment problems using artificial neural network. We presented the classical Hungarian algorithm to point the need for a reduced complexity and parallel computing. The proposed algorithm satisfies these needs at the cost of a partial assignment solution and a fair approximation of the cost. Even though the solution might not be complete, it is worth to consider this approach either for specific cases where final winners match with the correct assignment or seek to use it as a preprocessing with the Hungarian algorithm. Finally, we presented some examples of application of the assignment problem using both approaches. Further development of our model will include trying different penalization functions such as sigmoid functions. We shall also study the theoretical evolution of the accuracy in order to give a more precise evaluation of the advantage of using this neural network model for solving the assignment problem.

Acknowledgment

This work has been performed in the framework of the research minor program at Telecom Bretagne. In this context, we would like to thank Dr. Vincent Gripon for his support and contributions.

REFERENCES

[1] C. Papadimitriou and K. Steiglitz, Combinatorial Optimization: Algorithms and Complexity, ser. Dover Books on Computer Science Series. Dover Publications, 1998.

[2] M. Held and R. M. Karp, "The traveling-salesman problem and minimum spanning trees," Operations Research, vol. 18, no. 6, 1970, pp. 1138–1162.

[3] M. M. Zavlanos and G. J. Pappas, "Dynamic assignment in distributed motion planning with local coordination," IEEE Transactions on Robotics, vol. 24, no. 1, 2008, pp. 232–242.

[4] M. Balinski, "Signature methods for the assignment problem," Operations research, vol. 33, no. 3, 1985, pp. 527–536.

[5] M. S. Hung, "Technical NoteA Polynomial Simplex Method for the Assignment Problem," Operations Research, vol. 31, no. 3, 1983, pp. 595–600.

[6] K. Date and R. Nagi, "Gpu-accelerated hungarian algorithms for the linear assignment problem," Parallel Computing, vol. 57, 9 2016, pp. 52–72.

[7] V. Gripon and C. Berrou, "Sparse neural networks with large learning diversity," IEEE transactions on neural networks, vol. 22, no. 7, 2011, pp. 1087–1096.

[8] F. Schwenker, F. T. Sommer, and G. Palm, "Iterative retrieval of sparsely coded associative memory patterns," Neural Networks, vol. 9, no. 3, 1996, pp. 445–455.

[9] A. Aboudib, V. Gripon, and G. Coppin, "A Neural Network Model for Solving the Feature Correspondence Problem," in International Conference on Artificial Neural Networks. Springer, 2016, pp. 439–446.

[10] R. E. Burkard and E. Cela, "Linear assignment problems and extensions," in Handbook of combinatorial optimization. Springer, 1999, pp. 75–149.

[11] H. W. Kuhn, "The hungarian method for the assignment problem," Naval research logistics quarterly, vol. 2, no. 1-2, 1955, pp. 83–97.

[12] J. Munkres, "Algorithms for the assignment and transportation problems," Journal of the society for industrial and applied mathematics, vol. 5, no. 1, 1957, pp. 32–38.

[13] Operations Research, ser. Core business program. McGraw-Hill Education (India) Pvt Limited, 2008. [Online]. Available: https://books.google.com.hk/books?id=Kc6y14jtkYYC [accessed: 2017-02-10]

[14] D. König, "Über graphen und ihre anwendung auf determinantentheorie und mengenlehre," Mathematische Annalen, vol. 77, no. 4, 1916, pp. 453–465.

[15] A. Toet and H. de Waard, The Weapon-Target Assignment Problem. TNO Human Factors Research Institute, 1995.

An Intrinsic Difference Between Vanilla RNNs and GRU Models

Tristan Stérin
Computer Science Department
École Normale Supérieure de Lyon
Email: tristan.sterin@ens-lyon.fr

Nicolas Farrugia
Electronics Department
IMT Atlantique
Email: nicolas.farrugia@imt-atlantique.fr

Vincent Gripon
Electronics Department
IMT Atlantique
Email: vincent.gripon@imt-atlantique.fr

***Abstract*—In order to perform well in practice, Recurrent Neural Networks (RNN) require computationally heavy architectures, such as Gated Recurrent Unit (GRU) or Long Short Term Memory (LSTM). Indeed, the original Vanilla model fails to encapsulate middle and long term sequential dependencies. The aim of this paper is to show that gradient training issues, which have motivated the introduction of LSTM and GRU models, are not sufficient to explain the failure of the simplest RNN. Using the example of Reber's grammar, we propose an experimental measure of both Vanilla and GRU models, which suggest an intrinsic difference in their dynamics. A better mathematical understanding of this difference could lead to more efficient models without compromising performance.**

***Index Terms*—Recurrent Neural Networks; Gradient Backpropagation; Grammatical Inference; Dynamical Systems.**

I. Introduction

Recurrent Neural Networks (RNN) [1] are a class of artificial neural networks that feature connections between hidden layers that are propagated through time in order to learn sequences. In recent years, such networks, and especially variants such as Gated Recurrent Units (GRU) [2] or Long Short-Term Memory (LSTM) networks [3] have demonstrated remarkable performance in a wide range of applications involving sequences, such as language modeling [4], speech recognition [5], image captioning [6], and automatic translation [7]. Such networks often include a large number of layers (i.e., deep neural networks), each containing many neurons, resulting in a large set of parameters to be learnt. The main reason explaining this challenge are vanishing or exploding gradients while training parameters [8], [9], such problems being likely to emerge when learning any large set of parameters.

The conceptual leap from Vanilla RNN architectures to LSTM or GRU was initially justified by the inability of Vanilla RNN to learn long term sequential dependencies [3]. Theoretically, it is not clear whether this limitation of Vanilla RNN is indeed due to training issues, or to an intrinsic limitation in their architecture. In this paper, we propose to revisit this question by confronting GRU and Vanilla RNN by suggesting the existence of intrinsic theoretical differences between two models. We use the Embedded Reber Grammar and introduce an experimental measure based on dynamical systems theory, in order to highlight a limitation of Vanilla RNN architectures without encountering vanishing or exploding gradient issues.

The remainder of the paper is organized as follows. In Section II, we present the two RNN models that we evaluate, Vanilla RNN and GRU. Section III presents the Embedded Reber Grammar. In Section IV, we perform a set of experiments using both models, and highlight limitations of the Vanilla RNN while no issues with gradients can be demonstrated. in Section V, we introduce a discrepancy measure and show how it can be used to point out the limitations of the Vanilla RNN model. Finally, we give conclusions and perspectives in Section VI.

II. Recurrent Neural Network Models

In this section, we introduce the two models of recurrent neural networks we discuss in this paper, namely Vanilla RNNs and GRU.

A. Vanilla RNNs

Vanilla is the first model of recurrent artificial neural networks that was introduced [1]. Relying on very simple dynamics, this neural network is described with the following set of equations, indexed by time-step t:

$$\boldsymbol{h}_t = \sigma(U_h \boldsymbol{x}_t + W_h \boldsymbol{h}_{t-1}) \quad (1)$$

$$\boldsymbol{y}_t = O\boldsymbol{h}_t \quad (2)$$

where:

- $\boldsymbol{x}_t \in \mathbb{R}^n$ is the input of the RNN,
- $\boldsymbol{h}_t \in \mathbb{R}^k$ is called hidden state of the RNN, and acts as a memory of the current state the dynamics is into. When starting a sequence, it is set to the all zero vector ($\boldsymbol{h}_{-1} = 0$).
- $\boldsymbol{y}_t \in \mathbb{R}^p$ is the output of the RNN,
- The logistic function $\sigma(x) = \frac{1}{1+e^{-x}}$ is applied component-wise,
- U_h, W_h, O are the network's parameters.

Figure 1 depicts a *Vanilla* RNN with four input neurons, a hidden layer with five neurons and one output neuron. The output of such a neural network depends on both the input x_t and the hidden state h_{t-1} that stores information about the past values observed in the sequence.

B. GRU

GRU neural networks are a LSTM variant based on the following equations:

$$z = \sigma(U^z x_t + W^z h_{t-1})$$
$$r = \sigma(U^r x_t + W^r h_{t-1})$$
$$h' = tanh(U^{h'} x_t + W^{h'} (h_{t-1} \circ r))$$
$$h_t = (1 - z) \circ h' + z \circ h_{t-1}$$
$$y_t = O h_t$$

where:

- $x_t \in \mathbb{R}^n$ is the input vector,
- $h_t \in \mathbb{R}^k$ is the hidden state vector, $h_{-1} = 0$,
- $y_t \in \mathbb{R}^p$ is the output vector,
- $r \in \mathbb{R}^k$ is the "reset" vector, which is multiplied component-wise with the hidden state vector h_t when updating it, hence its name,
- $z \in \mathbb{R}^k$ is a combination vector, which acts as a barycenter vector that combines the previous hidden state and currently estimated one to produce the next one,
- The logistic function $\sigma(x) = \frac{1}{1+e^{-x}}$ is applied component-wise,
- $U^{z,r,h'}, W^{z,r,h'}, O$ are the network's parameters.

Both models are known to be Turing complete [10] and could theoretically achieve the same tasks. In practice, it is readily seen that it is much harder to encapsulate long term dependencies with Vanilla RNNs than with its LSTM-based counterpart.

III. Performance of Models on Regular and Embedded Reber's Grammar

Here, we introduce the grammatical inference problem associated with Reber's grammar as in [3] (Figure 2). The corresponding regular expression is $BPT^*V(PSE|VE) + BTS^*X(SE|XT^*V(PSE|VE))$.

We examine the ability of neural network models to infer this automaton from a set of examples in the grammar. Each letter is encoded using a one-hot encoding scheme, thus the input dimension n equals the number of different letters ($n = 7$). A word of length m is thus encoded as a sequence of vectors $x_0 \ldots x_{m-1}$. A valid word is a word for which the automaton ends in the rightmost state. For instance, $BTSSXXTTTVPSE$ is valid and $BTSSE$ is not. The output space is also of size 7 and gives a –non normalised– probability distribution on the following character given the past input sequence. The RNN output –after softmax– can be interpreted as follows:

$$Pr(x_{t+1}|x_0 \ldots x_t)$$

We first train a Vanilla RNN model on this task using a dataset comprising 250 Reber strings. Code can be found at https://github.com/brain-bzh/IARIA17_RNNs/blob/master/ReberGrammars/.

The results are depicted in Figure 3 under the form of heatmaps. Interestingly, this model was able to provide good predictions after training, as we retrieve the edges of the corresponding states in the automaton of Figure 2.

Figure 4 shows the heatmaps of the hidden vectors h_t. Here, a Vanilla RNN successfully infers some of the automaton's states, (e.g., $q2$ and $q5$). Hidden states are very similar even when sequences used to reach them are different.

Hence, a Vanilla RNN model can be trained to infer Reber's grammar. This result can be explained by the fact that it is sufficient to recall the two previous letters to infer which state the automaton is in.

We now consider the example of the Embedded Reber's grammar. An automaton corresponding to this grammar is depicted in Figure 5. In short, the Embedded Reber's grammar consists in two copies of Reber's grammar, except that all strings with a T (resp. P) in second position must have a T (resp. P) at the end, thus exhibiting a long term sequential dependency. We train a Vanilla RNN ($k = 18$) and a GRU model ($k = 10$) with about the same number of parameters ($\simeq 590$), using the same dataset comprising 2000 example sequences.

Figure 6 (resp. Figure 7) depicts the output given by a Vanilla RNN (resp. a GRU model) on the prediction task. This figures emphasizes the fact that Vanilla RNNs are unable to capture long term dependencies, whereas GRU successfully do so.

The confusion phenomenon observed in Figure 6 is already true for the hidden layer, as depicted in Figure 8. In the next sections, we investigate hypothesis regarding the origin of such differences of performance between the two models.

IV. Gradient's Coefficients Distribution

A commonly used argument to justify the performance difference between Vanilla RNNs and GRU models, as presented in [8], is related to the gradient instability when learning parameters of Vanilla RNNs, leading to gradient's coefficients that either explode or vanish. We tested this hypothesis by studying the statistical distributions of gradients when training both neural network models. Figure 9 represents the obtained distribution of absolute value of gradient's coefficients for both the training of Vanilla RNNs and the GRU model, over all the examples in the training set (embedded Reber's grammar). Both distributions are similar and discredit the hypothesis that instable gradient's coefficients are responsible for the unability of Vanilla RNNs to correctly infer the embedded Reber's grammar.

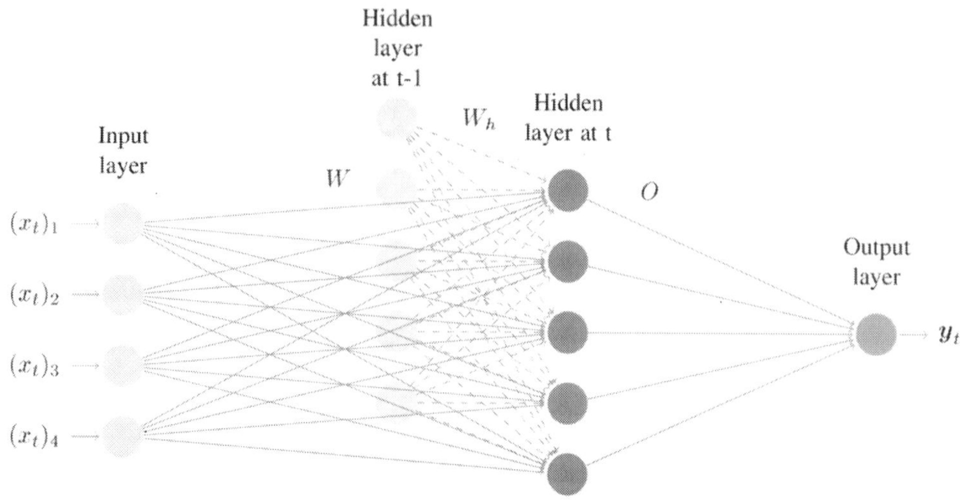

Fig. 1. Vanilla RNN with $n = 4$, $k = 5$ and $p = 1$.

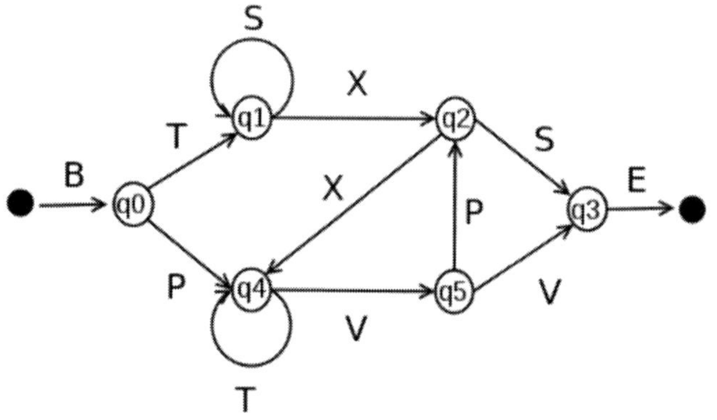

Fig. 2. Reber's grammar automaton.

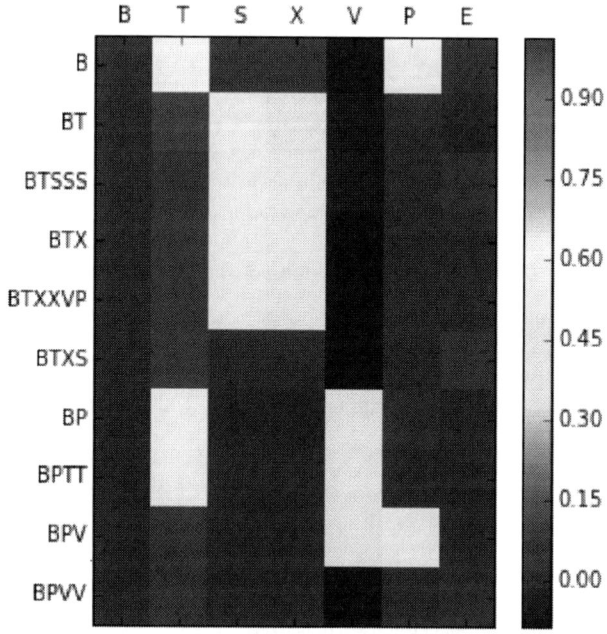

Fig. 3. Heatmaps of the output layer for different sequences on a 5-neurons Vanilla RNN model trained on Reber's gramm.

V. The (L,K)-Discrepancy

We now introduce a formal way to measure the discrepancy capability of a recurrent neural network. More precisely, we introduce a positive quantity that illustrates the ability a model has to propagate long term dependencies.

Definition V.1 ((l,k)-discrepancy)**.** Let us consider:

- Two integers $l, k \in \mathbb{N}$,
- A binary alphabet ($n = 2$), symbolically represented by **0** and **1** ,
- A RNN – either Vanilla RNN or GRU model – comprising k neurons,
- The words $u = \mathbf{0}\overbrace{\mathbf{0}\ldots\mathbf{0}}^{l-1}$ and $v = \mathbf{1}\overbrace{\mathbf{0}\ldots\mathbf{0}}^{l-1}$ differing only by their first bit,
- $\boldsymbol{h}_u$ and $\boldsymbol{h}_v$ the states where the model's hidden state lands after reading u and v.

Then the **(l,k)-discrepancy** $D(l, k)$ of the model is computed with the following process:

- Compute a numerous time (2000 in the following) $||\boldsymbol{h}_u - \boldsymbol{h}_v||_2$ for different random affectations of the model's parameters (sampled over $\mathcal{N}(0, 1)$ in the paper).
- Average these norms, it is $D(l, k)$.

The quantity $D(l, k)$ is integrally computed without training. It summarizes the capacity of the k-neurons network to distinguish between sequences of length l perfectly identical but their first bit.

Figure 10 depicts the evolution of $D(l, k)$ for various values of l and k. Code can be found at https://github.com/brain-

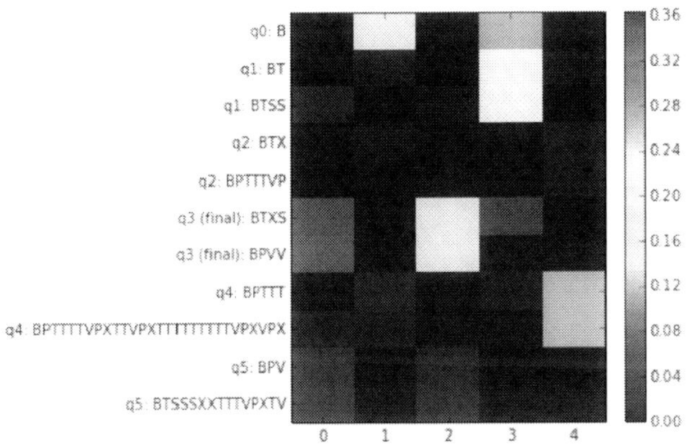

Fig. 4. Heatmaps of the hidden layer for a 5-neurons Vanilla on different observed sequences of a Reber's grammar. Corresponding automaton's states are also listed.

bzh/IARIA17_RNNs/tree/master/lk-discrepancy/.

It shows that as soon as l becomes large, the discrepancy ability of Vanilla RNNs becomes very close to 0, meaning that the two binary sequences are indistinguishable.

In comparison, Figure 11 depicts the discrepancy for the GRU model for various values of l and k. As we can see here, the discrepancy does not goes to 0 for large values of l, suggesting the ability of the dynamics of GRU to maintain long term information in the hidden state of the network.

These profiles provide an intuitive explanation of the results for the Reber's grammar: the Vanilla could succeed in the first problem because of the really short term memory required and definitely failed in the embedded case because of out-of-range dependencies.

VI. Conclusions and Future Research

Through Reber's grammar example we saw that Vanilla and GRU differenciate themselves more than just through learning and gradients arguments. This observation motivates future mathematical research to formally understand their intrinsic difference in term of dynamical systems. A good starting point could reside in the Echo States Network (c.f. [11]) theory and the mathematical tools it develops. Understanding this difference could lead to simpler RNN models than GRU/LSTM, less computationally heavy, and with better long term abilities.

Acknowledgements

This work was funded in part by the CominLabs project "Neural Communication".

References

[1] Pineda and F. J., "Generalization of back-propagation to recurrent neural networks", *Physical review letters*, vol.59, pp.19, 1987.
[2] Cho K., Merriënboer B., Bahdanau D. and Bengio Y., "On the Properties of Neural Machine Translation: Encoder-Decoder Approaches", arXiv, 2014.
[3] Hochreiter S. and Schmidhuber J., "Long short-term memory", *Neural Computation*, vol.9, pp.1735-1780, 1997.
[4] Mikolov T., Karafiát, M., Burget, L., Cernocký, J. and Khudanpur S., "Recurrent neural network based language model", *Interspeech*, vol.3, pp.2, 2010.
[5] Graves A., Mohamed, A. and Hinton G., "Speech recognition with deep recurrent neural networks", *2013 IEEE international conference on acoustics, speech and signal processing*, . IEEE, 2013.
[6] Karpathy, A., and Fei-Fei, L., "Deep visual-semantic alignments for generating image descriptions", *Proceedings of the IEEE Conference on Computer Vision and Pattern Recognition*, IEEE, 2015.
[7] Sutskever, I., Oriol V. and Quoc V. Le., "Sequence to sequence learning with neural networks", *Advances in neural information processing systems*, 2014.
[8] Bengio Y., Sinard P. and Frasconi P., "Learning Long-Term Dependencies with Gradient Descent is Difficult", *IEEE transactions on neural networks*, vol.5, pp.2, 1994.
[9] Pascanu, R., Tomas M. and Bengio, Y., "On the difficulty of training recurrent neural networks", *International Conference on Machine Learning*, vol.3, pp.28, 2013.
[10] T. Siegelmann H. and D. Sontag E., "On the Computational Power of Neural Nets", *Journal of computer and system sciences*, vol.50, pp.132-150, 1995.
[11] Jaeger H., "The "echo state" approach to analysing ang training recurrent neural networks", TechReport, 2001.

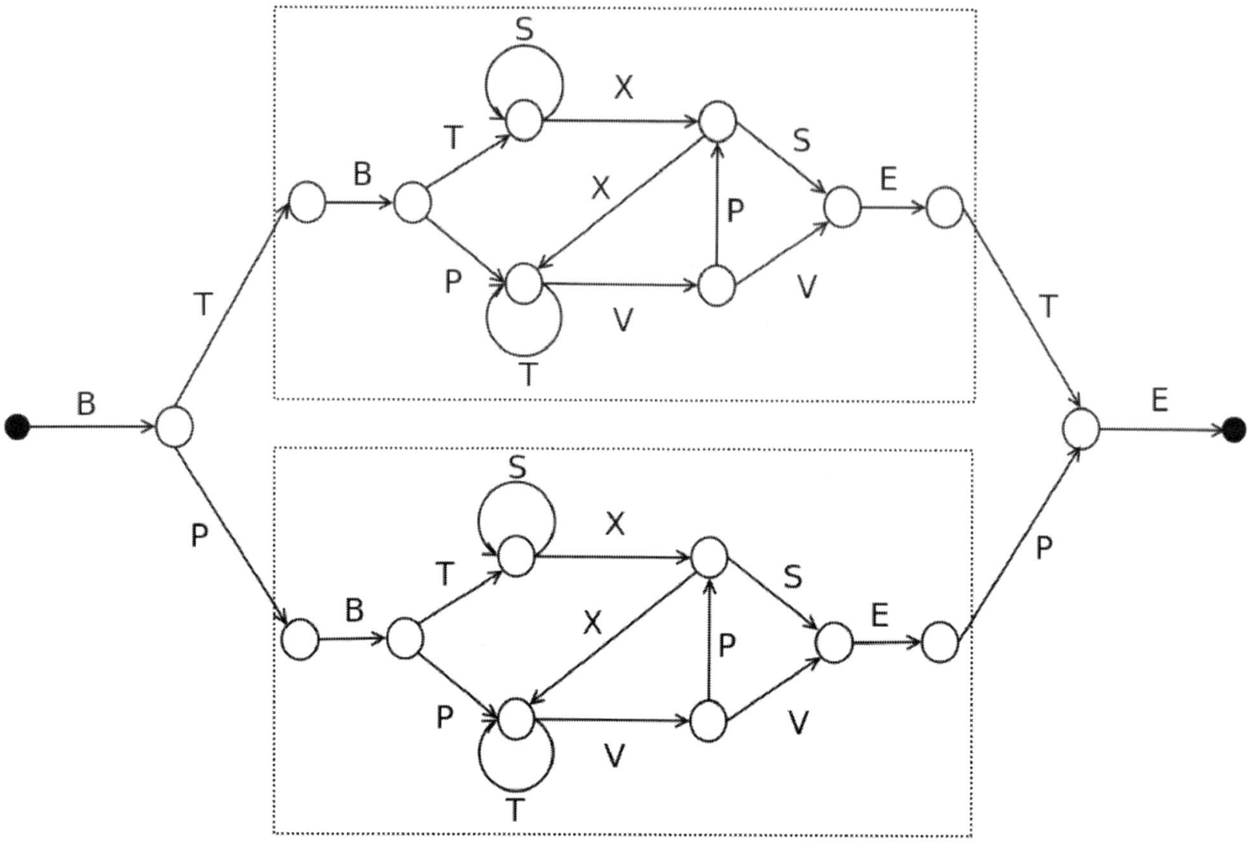

Fig. 5. A depiction of the automaton corresponding to the Embedded Reber's grammar.

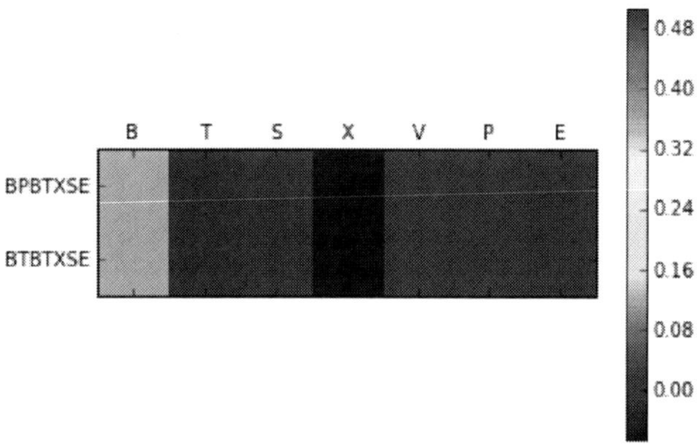

Fig. 6. Vanilla RNN prediction on several sequences of the Embedded Reber's grammar.

Fig. 7. GRU prediction on several sequences of the Embedded Reber's grammar. The expected letters are correct and reflect the fact the embedded Reber's grammar has been correctly inferred.

Fig. 8. Hidden layer of a 18-neurons Vanilla RNN after training on the embedded Reber's grammar.

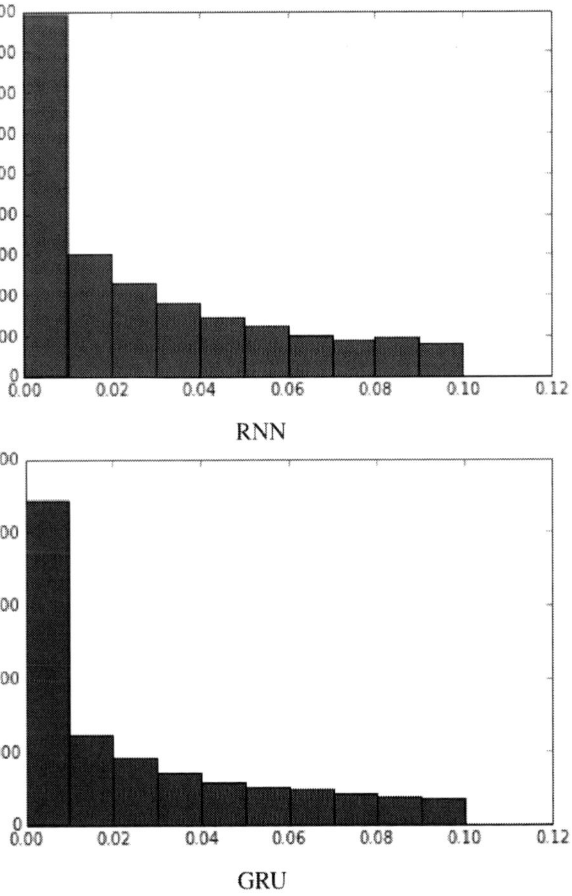

Fig. 9. Gradient's coefficients for both Vanilla RNNs and GRU models when learning the embedded Reber's grammar from 2000 examples.

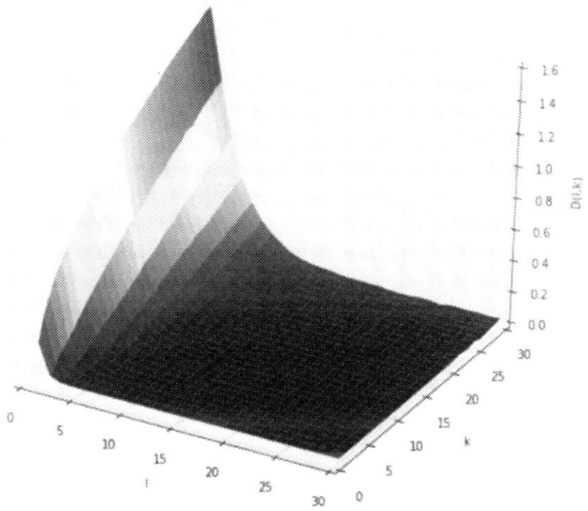

Fig. 10. Evolution of $D(l, k)$ for a Vanilla RNN.

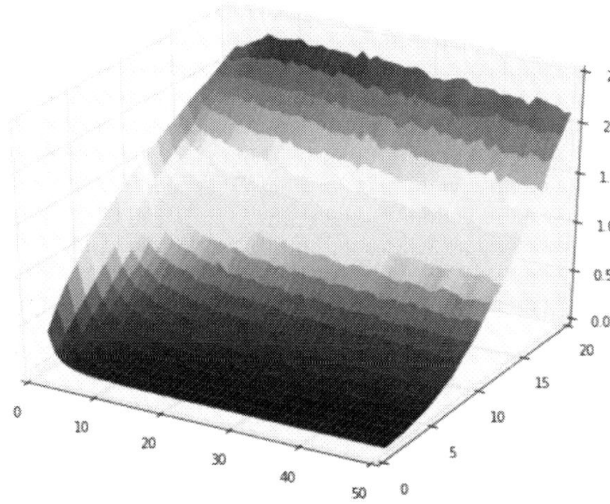

Fig. 11. Evolution of $D(l, k)$ for the GRU model.

Conversational Homes

Nick O'Leary, Dave Braines
Emerging Technology,
IBM United Kingdom Ltd,
Hursley Park, Winchester, UK
Email: nick_oleary|dave_braines@uk.ibm.com

Alun Preece, Will Webberley
School of Computer Science and Informatics,
Cardiff University, Cardiff, UK
Email: PreeceAD|WebberleyWM@cardiff.ac.uk

***Abstract*—As devices proliferate, the ability for us to interact with them in an intuitive and meaningful way becomes increasingly challenging. In this paper we take the typical home as an experimental environment to investigate the challenges and potential solutions arising from ever-increasing device proliferation and complexity. We show a potential solution based on conversational interactions between "things" in the environment where those things can be either machine devices or human users. Our key innovation is the use of a Controlled Natural Language (CNL) technology as the underpinning information representation language for both machine and human agents, enabling humans and machines to trivially "read" the information being exchanged. The core CNL is augmented with a conversational protocol enabling different speech acts to be exchanged within the system. This conversational layer enables key contextual information to be conveyed, as well as providing a mechanism for translation from the core CNL to other forms, such as device specific API requests, or more easily consumable human representations. Our goal is to show that a single, uniform language can support machine-machine, machine-human, human-machine and human-human interaction in a dynamic environment that is able to rapidly evolve to accommodate new devices and capabilities as they are encountered.**

***Keywords*–IoT; Controlled Natural Language; Conversational Interaction.**

I. Introduction

From an individual agent's perspective, the Internet of Things (IoT) can be seen as an increasingly large and diverse world of other agents to communicate with. Humans are agents too in this world, so we can observe four kinds of communication: (i) human-machine, (ii) machine-human, (iii) machine-machine, and (iv) human-human. There is a tendency to consider human-oriented (i, iv) and machine-oriented (ii, iii) interactions as naturally requiring different kinds of communication language; humans prefer natural languages, while machines operate most readily on formal languages. In this paper, however, we consider what the IoT world might look like where humans and machines largely use a common, uniform language to communicate. Our design goal is to support communication activities such as: the discovery of other agents and their capabilities, querying other agents and receiving understandable information from them, and obtaining rationale for an agent's actions. The proposed approach must be able to cope with rapid evolution of an IoT environment that needs to accommodate new devices, capabilities, and agent types. In Section II, we consider why human users might find such an environment more appealing when machines communicate using an accessible and human-friendly language, than when machines use a traditional machine-to-machine formalism. Section III substantiates our proposed approach using a series of vignettes, while section IV provides some initial experimental evidence that human-machine and machine-machine interactions can be facilitated via a CNL communication mechanism. Section V concludes the paper.

II. Background and Related Work

A key part of our approach is to consider the way in which humans "want" to interact with machines in the world. To help us gain insights into these latent human requirements we look towards existing trends and events occurring in the world and use these as inspiration to help us form our hypotheses about what a conversational environment for human-machine agents might entail. For example, in this work we consider recent interest in conversational technologies such as chatbots [1], conversational computing [2], and conversational agents [3]. The remainder of this section covers this human-motivated perspective and develops ideas first presented in [4].

A. Social Things

The advent of Twitter as a means of social communication has enabled a large number of otherwise inanimate objects to have an easily-accessible online presence. For example, Andy Stanford-Clark created an account for the Red Funnel ferries that service the Isle of Wight in the UK. The account [5] relays real-time information about the ferry arrivals and departures allowing a subscriber of the account to see if they are running on time.

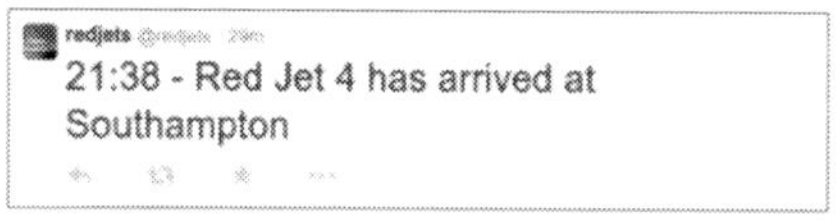

Figure 1: Redjet tweet example

Another similar example is an unofficial account for London's Tower Bridge [6]. Its creator, Tom Armitage, created a system that took the published scheduled of bridge opening and closing times and produced a Twitter account that relayed that information.

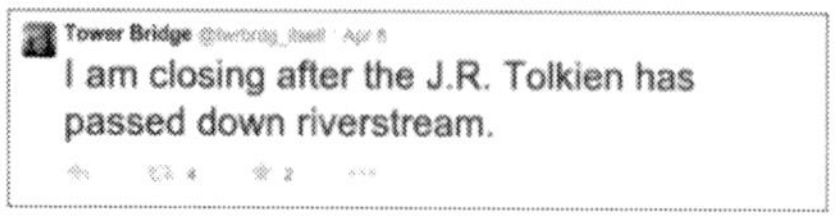

Figure 2: Tower Bridge tweet example

A key difference between the ferries and the bridge accounts is that the ferries are just relaying information, a timestamp and a position, whereas the bridge is speaking to us in the first-person. This small difference immediately begins to bring a more human nature to the account. But, they are ultimately simple accounts that relay their state to whomever is following them, providing an easily consumable feed of information on an existing platform.

This sort of thing seems to have caught on particularly with the various space agencies. We no longer appear able to send a robot to Mars, or land a probe on a comet without an accompanying Twitter account bringing character to the events. The Mars Curiosity Rover has had an account [7] since July 2008 and regularly shares images it has captured. There's always a sense of excitement when these inanimate objects start to have a conversation with one another. The conversations between the European Space Agency Philae lander [8] and its Rosetta orbiter [9], as the former began to lose power and had to shutdown, generated a large emotional response on social media. The lander, which was launched into space years before social media existed, chose to use its last few milliamps of power to send a final goodbye.

The reality, of course, is that the devices did not create these tweets. Communication with them remains the preserve of highly specialized engineers, and their personalities are a creation of their public relations agencies on this planet. There are however, examples of machine participation on social media provided by social bots [10]. On occasion, these entities can masquerade as human agents and alter the dynamics of social sense-making and social influence.

B. Seamlessness vs Seamfulness

The IoT makes possible a future where our homes and workplaces are full of connected devices, sharing their data, making decisions, collaborating to make our lives better [11]. Whilst there are people who celebrate this invisible ubiquity and utility of computing, the reality is going to be much more complicated.

Mark Weiser, Chief Scientist at Xerox PARC, coined the term "ubiquitous computing" in 1988 as recognition of the changing nature of our interaction with computers [12]. Rather than the overt interaction of a user sitting in front of a computer, ubiquitous computing envisages technology receding into the background of our lives.

Discussion of ubiquitous computing often celebrates the idea of seamless experiences between the various devices occupying our lives. Mark Weiser advocated for the opposite; that seamlessness was undesirable and a self-defeating attribute of such a system. He preferred a vision of "Seamfulness, with beautiful seams" [13].

The desire to present a single view of a system, with no joins, is an unrealistic aspiration in the face of the cold realities of Wi-Fi connectivity, battery life, system reliability and the status of cloud services. Presenting a user with a completely monolithic system gives them no opportunity to connect with, and begin to understand, the constituent parts. That is not to say all users need this information all of the time, but there is clearly utility to some users some of the time: when you come home from work and the house is cold, what went wrong? Did the thermostat in the living room break and decide it was the right temperature already? Did the message from the working thermostat fail to get to the boiler? Is the boiler broken? Did you forget to cancel the entry in your calendar saying you'd be late home that day? Without some appreciation of the moving parts in a system, a user cannot feel any ownership or empowerment when something goes wrong with it. Or worse yet, how can they avoid feeling anything other than intimidated by this monolithic system that responds in a manner akin to, "I'm Sorry Dave, I'm afraid I can't do that".

This is the justification for beautiful seams: they help you understand the edges of a device's sphere of interaction, but should not be so big as to trip you up. For example, such issues exist with the various IP connected light bulbs that are available today. When a user needs to remember which application to launch on their phone depending on which room they are walking into and which manufacturer's bulbs happen to be in there, the seams have gotten too big and too visible.

Designer Tom Coates has written on these topics [14]. He suggests the idea of having a chat-room for the home:

"Much like a conference might have a chat-room so might a home. And it might be a space that you could duck into as you pleased to see what was going on. By turning the responses into human language you could make the actions of the objects less inscrutable and difficult to understand..."

This relates back to the world of Twitter accounts for Things, but with a key evolution. Rather than one-sided conversations presenting raw data in a more consumable form, or Wizard-of-Oz style man-behind-the-curtain accounts, a chat-room is a space where the conversation can flow both ways; both between the owner and their devices, and also between the devices themselves.

C. Getting Things Communicating

For devices to be able to communicate they need to share a common language. Simply being able to send a piece of data across the network is not sufficient. As with spoken language, the context of an interaction is important too.

This model of interaction applies to both the data a device produces, as well as the commands it can consume. There are a number of technologies available for producing such a shared model. For example: HyperCat [15], a consortium of companies funded by the UK Government's innovation agency in 2014. It provides a central catalog of resources that are described using RDF-like triple statements. Each resource is identified by a URI allowing for ease of reference. URIs are a key component in building the World Wide Web and are well understood, but they are a technology used primarily by computers. They do not provide a human-accessible view of the model.

Furthermore, to enable a dynamic conversation, any such model needs to be adaptable to the devices that are participating, especially when one of those participants is a human being.

D. Talking to Computers

The most natural form of communication for most humans is that of their own spoken language, not some JSON or XML encoded format that was created with the devices as the primary recipient. Technical specialists can be trained to understand and use technical machine languages, but this overhead is not acceptable to more casual everyday users who may wish to interact with the devices in their home. In addition to this, we are living in an age where talking to computers is becoming less the preserve of science fiction: Apple's Siri, OK Google, Microsoft Cortana all exist as ways to interact with the devices in your pocket. Amazon Echo exists as a device for the home that allows basic interaction through voice commands. This means that there is now a plausible expectation that an everyday person could interact with complex devices in their home in a natural conversational manner.

Natural Language Processing (NLP) is one of the key challenges in Computer Science [16]. In terms of speech understanding, correctly identifying the words being spoken is relatively a well-solved problem, but understanding what those words mean, what intent they try to convey, is still a hard thing to do.

To answer the question "Which bat is your favorite?" without any context is hard to do. Are we talking to a sportsperson with their proud collection of cricket bats? Is it the zookeeper with their colony of winged mammals? Or perhaps a comic book fan is being asked to choose between incarnations of their favorite super hero.

Context is also vital when you want to hold a conversation. Natural language (NL) is riddled with ambiguity. Our brains are constantly filling in gaps, making theories and assumptions over what the other person is saying. For humans and machines to communicate effectively in any such conversational home setting, it is important that contextual information can be communicated in a simple, but effective, manner. This must be achieved in a manner that is accessible to both the human and machine agents in this environment.

III. Controlled Natural Language

To avoid a lot of the hard challenges of NLP, a CNL can be used. A CNL is a subset of a NL that uses a restricted set of grammar rules and a restricted vocabulary [17]. It is constructed to be readable by a native speaker and represents information in a structured and unambiguous form. This also enables it to be read and properly interpreted by a machine agent via a trivial parsing mechanism without any need for complex processing or resolution of ambiguity. CNLs range in strength from weaker examples such as simple style guides, to the strongest forms that are full formal languages with well-defined semantics. In our work, to identify a unifying language for both human and machine communication, we are focused on languages at the strong end of the scale, but we additionally wish to retain the requirement for maximal human consumability.

Ambiguity is a key issue for machine agents: whilst human readers can tolerate a degree of uncertainty and are often able to resolve ambiguity for themselves, it can be very difficult for a computer to do the same. CNLs typically specify that words be unambiguous and often specify which meaning is allowed for all or a subset of the vocabulary. Another source of ambiguity is the phrase or sentence structure. A simple example is concerned with noun clusters. In English, one noun is commonly used to modify another noun. A noun phrase with several nouns is usually ambiguous as to how the nouns should be grouped. To avoid potential ambiguity, many CNLs do not allow the use of more than three nouns in a noun phrase.

There are two different philosophies in designing a CNL. As mentioned previously a weaker CNL can be treated as a simplified form of NL with a stronger CNL as an English version of a formal language [18]. In the case of a simplified form of NL, it can allow certain degrees of ambiguity in order to increase human accessibility. It relies on standard NLP techniques, lexical-semantic resources and a domain model to optimize its interpretation.

The alternative is to treat a CNL as an entirely deterministic language, where each word has a single meaning and no ambiguity can exist. Whilst computationally very efficient, it can be hard for a human user unfamiliar with the particular lexicon and grammar to write it effectively. This is because it competes with the user's own intuition of the language. The closer a CNL is to corresponding NL, the more natural and easy it is to use by humans, but it becomes less predictable and its computational complexity increases. The converse is also true. The more deterministic the CNL is, the more predictable it is, but the more difficult it is for humans to use.

In summary, in the operational setting described in this paper a CNL is designed to support both human usage and machine processing. It provides:

1) A user-friendly language in a form of English, instead of, for example, a standard formal query language (such as SPARQL or SQL). Enabling the user to construct queries to information systems in an intuitive way.
2) A precise language that enables clear, unambiguous representation of extracted information to serve as a semantic representation of the free text data that is amenable to creating rule-based inferences.
3) A common form of expression used to build, extend and refine domain models by adding or modifying entities, relations, or event types, and specifying mapping relations between data models and terminology or language variants.
4) An intuitive means of configuring system processing, such as specifying entity types, rules, and lexical patterns.

A good balance between the naturalness and predictability of the CNL is fundamentally important, especially to the human users as the strength and formality of the language increases.

A. An Introduction to ITA Controlled English

In previous research, we have proposed a specific CNL that is a variant of "Controlled English" known as ITA Controlled English, or just "CE" in shorthand [19]. This has been researched and developed under the International Technology Alliance (ITA) in Network and Information Science [20]. CE is consistent with First Order Predicate Logic and provides an unambiguous representation of information for machine processing. It aspires to provide a human-friendly representation format that is directly targeted at non-technical domain-specialist users (such as military planners, intelligence analysts or business managers) to enable a richer set of reasoning capabilities [21] [22].

We assert that CE can be used as a standard language for representation of many aspects of the information representation and reasoning space [23]. In addition to more traditional areas such as knowledge or domain model representation and corresponding information, CE also encompasses the representation of logical inference rules, rationale (reasoning steps), assumptions, statements of truth (and certainty) and has been used in other areas such as provenance [24] and argumentation [25].

In the remainder of this section we give a number of examples of the CE language. These are shown as embedded sentences in this style. All of these sentences are valid CE and therefore directly machine processable as well as being human readable.

The domain model used within CE is created through the definition of concepts, relationships and properties. These definitions are themselves written as CE conceptualise statements:

conceptualise a ~ device ~ D.
conceptualise an ~ environment variable ~ E.

These statements establish the concepts within the CE domain model enabling subsequent instances to be created using the same CE language:

there is an environment variable named 'temperature'.

A slightly more advanced example would be:

conceptualise a ~ controlling thing ~ C that
is a device and
~ can control ~ the environment variable E.

This defines "controlling thing" as a sub-concept of "device" and that it can have a "can control" relationship with an "environment variable". This therefore allows statements such as:

there is a controlling thing named 'thermostat' that
can control the environment variable
'temperature'.

In the latter conceptualise statement, "can control" is an example of a CE verb singular relationship. Functional noun relationships can also be asserted:

conceptualise a ~ device ~ D that
has the value E as ~ enabled ~.

These two types of relationship construct allow a concept and its properties to be richly defined in CE whilst maintaining a strict subset of grammar. The use of verb singular and functional noun forms of properties provides a simple, but effective, mechanism to enable the conceptual model designer to use a language that is more natural and appealing to the human agents in the system.

The "is a" relationship used within conceptualise sentences defines inheritance of concepts, with multiple inheritance from any number of parents being a key requirement. It also allows any instance to be asserted as any number of concurrent concepts; an essential tool when attempting to capture and convey different contexts for the same information.

Whilst the examples given above are deliberately simplistic the same simple language constructs can be used to develop rich models and associated knowledge bases. The CE language has been successfully used in a wide range of example applications [26]. CE has been shown working with a reasonable number of concepts, relationships, queries and rules and has been used to model and interact with complex real-world environments with a high level of coverage and practical expressivity being achieved.

In our previous research into the application of the CE language we have observed that by gradually building up an operational model of a given environment, it is possible to iteratively define rich and complex semantic models in an "almost-NL" form that appeals to non-specialist domain users. For example, if the concept "device" was extended to include location information, the following query could be used to identify all devices of a particular type within a particular location:

for which D is it true that
(the device D is located in the room V) and
(the device D can measure
the environment variable 'temperature') and
(the value V = 'kitchen').

Note that we do not expect casual users to write CE queries of this complexity; the later conversational interaction section will show how users can do this in a more natural form.

The model can be extended with rules that can be used to automatically infer new facts within the domain. Whenever such facts are inferred the CE language is able to capture rationale for why a particular fact is held to be true:

the room 'kitchen'
is able to measure
the environment variable 'temperature' and
is able to control
the environment variable 'temperature'
because
the thermometer 't1'
is located in the room 'kitchen' and
can measure
the environment variable 'temperature' and
the radiator valve 'v1'
is located in the room 'kitchen' and
can control
the environment variable 'temperature'.

From these basic examples you can see how the CE language can be used to model the basic concepts and properties within a given domain (such as an operating environment for IoT devices). Through assertion of corresponding instance data and the use of queries and rules it is possible to define the specific details of any given environment. It should also be clear to the reader that whilst human-readable the core CE language is quite technical and does not yet meet the aspiration of a language that would appeal to everyday casual users. The language itself can be improved, and as reported in earlier research there is the ability to build incrementally usable layers of language on top of the CE core language [27]. However, in addition to all of these potential advances in the core language there is also a key innovation that has been recently developed, which is to build a rich conversational protocol on top of the CE language [28]. This provides a mechanism whereby casual users can engage in conversation with a CE knowledge base using their own NL in a manner similar to human-human conversation.

B. Conversational Interaction

To enable a conversational form of CE, earlier research [29] has identified a requirement for a number of core interaction types based on speech-act theory:

1) A confirm interaction allows a NL message, typically from a human user, to be provided, which is then refined through interaction to an acceptable CE representation. This is useful for a human user who is perhaps not fully trained on the CE grammar. Through multiple such interactions, their experience builds and such interactions become shorter.
2) An ask/tell interaction allows a query to be made of the domain model and a well-formulated CE response given.
3) A gist/expand interaction enables the CE agent to provide a summary form ("gist") of a piece of CE, possibly adapted to a more digestible NL form. Such a gist can be expanded to give the underlying CE representation.
4) A why interaction allows an agent in receipt of CE statements to obtain rationale for the information provided.

This "conversational layer" in built within the core CE environment and is defined using the CE language. Within the CE model, these interactions are modeled as sub-types of the card concept.

```
conceptualise a ~ card ~ C that is an entity and
    has the timestamp T as ~ timestamp ~ and
    has the value V as ~ content ~ and
    ~ is to ~ the agent A and
    ~ is from ~ the agent B and
    ~ is in reply to ~ the card C.
```

The concept of an agent is introduced to represent the different parties in a conversation. This model provides a framework for such agents to interact by CE statements. By developing a conversational protocol using the CE language it enables the same language to be used for the domain in question (e.g., IoT devices in the home), as well as the act of communication. This means that agents with different operational domains can still communicate using a standard conversational model, so even if they cannot decode the items being discussed they are at least able to participate in the conversation. This idea is central to the proposed approach for conversationally enabled human and machine agents in an IoT context described in this paper.

C. Agent and ce-store interaction

In our ongoing experiments using the CE language we are able to define models, build knowledge bases, build machine agents and enable conversational interaction between them using some key components, which we will refer to here as ce-store. The Java-based implementation of the full ce-store [30] is publically available from github and an additional javascript-based version [31] is also available, specifically engineered to enable operation at the edge of the network, i.e., in a mobile browser environment.

For example, the domain model shown earlier in this paper is created through CE, (including the concepts, relationships and instances) and held within an instance of the ce-store, also referred to as a CE knowledge base. This store can either be maintained at a central point in the architecture, or distributed across systems through a federated set of separate ce-store instances. A centralized store provides a more straightforward system to maintain and ensures a single, shared model. Distributing the store allows for more localized processing to be done by the agents without having to interact with the system as a whole. Distributing the store also enables different agents to have different models, and for models to be rapidly extended "in the field" for only those agents which require those changes.

The choice of agent architecture influences how the store should be structured. When considering the types of conversation a chat-room for the home may need to support, there are two possible approaches.

1) The human user interacts with a single agent in the role as a concierge for the home. This agent uses the CE knowledge base to maintain a complete situational awareness of the devices in the home and is able to communicate with them directly (see Figure 3). Interactions between concierge and devices do not use CE; only the concierge has a CE knowledge base.
2) The human user interacts with each device, or set of devices, individually. There may still be an agent in a concierge style role, but conversations can be directed at individual devices of interest as required (see Figure 4). Here, the concierge and all devices can communicate using CE and all have their own CE knowledge bases.

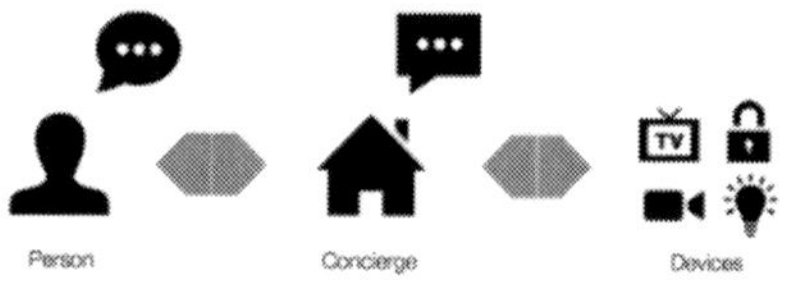

Figure 3: The human user interacts (via CE) only with the concierge

Whilst the former would be sufficient to enable purely human-machine interaction, one of the goals of this work is to enable the human to passively observe the interaction of the devices in the home in order to help the human gain awareness of how the system is behaving. This will better enable the human user to see normal behavior over time and therefore prepare them for understanding anomalous situations when they arise.

Figure 4: The human user can interact (via CE) directly with all devices and with devices via the concierge

As such, the latter approach is more suited for these purposes, perhaps with a concierge agent who is additionally maintaining the overall situation awareness from a machine-processing perspective.

D. Modelling the Conversation

In our proposed conversational homes setting there are a number of styles of interaction a human may wish to have with the devices in their home. This section considers four such styles and how they can be handled within a CE environment.

1) Direct question/answer exchanges: This is where a user makes a direct query as to the current state of the environment or one of the devices therein. For example: "What is the temperature in the kitchen?"

Through the existing conversational protocol and embedded simple contextual NL processing a machine agent is able to break down such a statement to recognize its intent. By parsing each word in turn and finding matching terms with the ce-store it can establish:

- it is a question regarding a current state ("What is ...")
- it is regarding the temperature environment variable instance
- it is regarding the kitchen room instance

At this point, the machine agent has sufficient information to query the ce-store to identify what devices in the model are in the right location and capable of measuring the required variable. If such a device exists, it can be queried for the value and reported back to the user. Otherwise, a suitable message can be returned to indicate the question cannot be answered, ideally conveying some indication of why not.

If the question is ambiguous, for example by omitting a location, the agent can prompt the user for the missing information. The concept of ambiguity for this kind of question is also captured in CE, for example by stating that for such an environment variable a location must be specified, perhaps even with a default location that can be assumed. With this knowledge available in CE the agent is able to determine that extra information is still required and can request this from the user as part of the conversation. The agent maintains information regarding the state of the conversation such that prompts can be made without requiring the user to repeat their entire question with the additional information included. By using the conversational protocol on top of the core CE language the human user and the device are able to converse in NL, for example:

User: *What is the temperature?*
Agent: *Where? I can tell you about the kitchen, the hall and the master bedroom.*
User: *The kitchen.*
Agent: *The temperature in the kitchen is 22C*

Other simple question types can be handled in this way, such as "where is...".

2) Questions that require a rationale as response: This is where a user requires an explanation for a current state of the system "Why is the kitchen cold?"

As with a direct question, an agent can parse the question to identify:

- it is a question asking for a rationale ("Why is ...")
- it has a subject of kitchen
- it has a state of cold that, through the CE model, is understood to be an expression of the temperature environment variable.

To be able to provide a response, the model supports the ability to identify what can affect the given environment variable. With that information it can examine the current state of the system to see what can account for the described state. For example, "the window is open" or "the thermostat is set to 16C".

3) An explicit request to change a particular state: This is where a user, or a machine agent, makes an explicit request for a device to take an action "Turn up the thermostat in the kitchen"

To identify this type of statement, the model maintains a set of actions that can be taken and to what devices they can be applied. By incrementally matching the words of the statement against the list of known actions, a match, if it exists, can be identified. Further parsing of the statement can identify a target for the action.

```
conceptualise an ~ action ~ A that
  ~ is reversed by ~ the action B and
  ~ can affect ~ the controlling thing M.

if (the action A is reversed by the action B)
then (the action B is reversed by the action A).
```

This demonstrates the ability to define a rule. These are logic constructs with premises and conclusions that get evaluated by the ce-store against each new fact added. Where a match in the premises is found, new facts are generated using the conclusions (with corresponding rationale). In this simple case it allows two-way relationships to be established without having to explicitly define the relationship in both directions.

```
there is an action named 'turn on'.
there is an action named 'turn off'.
the action 'turn on' is reversed by the action 'turn off'.
```

When a device receives an action, the trigger concept can be used to chain further sequences of actions that should occur. For example, when applied to a thermostat, the action "turn up" should trigger the action "turn on" to be applied to the boiler.

```
there is a trigger named ' tr1' that
  has 'turn up' as action and
  has 'boiler' as target device and
  has 'turn on' as target action.

the thermostat 'ts1' will respond to the trigger 'tr1'.
```

There is a natural point of contact here, with the popular 'If This Then That' framework (IFTTT) [32], specifically in that the use of conversational interactions could provide a nice way to implement IFTTT functionality. In future work we may consider the extent to which CE could be applied in IFTTT scenarios, and used to support a user-friendly form of programming for real-world objects, devices and situations.

4) An implicit desire to change a state: The styles considered so far have been explicit in their intent. There is another form whereby a statement is made that states a fact, but also implies a desire for an action to be taken.

This relies on Grice's Maxim of Relevance [33]. In the context of a conversation with the devices in a house, a statement such as "I am cold" should be taken as a desire for it to be warmer. The underlying information that can allow this Gricean inference to be implemented by machine agents using a simple algorithm is shown below:

```
there is a physical state named 'cold' that
  is an expression of
    the environment variable 'temperature' and
  has 'warmer' as desired state.

there is a desired state named 'warmer' that
  has 'temperature' as target and
  has 'increase' as effect.
```

Once the intention of the statement has been identified, the store can be queried to find any actions that satisfy the requirement. These actions can then be offered as possible responses to the statement, or possibly automatically enacted.

Through these four simple dialogue examples we have demonstrated that through the use of a CE knowledge base and a set of machine agents using the conversational protocol a human user could carry out basic interactions with the devices in their home (human-machine). We have also shown how those devices convey key information back to the user, or ask follow on questions to elicit additional information (machine-human). These same interactions using the same CE language can be used to enable direct communications between machine agents regardless of human involvement (machine-machine). Whilst we have not explicitly demonstrated human-human communication it is clear that this can easily be supported within a system such as this, for example, by enabling different human users within the home to use the same chat environment to converse with each other directly and then easily direct their questions or actions to machine agents when needed.

It is the use of this common human-readable CE language that enables the passive observation of system state and agent communications at any time without development of special tooling to convert from machine specific representation formats to something that human users can directly read. The CE language enables machine or human users to change or extend the conceptual models against which the system is operating as well as allowing them to define new knowledge, queries or rules.

Whilst it would be possible to demonstrate the same capabilities using more traditional Semantic Web languages they would be aimed at machine processability rather than human consumability and would therefore require additional components to be developed to allow conversational interaction and the inclusion of the human users in the conversation.

IV. Evaluation

As set out in the introduction, our hypothesis is that CNL can enable machine-machine, machine-human, human-machine and human-human interaction in a dynamic environment. The previous section has given illustrative examples of how we envisage the approach working in a range of use cases. Through a series of experiments, we are building an evidence base to show the feasibility and effectiveness of the approach, in two respects: (i) that humans without any significant degree of training are able to engage in dialogues using a combination of NL and CNL; and (ii) that the approach supports environments that can rapidly evolve to accommodate new devices and capabilities as they are encountered.

To gather evidence for (i), we have to date run a series of trials in controlled conditions, focusing on the proposition that users with little or no training in the use of CE can productively interact with CE-enabled agents. We reported the results of the first of these studies in [29]. Twenty participants (undergraduate students) were assigned a task of describing scenes depicted in photographs using NL, and given feedback in the form of CE statements generated via NLP by a software agent. The agent had been constructed rapidly to perform simple bag-of-words NLP with a lexicon provided by having four independent people provide scene descriptions in advance of the experiment. The results were promising; from 137 NL inputs submitted by the 20 subjects, with a median of one sentence for each input, a median of two CE elements was obtained by NLP for each input. In other words, with no prior training in the use of CE or prior knowledge of the domain model constructed for the scenes, users were able to communicate two usable CE elements (typically an identified instance and a relationship) per single-sentence NL input.

The ability of the CE agent to extract meaningful elements from the user's input and confirm these in CE form was constrained by the rapid manner in which the background domain knowledge base had been constructed. In effect, the agent's limited knowledge about the world led to results that were characterized by high precision, but relatively low recall, since the agent was engineered only to be "interested" in a narrow range of things. In this respect, however, we see these results as applicable to our "conversational homes" scenarios, where the concerns of home-based devices and the affordances users expect them to provide will be similarly narrow. Further experiments are planned in settings more closely aligned with the examples in the previous section.

In terms of our requirement (ii), that the approach supports environments which can rapidly evolve to accommodate new devices and capabilities as they are encountered, we have constructed and demonstrated experimental prototypes for sensing asset selection for users' tasks, as described in [34]. Again, while these prototypes are not exactly aligned with the scenario of home automation (instead being more concerned with sensing systems such as autonomous aerial vehicles and ground systems) these experiments have shown that the CE-based approach supports the rapid addition of new knowledge. This includes not only of types of asset, but also of asset capabilities (that can be used to match assets to tasks). In many ways, the home setting is simpler than, say, an emergency response or search-and-rescue scenario, so we believe that the positive outcomes of these experiments are translatable into the domestic context.

An arguable difference between the home versus emergency response or search-and-rescue settings is the degree of training that a user can reasonably be expected to have obtained in the use of the available devices. In the home setting, this must always be minimal. In the other setting, however, minimal training is still desirable, since users should not necessarily be experts in the operation of sensing systems [35]. In any case, we argue that this usability point is addressed under (i) above. Also, in many cases, the addition of knowledge about new devices and their capabilities will typically be provided by the originators of the devices rather than end-users, though our approach does not preclude a "power" user from providing additional knowledge to their local environment.

V. Conclusion

In this paper we have explored the use of conversations between humans and machines, motivated by a desire for "beautiful seams". We assert that this approach could enable better understanding of complex system such as a set of IoT devices in a home. In this paper, we have shown how semantic representations can be used in a human-friendly format through the use of a CNL technology known as ITA CE. Through the use of a conversational protocol built on top of the core CE language we show how human and machine agents are able to communicate using this single language. Examples of the CE language are provided throughout the paper showing how different concepts can be constructed and the subsequent data for the knowledge base can be provided in the same CE language. Through a set of four typical types of interaction we show how human users can interact with the devices in such an environment, and we note that whilst we have focused these four examples on a human-machine interaction, the exact same approach applies to machine-machine as well. Some additional discussion around what machine-human and human-human forms would look like is mentioned. Future work may include conducting experiments in the conversational home setting, aiming to replicate the results from our earlier work where human users without training were able to use the conversational protocol and the CE language to communicate key features within the domain of interest.

Acknowledgment

This research was sponsored by the U.S. Army Research Laboratory and the U.K. Ministry of Defence under Agreement Number W911NF-16-3-0001. The views and conclusions contained in this document are those of the authors and should not be interpreted as representing the official policies, either expressed or implied, of the U.S. Army Research Laboratory, the U.S. Government, the U.K. Ministry of Defence or the U.K. Government. The U.S. and U.K. Governments are authorized to reproduce and distribute reprints for Government purposes notwithstanding any copy-right notation hereon.

References

[1] R. Dale, "The return of the chatbots," *Natural Language Engineering*, vol. 22, no. 5, pp. 811–817, 2016.

[2] M. Witbrock and L. Bradeško, "Conversational computation," in *Handbook of Human Computation*. Springer, 2013, pp. 531–543.

[3] J. Lester, K. Branting, and B. Mott, "Conversational agents," *The Practical Handbook of Internet Computing*, pp. 220–240, 2004.

[4] N. O'Leary. (2014) Conversational iot. [Online]. Available: http://knolleary.net/2014/12/04/a-conversational-internet-of-things-thingmonk-talk/

[5] A. Stanford-Clark. (2008) Redjets on twitter. [Online]. Available: https://twitter.com/redjets

[6] T. Armitage. (2008) Tower bridge on twitter. [Online]. Available: https://twitter.com/twrbrdg_itself

[7] (2008) Mars curiosity on twitter. [Online]. Available: https://twitter.com/MarsCuriosity

[8] (2010) Philae lander on twitter. [Online]. Available: https://twitter.com/Philae2014

[9] (2011) Rosetta probe on twitter. [Online]. Available: https://twitter.com/ESA_Rosetta

[10] E. Ferrara, O. Varol, C. Davis, F. Menczer, and A. Flammini, "The rise of social bots," *Communications of the ACM*, vol. 59, no. 7, pp. 96–104, 2016.

[11] L. Atzori, A. Iera, and G. Morabito, "The internet of things: A survey," *Computer networks*, vol. 54, no. 15, pp. 2787–2805, 2010.

[12] M. Weisser, "The computer for the twenty-first century," *Scientific American*, vol. 265, no. 3, pp. 94–104, 1991.

[13] M. Chalmers, "Seamful design and ubicomp infrastructure," in *Proceedings of Ubicomp 2003 Workshop at the Crossroads: The Interaction of HCI and Systems Issues in Ubicomp*. Citeseer, 2003.

[14] T. Coates. (2014) Interacting with a world of connected objects. [Online]. Available: https://medium.com/product-club/interacting-with-a-world-of-connected-objects-875b4a099099#.nd00bbs5n

[15] Hypercat. [Online]. Available: http://hypercat.io

[16] M. Bates and R. M. Weischedel, *Challenges in natural language processing*. Cambridge University Press, 2006.

[17] T. Kuhn, "A survey and classification of controlled natural languages," *Computational Linguistics*, vol. 40, no. 1, pp. 121–170, 2014.

[18] R. Schwitter, "Controlled natural languages for knowledge representation," in *Proceedings of the 23rd International Conference on Computational Linguistics: Posters*. Association for Computational Linguistics, 2010, pp. 1113–1121.

[19] D. Mott, "Summary of ita controlled english," *ITA Technical Paper, http://www. usukita. org*, 2010.

[20] A. Preece and W. R. Sieck, "The international technology alliance in network and information sciences," *IEEE Intelligent Systems*, vol. 22, no. 5, 2007.

[21] D. Mott, C. Giammanco, M. C. Dorneich, J. Patel, and D. Braines, "Hybrid rationale and controlled natural language for shared understanding," *Proc. 6th Knowledge Systems for Coalition Operations*, 2010.

[22] T. Klapiscak, J. Ibbotson, D. Mott, D. Braines, and J. Patel, "An interoperable framework for distributed coalition planning: The collaborative planning model," *Proc. 7th Knowledge Systems for Coalition Operations*, 2012.

[23] D. Braines, D. Mott, S. Laws, G. de Mel, and T. Pham, "Controlled english to facilitate human/machine analytical processing," *SPIE Defense, Security, and Sensing*, pp. 875 808–875 808, 2013.

[24] J. Ibbotson, D. Braines, D. Mott, S. Arunkumar, and M. Srivatsa, "Documenting provenance with a controlled natural language," in *Annual Conference of the International Technology Alliance (ACITA)*, 2012.

[25] F. Cerutti, D. Mott, D. Braines, T. J. Norman, N. Oren, and S. Pipes, "Reasoning under uncertainty in controlled english: an argumentation-based perspective," *AFM*, 2014.

[26] D. Braines, J. Ibbotson, D. Shaw, and A. Preece, "Building a living database for human-machine intelligence analysis," in *Information Fusion (Fusion), 2015 18th International Conference on*. IEEE, 2015, pp. 1977–1984.

[27] D. Mott and J. Hendler, "Layered controlled natural languages," in *3rd Annual Conference of the International Technology Alliance (ACITA)*, 2009.

[28] A. Preece, D. Braines, D. Pizzocaro, and C. Parizas, "Human-machine conversations to support multi-agency missions," *ACM SIGMOBILE Mobile Computing and Communications Review*, vol. 18, no. 1, pp. 75–84, 2014.

[29] A. Preece, C. Gwilliams, C. Parizas, D. Pizzocaro, J. Z. Bakdash, and D. Braines, "Conversational sensing," in *SPIE Sensing Technology+ Applications*. International Society for Optics and Photonics, 2014, pp. 91 220I–91 220I.

[30] D. Braines. (2015) Ita controlled english store (ce-store). [Online]. Available: https://github.com/ce-store

[31] W. Webberley. (2016) Cenode.js. [Online]. Available: http://cenode.io/

[32] If this then that. [Online]. Available: https://ifttt.com/

[33] H. P. Grice, "Logic and conversation," *1975*, pp. 41–58, 1975.

[34] A. Preece, D. Pizzocaro, D. Braines, and D. Mott, "Tasking and sharing sensing assets using controlled natural language," in *SPIE Defense, Security, and Sensing*. International Society for Optics and Photonics, 2012, pp. 838 905–838 905.

[35] A. Preece, T. Norman, G. de Mel, D. Pizzocaro, M. Sensoy, and T. Pham, "Agilely assigning sensing assets to mission tasks in a coalition context," *IEEE Intelligent Systems*, vol. 28, no. 1, pp. 57–63, 2013.

Towards A Distributed Federated Brain Architecture using Cognitive IoT Devices

Dinesh Verma
Distributed Cognitive Systems,
IBM T. J. Watson Research Center
Yorktown Heights, NY, U.S.A.
e-mail: dverma@us.ibm.com

Graham Bent
Emerging Technology Services
IBM UK
Hursley Park, Hants, UK
e-mail: gbent@uk.ibm.com

Ian Taylor
Cardiff University, Cardiff, Wales, UK
& University of Notre Dame, USA
email: TaylorIJ1@cardiff.ac.uk

Abstract—**Cognitive Computer Systems (CCS) like IBM Watson implement a brain-like system in a centralized location. Limitations of current networks and organization structure necessitate the development of a distributed cognitive system, in effect a distributed federated brain. This distributed federated brain is composed of the different types of devices in the system, ranging from hand-held devices at the edge of the network to large systems in the cloud. It needs to demonstrate the properties of resilience, proactivity, agility and collaboration. In this vision, we discuss the factors that drive the need for the distributed brain, its technical requirements, and propose an architecture to attain the concept of a distributed brain for military coalition operations. We provide a roadmap that can attain this vision, moving intelligence from a centralized cloud location to a distributed collection of smart devices which are connected together using a cognitive Internet of Things technology.**

Keywords-distributed brain, IoT, distributed analytics, distributed learning, cognitive computing, symbolic vector representations

I. INTRODUCTION

Cognitive computing [1] refers to an approach for developing computer systems that augment human capabilities in a seamless manner. A Cognitive Computing System (CCS) consists of humans and software that work together, with the computer systems showing characteristics of a human brain to assist humans in an intuitive manner. CCS's improve their capabilities over time, learning from the environment and changing their characteristics without requiring manual programming or reprogramming. The IBM Watson Jeopardy [2] machine is a well known example of a CCS, but not the only cognitive system being worked upon. A CCS can be envisioned as the cyber-equivalent of a human brain implemented in software. A CCS can be viewed as a specialized instance of the broader notion of distributed cognition [3] which refers to a socio-technical system in which cognitive processing routines are distributed across the constituent social and technological elements

Most current industrial CCS's adopt a cloud-centric approach, with the brain component such as a deep learning algorithm being a centralized entity. Data, whether for training purposes, or for analysis, is uploaded to a central site, where the brain software processes it. While the centralized approach has proven successful in several domains, it does suffer from a number of limitations. When the data volume is large, the delays and costs associated with uploading the information to a central site, whether to a cloud site or a data center, may render cognitive computing solutions slow and expensive. As the processing power of distributed devices increases over time, decentralized cognitive solutions have the potential to become more responsive, scalable and inexpensive. Thus, there is a need to move from the paradigm of a centralized brain to a distributed brain. Furthermore, in many cases, the distributed brain may leverage assets across several administrative domains resulting in a federated distributed brain.

In this paper, we examine the challenge of creating a distributed federated brain, and propose an architecture and a roadmap for attaining this vision. The rest of the paper is organized as follows. Section II provides the motivating factors behind the need for a distributed federated brain. Section III provides a definition of the distributed federated brain, and discusses the technical challenges that need to be addressed to attain this vision. The following Section proposes a high level architecture which can be used to create a distributed brain. Section V discusses the concept of cognitive Internet of Things (IoT) and approach proposed for the physical realization of the distributed brain. Section VI discusses a possible evolution of the capabilities of such a system. Finally, Section VII lays out a roadmap for how the cognitive capabilities of the 'distributed federated brain' may increase over time.

II. MOTIVATIONS FOR DISTRIBUTED CCS

While the concept of a CCS has primarily focused on a centralized processing paradigm. When all entities within a network are connected together with a high speed reliable inexpensive network, centralized CCS has many advantages. However, there are many situations where such network connectivity is not present. Furthermore, there are several conditions under which a centralized CCS may underperform compared to a distributed CCS, even where the network connectivity is favorable.

Situations where network connectivity can be problematic include environments with mobile endpoints, including automobiles, ships, drones, trains and robotic mules, which need to move over a wide geographical area. Connectivity to a cloud site for such devices can only be provided by wireless communication networks such as cellular or satellite. These networks have high latencies and can be very expensive when a large amount of data needs to be transmitted.

In some areas, even cellular or satellite communications may be absent or be of poor quality. Mountainous terrains, hilly areas, or underground mines are likely to have poor network connectivity. There are many areas in the world where networking infrastructure is inadequate. In military coalition operations, which occur in areas with poor infrastructure, connectivity to a backend cloud system can be very sporadic and frequently absent. Any cognitive capabilities in these situations have to be provided in a manner that does not depend on continuous network connectivity to a cloud site.

Even when adequate network connectivity to cloud servers is available, there are many scenarios where a distributed CCS approach will be better. For instance, when devices are generating a significant amount of data, extracting insights from the data can be computed more efficiently near the location of data generation, as opposed to moving the data to a central location. As an example, consider a CCS which relies on video input to train itself. The code which extracts patterns from the video data, or finds interesting events in the video code, is likely to be much smaller, e.g. around a few Megabytes in size compared to streaming high resolution video, which at the rate of 4-8Mbps and can easily run into tens of Gigabytes. In these cases, it will be more efficient to move the code near the source of data, and extract patterns near the point where data is generated. The smaller of the two elements needed for cognition, code implementing intelligence or data which needs examination, needs to be moved for optimal performance.

Another scenario where distributed CCS is needed despite sufficient network connectivity occurs in relation to issues of regulatory compliance. Many types of data, e.g. healthcare data, are subject to regulations which may prevent it being sent to a central location for processing. Several countries restrict information on their citizens to be moved across borders. Extracting insights from data, subject to such restriction, requires a distributed cognitive infrastructure.

In some cases, security, privacy and licensing concerns may prevent the movement of data to a central location. In other cases, cost considerations may lead to a distributed cognitive infrastructure i.e. if a distributed cognitive system reduces the workload on the cloud site, it reduces the cost of cloud hosting. Furthermore, given the increasing processing capacity of end points like smart-phones, drones and robotic mules, this reduction in cost can be performed without impacting the cognitive capabilities of the system.

Because of the above motivating factors, we need to develop technologies that can enable distributed cognition that can leverage, but not be reliant on, a centralized infrastructure. The reasons for distributed cognition have a strong commonality with the driving forces behind approaches such as fog computing [4] or mobile edge computing [5].

III. Definition and Technical Challenges

With the explosion in low cost phones, wearable devices and the IoT, future computing environments will have a diverse set of small elements capable of computation, storage and communication. Leveraging cognitive software on all of these devices leads to the concept of the distributed federated brain. The distributed federated brain is a socio-technical hybrid system capable of taking proactive actions based on the current and anticipated future situation on the ground. It is composed from the different types of devices present in the environment (sensors, hand-held devices, UAVs, robots, backend cloud computing sites, data center server farms etc.), along with the people who use those devices. This system provides a self-organizing self-healing predictive analytics capability, which is capable of functioning as a whole even when connectivity to the backend systems is missing. It will leverage all the services offered by a wired backend infrastructure (e.g. a backend cloud system, data center or available cellular network infrastructure) but it will not be critically dependent on a continuous form of connectivity to the backend.

The distributed federated brain operates seamlessly across networks and systems belonging to different organizations. In the context of military coalition operations, it uses assets belonging to coalition members or sub-groups within a single coalition member, while complying with any policies and guidelines required by individual coalition members. In the context of a civilian infrastructure, the brain uses assets across several enterprises and consumers, taking into account any restrictions imposed by the owners of the assets.

The distributed brain can analyze the situation on the ground in real-time, anticipate the situation likely to happen in the future, and determine whether the situation requires human involvement. If the situation does not require human involvement, the brain would undertake the most appropriate automatic action to the situation. When the situation needs human involvement, the brain will recommend alternative courses of actions, along with their pros and cons.

The brain is frequently charged with performing tasks that require creating dynamic groups on a short notice. Such dynamic groups may be transient and short-lived (days or hours), but could also last for a longer period (months). Differences in the pedigree of disparate systems belonging to different organizations necessitate the development of approaches that work with partial visibility, partial trust, and cultural differences, while simultaneously dealing with the challenges of a dynamically changing situation in which power, computation and connectivity may be severely constrained.

The 'distributed brain', therefore, needs to have several key properties. It must be self-healing and resilient, since it has to operate in an environment where elements may lose connectivity to backend systems, and any of the small component systems may disappear in an unpredictable manner. It has to react rapidly to changing situations on the ground, so it must be predictive and proactive in the decisions it makes. To deal with a dynamic environment, the system must be self-configuring, agile and adaptive. Since it is dynamically assembled from a large number of independent components, it needs to be a cooperative and collaborative collective of individual components. Humans and machines have different types of analytic and cognitive capabilities. The 'distributed brain' must integrate human analytics capabilities into the machine analytics capability in a seamless manner.

A number of challenges confront the attempt to develop the distributed brain. Some insight into the nature of these challenges is provided by a consideration of the following four attributes:

Composability: How do we compose smaller elements into a larger aggregate that works like a seamless whole? What are the principles that link the attributes of a component to the larger whole, and how can we compose components belonging to different organizations with partial visibility and control in an environment with limited resources?

Interactivity: How do different computing elements and people interact with each other, both with other members of the groups and to external stimuli from the environment? How should we model and understand the interactions between different elements and information sources? How do different sub-brains work together as a larger aggregate brain?

Optimality: How can elements work together to obtain the optimal results in an environment with constrained resources? How can analytics be performed so that optimal performance is obtained automatically, instead of requiring complex manual optimization?

Autonomy: How can elements work together in a proactive manner understanding future situations sufficiently well to operate with a degree of autonomous behavior? How can a system determine that autonomous operation is inappropriate and human intervention is needed? How can different elements simplify the cognitive burden involved to best assist humans in the loop when intervention is needed?

The four attributes are not independent, and progress along any one attribute can positively address the attainment of the other attributes. If we want to decompose the problem further into relatively independent technical topics, we can identify six key topics which can collectively provide approaches to obtain the four attributes identified above. These six key topics are:

- *Software Defined Federations*: understand the principles by which different elements across a federated environment could be composed to form a virtualized larger element, and the properties of different types of architectures that enable such composition.
- *Generative Policy Models*: explore architectures and algorithms which enable devices in a federated environment to automatically determine their own operational policies, under the loose guidance of a higher level manager, but not be a slave to the higher level manager.
- *Agile Composition*: understand the architectures and principles which will allow different digital assets, such as code or data, to find each other in an optimal manner to generate insights.
- *Complex Adaptive Human Systems*: understand the properties of groups of humans working with machines, and understand how such groups would react to external stimuli and interact with other groups.
- *Instinctive Analytics*: create new techniques by which data and services can be automatically advertised, discovered and matched together to create analytics workflows that are autonomous and optimal.
- *Anticipatory Situational Understanding*: create new analytics approaches that can attain proactive situation understanding by autonomous systems and help create intelligent advisors for human-in-the-loop systems.

These six key topics are being investigated by an alliance of several universities, industrial and government research laboratories from the UK and the USA as part of the International Technology alliance in Distributed Analytics and Information Sciences (DAIS ITA) [6].

IV. ARCHITECTURE ENABLING DISTRIBUTED BRAIN

The ultimate goal of DAIS ITA is to investigate the basic science that would enable the creation of a distributed CCS that can perform analytics on demand across heterogeneous networks of interconnected devices. Some of the capabilities of such a system will be to (i) understand user requests for analysis, (ii) seamlessly compose the desired analytics functions from other functions and services available in the network, (iii) identify the right data set needed for the analytics, and (iv) bring together the data and analytics required to perform the function.

One approach that is being considered is a CCS architecture inspired by the cloud computing paradigm [7], comprising (i) a cognition layer, (ii) a platform layer, (iii) infrastructure layer and (iv) a management layer, with the six key topics mapping onto the layers as shown in Figure 1.

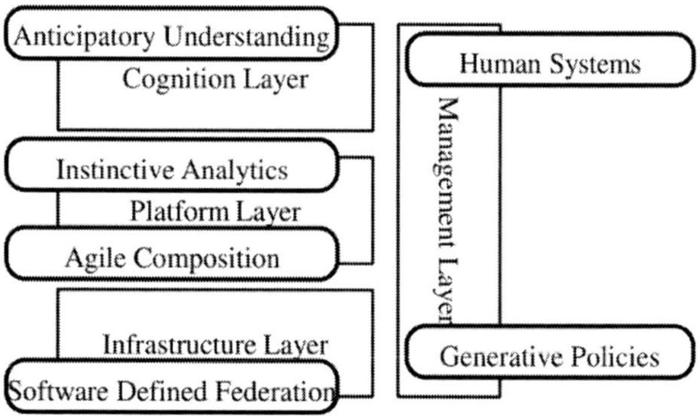

Figure 1. Key Topics in relation to layered architecture

An alternative approach maintains the CCS architecture, but considers the challenge from the perspective of an interacting network of cognitive micro-services. Our micro-services are cognitive in the sense that they comply with established principles of cognition such as those defined by the Core Cognitive Criteria (CCC) [8] which to a large extent incorporates the four key attributes of *composability, interactivity, optimality* and *autonomy* described above. In this approach micro-services are considered as semantic concepts and can be processed as such. It is in this sense our distributed CCS can truly be described as a 'distributed federated brain.

Our challenge is to develop an approach where micro-services are self-describing, can self-discover other micro-services (including data services, network services, policy and security services) and where micro-services are self-allocating and self-provisioning in the sense that they can optimally position themselves or be invoked within a network to perform the tasks demanded by users. To achieve these goals, we require a common way to represent our cognitive services and their capabilities. Distributed cognitive processing is then the patterns of information flow and influence that occur across the network. The resulting cognitive phenomena are a property of the larger systemic organization, rather than a property of the individual micro-services.

V. EXAMPLE OF A COGNITIVE IOT

To illustrate how our 'distributed federated brain' concept might be realized, we consider how it can be applied to micro-service architectures in IoT context. Micro-services are an approach to developing a single application as a suite of small services, each deployed and running independently while communicating with each other via lightweight mechanisms. They typically require minimum centralized management and may be written in different programming languages and use different data storage technologies. They are widely adopted in the industry by companies like Netflix and Amazon, with a large number of developers, to streamline the software development lifecycle. They are also the basic building blocks of the IoT and can also be immensely useful in military and coalition scenarios being considered by the DAIS ITA, where each of the individual services may belong to different partners but a common goal needs to be achieved by composing them dynamically.

Applications that use micro-service architectures, may be composed of hundreds or even thousands of micro-services [9]. To be able to learn feasible composition of micro-services, dynamically compose new workflow graphs, and run learning algorithms on these workflows, we propose that micro-services self-describe in the form of vectors that capture not only the functionality that the service offers but also how it may be composed with other available services in the network, i.e., the feasible sequences of the service calls. These vector representations need to capture not just the semantic meaning of the service composition of which the micro-service is a part but also the order in which the micro-services are called. One possible representation is to use vector symbolic architectures such as the Holographic Reduced Representations (HRR) [10] which use convolution algebra for compositional distributed representations, a form of symbolic binding and unbinding. Other potential vector representations include binary spatter coding (BSC) or random permutation (RP) [11]. These types of representation have been demonstrated to be capable of supporting a wide range of cognitive tasks including reasoning [12], semantic composition [13], analogical mapping [14] and representing word meaning and order [15]. HRR's form the basis of the Semantic Vector Pointer Unified Network Architecture (SPAUN) [16] which claims to be a biologically plausible implementation of spiking neural network computation in a brain like manner, and can be used in military coalition contexts[17].

In our distributed brain model, we envisage micro-services being distributed across a heterogeneous network with micro-services being owned by different organizations. Rather than searching for micro-services and then centrally compiling a workflow, as in the standard service oriented architecture model, in our proposed model each micro-service learns its role (i.e. position in the workflow) in each of the service workflows in which it has been invoked and binds this into its own symbolic vector representation (this is an online learning task). Essentially, the resulting vector is the micro-service's memory of all of the workflow contexts in which it has been used. A user can request a high level task to be performed by declaratively specifying the precise service composition they require using a symbolic vector representation of the workflow. Alternatively, we are investigating how users can specify the service requirement (e.g. using natural language request) and the nearest matching service compositions are discovered automatically using semantic matching to automatically compute the corresponding symbolic vector representation. The resulting vector is broadcast to all nodes on the network that are capable of invoking micro-services and the micro-services respond by configuring themselves (self–provision and self-allocate) to match the request. Details of the online learning, matching and self-organization are described in [18].

VI. EVOLUTION OF COGNITIVE COMPUTING SYSTEMS

From an evolution perspective, we can envision how CCS's will progress over time. This is illustrated in Figure 2.

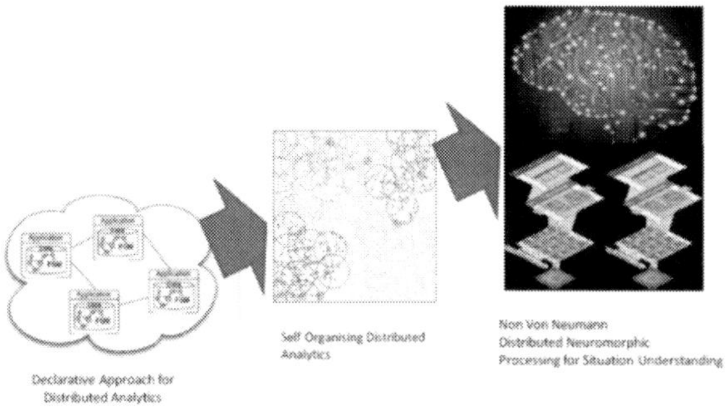

Figure 2. Evolution of a distributed federated brain

Our approach begins with the declarative approach described above, in which users request analytic services which are self-composed from multiple cognitive micro-services. Using extensions of the vector symbolic representations we are investigating the mechanisms by which these micro-services can best organize themselves not only in in response to user demand but also within the constraints of network availability, location of data, policy and security requirements. We envisage this self-organization to include the four principles of *composability*, *interactivity*, *optimality* and *autonomy* outlined above, including the capability to for cognitive micro-services to learn from their environment and to exhibit proactive situation understanding and adapt accordingly.

The use of vector symbolic representation in the SPAUN architecture suggests that a future distributed federated brain may operate as a highly parallel non Von Neumann machine where the micro-services are themselves implemented as neuromorphic machines using spiking neural network processing. Such machines, which mimic the processing capabilities of the neo-cortex, have the distinct advantage of being extremely low power, operate at much lower frequencies than conventional microprocessors and potentially have less stringent bandwidth and latency requirements for inter service communication [14, 15]. Using a symbolic vector representation lends itself to both a conventional computing paradigm and to a neuromorphic computing model or a hybrid approach. For this reason, we believe that this is a fruitful area of research that will produce valuable insights as we move towards our goal of a distributed federated brain.

VII. A ROADMAP FOR LEARNING IN CCS

While the current state for cognitive computing systems is that of a centralized environment, the eventual state will be that of a fully distributed cognitive system with a peer to peer relationship among different nodes in the system. Learning is a core capability of such systems. From a learning perspective, the roadmap in Figure 3 shows one way in which cognitive systems may progress in their learning capabilities over time.

The working of any cognitive computing system can be defined into two distinct functions, the first being that of analyzing data to understand the patterns that lie within it, and the second one trying to assess the current situation on the ground, as to whether it matches one of the previously encountered patterns. We can refer to the first step as learning and the second as inference.

From a physical infrastructure perspective, we can divide the devices into two categories, cloud and edge. The cloud consists of a central location, while the edge consists of devices not in the cloud. Depending on the physical topology of the system, the edge may consist of mobile devices, sensors, gateways or other network devices.

In the roadmap shown in Figure 3, the current state is that of cloud based cognition in which the edge devices are just feeders of data. They send in information to the cloud based site, and the cloud performs both learning and inference for them.

The next stage of distributed cognition in CCS consists of the situation when learning happens in the cloud, while inference happens in the edge devices. In this stage, the cloud interprets all the data that it receives to create models of knowledge, e.g. a trained neural network, or a calculated decision tree, and sends that model to the edge devices that are not in the cloud. The edge devices use those models of knowledge to perform the task of inference.

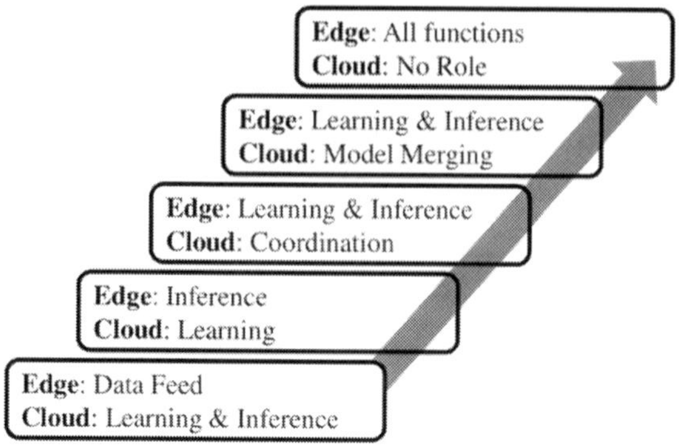

Figure 3. Roadmap for CCS Capabilities

Note that in this stage of CCS, none of the individual elements at the edge is cognitive on its own. However, when they are taken together, and the capabilities in edge devices combined with the capabilities in the cloud, cognitive computing capabilities are realized. A higher-level cognitive function is realized by the coordinated activity of distinct elements, each engaged in its own form of processing, some of which is cognitive (e.g. learning in the cloud) and some of which is not cognitive (functions at the edge-devices).

In the third stage, the edge devices perform both tasks of inference and learning, but rely on the cloud for coordinating their learning. The cloud can provide coordination such as directing different edge nodes to learn about different types of information, and then share the learnt models with each other. As an example, the cloud may instruct one edge node to learn models for identifying cars, another to learn models for identifying trucks, and yet another to learn models for identifying planes. The models can then be exchanged among the edge-devices, each of whom benefit from the models learnt by the other edge devices. In this stage, cognitive functions are enabled at the edge, while the task in the cloud, that of coordination, can be considered non-cognitive (standard computer processing). The net result is a distributed cognitive computing system.

In the next stage, the edge devices learn models that may potentially be for the same type of information. Since models learnt by one edge device may not always match with the models of the other edge device, a merging of the models needs to be performed. The cloud provides this capability for merging models. In this stage, both the edge devices as well as the cloud based system are performing cognitive processing. Distributed cognition is obtained by a combination of many different cognitive elements, some on the edge and some in the cloud.

In the final stage of distributed cognition, the role of the cloud can be dispensed with, and the merging of the models happens using peer to peer information exchanges among the edge devices.

Acknowledgment

This research was sponsored by the U.S. Army Research Laboratory and the U.K. Ministry of Defence under Agreement Number W911NF-16-3-0001. The views and conclusions contained in this document are those of the authors and should not be interpreted as representing the official policies, either expressed or implied, of the U.S. Army Research Laboratory, the U.S. Government, the U.K. Ministry of Defence or the U.K. Government. The U.S. and U.K. Governments are authorized to reproduce and distribute reprints for Government purposes notwithstanding any copy-right notation hereon.

References

[1] J. Kelly III & S. Hamm, Smart Machines: IBM's Watson and the Era of Cognitive Computing. Columbia University Press, 2013.

[2] D. Ferrucci, Introduction to "this is watson". IBM Journal of Research and Development. vol 56, no 3, May 2012.

[3] J. Hollan, E. Hutchins & D. Kirsh, Distributed cognition: Toward a new foundation for human-computer interaction research. ACM Transactions on Computer-Human Interaction (TOCHI), vol. 7(no 2), pp. 174-196, 2000.

[4] F. Bonomi, R. Milito, J. Zhu and S. Addepalli, Fog computing and its role in the internet of things, Proc. First ACM workshop on Mobile cloud computing, Aug 2012

[5] A. Ahmed and E. Ahmed, A survey on mobile edge computing. Proc. IEEE International Conference on Intelligent Systems and Control (ISCO), Jan 2016.

[6] T. Pham, G. Cirincione, A. Swami, G. Pearson, & C. Williams, Distributed analytics and information science. In IEEE International Conference on Information Fusion (Fusion), July 2015.

[7] W. Kim, Cloud computing architecture. International Journal of Web and Grid Services. Jan 2013.

[8] C. Eliasith, How to build a brain, Oxford University Press 2013

[9] Microservices. https://developer.ibm.com/cloudarchitecture/2016/10/20/meeting-microservices/

[10] T. A. Plate, Holographic reduced representations.IEEE Transactions on Neural Networks, 6 , 623–641.(1995)

[11] P. Kanerva, Hyperdimensional Computing: An Introduction to Computing in Distributed Representation with High-Dimensional Random Vectors, Cogn Comput (2009) 1:139–159 DOI 10.1007/s12559-009-9009-8, January 2009

[12] D. Widdows and T. Cohen, Reasoning with Vectors: A Continuous Model for Fast Robust Inference, Log J IGPL; 23(2):141–173 October 2015.

[13] A. Neelakantan, B. Roth, A. McCallum, Compositional Vector Space Models for Knowledge Base Inference, Knowledge Representation and Reasoning: Integrating Symbolic and Neural Approaches: Papers from the 2015 AAAI Spring Symposium

[14] R.W. Gayler and S.D. Levey, A distributed basis for analogical mapping,

[15] M.N. Jones and D.J.K. Mewhort, Representing word meaning and order information in a composite holographic lexicon, Psychological Review 2007, Vol. 114, No. 1, 1–37

[16] C. Eliasmith et. al,. A large-scale model of the functioning brain. Science. vol 30 no. 338, pp. 1202-1205, Nov. 2012.

[17] F. Bergamaschi et al, Smart coalition systems: a deep machine learning approach, Human-machine Interface and Machine Learning Approaches II, SPIE Conference 10190, April 2017 (in prep)

[18] P.A. Merolla et al., A million spiking-neuron integrated circuit with a scalable communication network and interface. Science. 345 (6197): 668. doi:10.1126/science.1254642. PMID 25104385.

Machine Intelligence and the Social Web: How to Get a Cognitive Upgrade

Paul R. Smart

Electronics & Computer Science
University of Southampton
Southampton, UK
email: ps02v@ecs.soton.ac.uk

***Abstract*—The World Wide Web (Web) provides access to a global space of information assets and computational services. It also, however, serves as a platform for social interaction (e.g., Facebook) and participatory involvement in all manner of online tasks and activities (e.g., Wikipedia). There is a sense, therefore, that the advent of the Social Web has transformed our understanding of the Web. In addition to viewing the Web as a form of information repository, we are now able to view the Web in more social terms. In particular, it has become possible to see the Web as providing access to the human social environment. This is important, because issues of social embedding and social interaction have been seen to contribute to the emergence of human cognitive capabilities. The ability of the Web to provide access to the human social environment thus raises an important question: Can humanity play a productive role in the emergence of advanced forms of machine intelligence by virtue of their interactions and engagements with the online realm? The present paper attempts to show why this question is worth asking. It also attempts to highlight some of the ways in which Web-based forms of contact with the human social environment may be relevant to research into machine intelligence.**

***Index Terms*—social web; social intelligence; language; machine intelligence; machine learning.**

I. INTRODUCTION

The World Wide Web (Web) is a technology that was created by humanity, and its implications for humanity—e.g., its effects on human cognitive and social processes—are, to a large extent, the primary focus of our current interest and concern [1]. Such a preoccupation is, of course, perfectly understandable. It is natural for us to wonder (and sometimes worry) about the implications of the Web for our species, especially when it comes to the effect of the Web on our cognitive capabilities. For such capabilities are the hallmark of our species: it is our cognitive profile that sets us apart from other forms of terrestrial life, and it is such capabilities that enable us (and only us) to actively shape the course of our cognitive destiny—to engineer something like the Web, and then worry about its cognitive consequences.

The present paper attempts to approach the Web from a somewhat different perspective. Rather than attempt to consider the implications of the Web for future forms of *human* intelligence, it aims to consider the implications of the Web for future forms of *machine* intelligence. In order to lay the foundation for this appraisal, it is important that we first recognize the status of the Web as a social environment, or at least as an environment that provides an important form of informational contact with the human social environment. Such a claim is unlikely to require much in the way of a detailed defence. There can be little doubt that the Web has come to play a significant role in supporting all manner of social activities and processes. One need only reflect on the popularity of systems such as Facebook, Instagram, Twitter and Snapchat to appreciate the status of the Web as a form of social technology, i.e., as a technology that can be used to support and enable various forms of social interaction and engagement. This does not mean, however, that the social significance of the Web is exhausted by systems that support human–human communication. Beyond the social networking and instant messaging systems, we thus encounter a rich array of systems where issues of social participation are of paramount importance. These include systems that rely on large-scale social participation to yield substantive bodies of online content (e.g., Wikipedia). It also includes so-called human computation systems [2], which rely on social participation for the purposes of completing computationally difficult or intractable tasks. In general, the contemporary Web is dominated by an array of systems that enable human users to generate, edit and organize online content. Such systems are, of course, the familiar socio-technical denizens of what we now refer to as the Social Web.

Why should the social properties of the Web, however we choose to define them, be of any interest or relevance to the emergence of advanced forms of machine intelligence? To answer this question, it will help to introduce two substantive strands of empirical and theoretical research: one focused on the evolution of human intelligence, the other, on the ontogenetic development of human cognitive capabilities.

Evolutionary matters first. Humans, it should be clear, are prodigious cognizers, capable of traversing cognitive terrains that other organisms seem congenitally ill-equipped to navigate. What is it that explains this remarkable difference between ourselves and every other species that has inhabited Planet Earth? Surely not the properties of the physical environment in which we are embedded; for we are not alone in having to cope with the problems the physical world throws at us. An alternative possibility is that our particular form of intelligence is tied to the properties of the social environment in which we are embedded. It is thus the peculiar features of the *human social environment* that best explains the evolutionary emergence of the human mind. This idea actually comes in a variety of flavours, including the social brain hypothesis [3], the machiavellian intelligence hypothesis [4], the cultural intelligence hypothesis [5], and the social intelligence hypothesis [6]. The specific details of these hypotheses need not concern us here: what is important, for present purposes, is simply the idea that a considerable body of work associates the evolutionary emergence of human intelligence with the peculiar properties of the human social environment.

The importance of the human social environment has also been highlighted by work that seeks to explain the development of human cognitive capabilities. "[S]ociality," it has been suggested, "lies at the heart of cognitive development" [7, p. 7]. This is a view whose lineage can be traced to the work of the Soviet psychologist, Lev Vygotsky. Vygotsky argued that it is the nature of our interaction with socially-significant others that holds the key to understanding human cognition (see [8]). In the absence of our ability to interact and engage with other human agents, we would, Vygotsky suggests, be unable to acquire the sorts of abilities that are the hallmark of human cognizing. Similar sentiments are expressed by those who emphasize the importance of enculturation to human cognitive development. Tomasello [9], for example, suggests that:

> ...if a human child were raised from birth outside of human contact and culture, without exposure to human artifacts or communal activities of any kind, that child would develop few of the cognitive skills that make human cognition so distinctive... [9, p. 359]

The general idea, then, is that a capacity for social interaction, and an ability to exploit the products of human culture, are of crucial importance when it comes to understanding the distinctive shape of the human cognitive economy. Once we combine this idea with the earlier claim regarding the role of the human social environment in human cognitive evolution, it is easy to see how the putative social properties of the Web might pique the interests of the machine intelligence community. For inasmuch as we accept the claim that the Web affords an unprecedented form of access to the human social environment, then it seems that we are provided with a novel opportunity to expand the cognitive repertoire of systems that inhabit the online realm. The argumentative basis for this claim is as follows:

- P1: The Web provides an important form of contact with the human social environment.
- P2: The development of human intelligence is tied to the fact that we are socially-situated agents that are embedded within the human social environment.
- C1: The Web is poised to play a productive role in the emergence of advanced forms of machine intelligence by virtue of the kind of contact it provides with the human social environment.

The present paper aims to marshal support for the claim that the Web provides an important form of contact with the human social environment. It also attempts to highlight some of the ways in which such forms of contact may be relevant to research into machine intelligence. The paper makes no attempt to evaluate the extent to which the (contemporary) Web is able to yield actual advances in machine intelligence—such efforts must, of course, await the results of empirical research. Instead, the aim of the present paper is more to identify a number of avenues for future research and explain why such avenues are worth pursuing.

II. THE HUMAN CLOUD

Elizabeth Shaw: *How do you...? How do you know that?*
David: *I watched your dreams.*

—Prometheus, 20th Century Fox, 2012

As the Web has developed, it has yielded an unprecedented form of access to the human social environment. The Social Web has, of course, played a particularly important role in this transition. With the advent of social networking sites, microblogging services, and media sharing systems, the online environment seems to afford ever-deeper insights into the dynamics of human social behavior [10]. Beyond this, however, the Web is a technology that has become deeply embedded in society, playing a crucial (and sometimes indispensable) role in all manner of social activities and processes. In the extreme case, such forms of socio-entanglement may lead to the conclusion that the Web has become an intrinsic part of society—part of the physical machinery that (at least in part) realizes a rich array of social processes (see [11]).

When we look at the Web through human eyes, what we see is a global space of networked information assets and computational resources. It is a space of almost unimaginable scale and complexity. But now imagine that you are a machine agent that is embedded in this space. From this new perspective, you can see yourself, perhaps, as having access to the social environment in which we—us humans agents—live. It is, perhaps, an imperfect form of access—you only see the digital shadows of the human agents that inhabit the offline world. But it is arguably a form of access, nevertheless.

As a means of helping to effect this shift of perspective, consider the claim that our current arsenal of Internet-enabled devices—our phones, watches, tablets and so on—serve as bidirectional 'plug points' [12]. In one sense, such devices enable us to 'plug into' the online environment, typically for the purposes of pursuing some cognitive, social or epistemic objective. In another sense, however, these devices also enable the machines of the online world to plug into us! We are thus the resources that exist at the edge of the Web, just as (from our human perspective) it is the machines that are available at the end of an HTTP request.

Such forms of bidirectional contact lie at the heart of what has been referred to as the "human cloud" [13]. The human cloud, in this case, is the human counterpart of the conventional 'cloud', i.e., the suite of online resources and services that are the typical targets of cloud computing initiatives [14]. In essence, the notion of the human cloud encourages us to see the human social environment as a kind of computational resource—one that can be used to assist with certain kinds of information processing activity and (perhaps) the storage of certain kinds of information. A number of engineering efforts are relevant to this cloud-based view of the human social environment. Such efforts include the use of service-oriented protocols to discover and access human agents [15], the extension of traditional Web service description languages to accommodate the possibility of human involvement [15], and the emergence of programming frameworks that are specifically geared to deliver "complex computation systems incorporating large crowds of networked humans and machines" [16, p. 124].

The concept of the human cloud is important because it helps to highlight some of the ways in which machine-based systems can draw on the human social environment as a means of solving certain kinds of problem. Thus just as we humans rely on the online environment to support our problem-solving efforts, so too, perhaps, we can see machine-based systems as 'tapping' into the human cloud as a means of bolstering their 'cognitive' performance profiles. In some cases, such forms of socio-technical coupling can be seen to yield hybrid problem-solving organizations whose computational capabilities surpass those of their constituent (human and machine) elements. The forms of socio-technical entanglement that are enabled by the Web thus provide a range of novel opportunities to support large-scale problem-solving efforts that combine the distinctive strengths (and perhaps weaknesses) of both human agents and conventional computational systems [2][17][18].

There is, however, another point that is worth mentioning here. It relates to the way in which various forms of human–machine interaction can play a productive role in extending the reach of machine-based cognitive capabilities. By reaching out to the human cloud, for example, resources that were previously too ill-structured to support machine learning can sometimes be transformed into something that is much better aligned with the requirements of machine learning algorithms. Consider, for example, the way in which the addition of descriptive tags and annotations to a set of image resources can assist with the development of automated image classification (machine vision) systems [19]. Such possibilities are explicitly recognized by those who seek to engage human subjects in computationally-difficult tasks. With respect to citizen science systems, for example, Lintott and Reed [20] note that one of the limiting factors in the development of automated processing solutions is the availability of sufficiently well-structured training data sets, and that one of the key advantages of citizen science projects is the provision of such data sets. Similarly, when it comes to a class of systems known as Games With A Purpose (GWAPs), von Ahn and Dabbish [21] are keen to stress the role of human contributions in giving rise to evermore intelligent (and human-like) forms of machine-based processing:

> By leveraging the human time spent playing games online, GWAP game developers are able to capture large sets of training data that express uniquely human perceptual capabilities. This data can contribute to the goal of developing computer programs and automated systems with advanced perceptual or intelligence skills. [21, p. 67]

III. Learning From Experience

Roy Batty: *If only you could see what I've seen with your eyes!*

—Blade Runner, Warner Bros., 1982

The concept of the human cloud helps to highlight the status of the human social environment as a form of complementary computational resource—one that can be used to circumvent the limitations of more conventional forms of (silicon-based) computational processing. This is clearly important when it comes to our ability to support novel kinds of problem-solving organization. However, it also serves as a reminder that human agents are the locus of particular forms of skill and expertise that are often grounded in the extensive experience we have with particular domains. It is here that the Web provides us with an opportunity to extend the reach of machine-based capabilities. The basic idea is that the Web can be used as a form of *social observatory*—one which enables machines to observe the human social environment and acquire information about various forms of human competence. From this perspective, the Web can be seen to support a particular form of *social learning*: it enables us to treat the human social environment as a source of information and knowledge that can be mined and monitored in order to reduce the 'experiential gap' that otherwise limits the cognitive and epistemic reach of intelligent systems.

To help us understand this claim in a little more detail, consider the effort to develop self-driving cars. Such efforts clearly depend on advances in our ability to engineer sophisticated forms of information processing, especially in the visual domain. However, they also rely on advanced control systems that are able to respond in an intelligent manner to a multitude of road-relevant situations. In order to emulate the behavior of human road users, it thus seems important to capture some of the knowledge that human drivers have acquired as a result of their experience behind the wheel. Such experience underlies our ability to anticipate the likely behavior of other road users, our ability to behave appropriately at an intersection, our ability to adjust our driving behavior given specific meteorological conditions, and so on. An experienced human driver thus embodies a wealth of knowledge and experience that is clearly pertinent to the design of autonomous vehicles, and this is especially so if (as seems likely) we encounter a transitional era in which self-driving vehicles must share the road with human-driven vehicles.

How do we go about building cars that possess the behavioral competence and road-related *savoir faire* exhibited by the typical human driver? One option is to enlist the use of conventional knowledge elicitation techniques [22] in order to create formal models of the relevant body of human knowledge. The problem with this approach is that it is likely to require substantial time and effort, especially when one considers the complexity of the target domain and the diversity of driving practices exhibited by both individuals and cultural groups (consider the norms and conventions that appear to characterize the behavior of British and Italian drivers!).

Here is another approach: track the behavior of human-driven vehicles as they move around the road network and attempt to extract and formalize interesting regularities from the resultant body of 'experiential data'. Such data sets are likely to be particularly valuable in cases where it is possible to track the precise behavior of vehicles at particular locations, such as at an intersection, a roundabout or a notorious black spot. Additional value comes from the ability to track other kinds of information, such as the use of driver signalling mechanisms (e.g., the use of indicators and headlights) and information about prevailing meteorological conditions (e.g., the presence of fog).

The main point of this example is that it helps us see how a particular form of access to the human social environment can provide insight into bodies of experientially-grounded knowledge, some of which may be relevant to the attempt to engineer intelligent systems. The vision is thus one in which advanced forms of machine intelligence come about as the result of a deliberate attempt to monitor and learn from the human social environment. According to this vision, machine intelligence is, in some sense, parasitic on human experience: it relies on the experience that humans have in order to short-circuit the acquisition of particular forms of cognitive and behavioral competence.

It is here that we encounter an interesting point of contact with research in the Web Science community. For inasmuch as we accept the idea that the Web provides access to the human social environment, then it seems that we should be able to mine the Web for certain kinds of knowledge. This is the general idea behind a body of work that goes under the heading of *experiential knowledge mining* [23]. Experiential knowledge mining is defined as "the process of acquiring experiential knowledge, as opposed to a priori knowledge, from a variety of multimedia sources that describe human experiences of various sorts" [23, p. 33]. In a Web context, such forms of knowledge acquisition aim to shed light on (among other things) the norms and conventions that surround particular patterns of human behavior. A similar sort of claim is sometimes encountered in the nascent sub-discipline of computational social science [10]. In this case, the Web is seen to provide an unprecedented opportunity to learn about the human social environment, enabling us to acquire the sorts of insights that other approaches may be unable to provide.

IV. Active Learning

Caleb: *Did you program her to flirt with me?*
Nathan: *If I did, would that be cheating?*

—Ex Machina, Universal Pictures, 2015

We have seen that the Web provides us with an unprecedented opportunity to observe the human social environment (or at least aspects thereof). But the notion of the Web as a form of social observatory comes with an attendant risk. The risk is that we lose sight of the way in which online systems can play an active role in shaping the course of their own cognitive development. When we view the Web as a form of social observatory, there is a danger that we see machines as the purely passive observers of some distant and perhaps impervious social realm. This is a highly impoverished view of social learning, and it is one that seems at odds with the profile of human learning.

There is, however, no reason why we should restrict ourselves to this purely passive view of machine learning. There are, in fact, a number of ways in which we can view machines as playing a more active role in the learning process. One example of this comes from work into what is conveniently called *active learning* [24]. Active learning is a form of machine learning in which the machine attempts to actively intervene in the learning process, structuring its training experiences in a manner that yields the best learning outcome. Such forms of active intervention have been shown to yield a number of pedagogical pay-offs. For example, active learning has been shown to improve the efficiency of the learning process by reducing the number of training examples that are required to reach near-optimal levels of performance [25].

A good example of active learning in a Web context is provided by Barrington et al. [26]. Barrington et al. describe the use of an online game, called Herd It, in which groups of human individuals annotate a musical resource with descriptive tags. These annotations are used to train a supervised machine learning system that ultimately aims to perform the annotation task independently of the human agents. All this, of course, is broadly in line with the general shape of machine learning methods. But what makes Barrington et al.'s system of particular interest is the way in which the machine actively *directs* the course of its own learning. It does this by actively selecting the musical resources that will be the focus of future tagging efforts by the human game players. This is important, because it gives the machine an opportunity to select those forms of feedback that are likely to be of greatest value relative to its subsequent cognitive development. In the words of Barrington et al. [26], "the machine learning system actively directs the annotation games to collect new data that will most benefit future model iterations" (p. 6411).

A consideration of active learning thus expands our understanding of the forms of contact that the Web provides with the human social environment. Rather than seeing the Web simply as a form of social observatory—one that permits a largely passive form of observational contact with humanity—we can now entertain a more active (and interactive) view of the Web. On this view, the Web provides machines with an opportunity to structure their contact with the human social environment, enabling machines to influence human behavior in a manner that befits the demands of a particular cognitive task.

V. The Gift of Language

Louise: *It's not a weapon, it's a gift—their language.*

—Arrival, Paramount Pictures, 2016

Given that much of the content of the Web is expressed in the form of natural language, it is perhaps unsurprising that the advent of the Web has led to something of a renaissance in language-related computational research. Such interest is evidenced by research into Natural Language Processing (NLP) (e.g., [27]), information extraction [28], and sentiment analysis [29]. It is also evidenced by the effort to develop various forms of language-enabled agents, i.e., computational agents that are able to exhibit proficiency in the use of natural language expressions. This includes work relating to so-called social bots [30], chatbots [31] and conversational agents [32]. The reason for this renewed interest in language-related technologies is, at least in part, due to the wealth of linguistic content that is available in the online realm. Such content provides us with a substantive body of empirical data that can be used to inform large-scale analytic efforts. It should also be clear that the Web has transformed the incentives that drive research and development in this area—consider, for example, the potential use of Twitter feeds as a means of predicting the outcome of political elections [33].

How does this renewed interest in linguistic analysis impact the present discussion on machine intelligence? The most obvious answer to this question is that machines will become increasingly proficient in understanding human language, and as a result of this understanding, they will be better placed to exploit our orthographic contributions to the online realm (e.g., they will have an improved ability to distil information and knowledge from resources such as Wikipedia, Twitter, Facebook and so on). It should also be clear that enhancements in linguistic proficiency often go hand-in-hand with improvements in communicative ability. There can be little doubt that such communicative abilities play an important role in extending the cognitive reach of an agent community. Indeed, we can view communication as a form of networking capability that enables agents to 'connect' with a range of cognitively-relevant resources. This applies as much to human agents as it does to their synthetic counterparts. As noted by Merlin Donald [34], when it comes to human language, "Individuals in possession of reading, writing, and other visuographic skills...become somewhat like computers with networking capabilities; they are equipped to interface, to plug into whatever network becomes available" (p. 311).

The communicative function of language is no doubt important when it comes to future forms of machine intelligence. But there is another view of language that is of potential significance here. This view is sometimes referred to as the supracommunicative view of language [35][36]. The general idea, in this case, is that language plays a role in transforming the cognitive capabilities of the language-wielding agent. Echoes of this view are apparent in the work of the philosopher, Daniel Dennett [37]. He suggests that our ontogenetic immersion in a linguistic environment contributes to an effective reorganization of the human cognitive economy, such that the parallel-processing dynamics of the biological brain are transformed into something that more closely resembles a conventional (symbol-manipulating) computational machine. Strikingly, Dennett proposes that some of the most distinctive features of human cognition (including the phenomenon of human consciousness) emerge as a result of our attempts to get to grips with the linguistic domain. Inasmuch as we accept these claims, it should be clear that a simple *communicative* view of language is unlikely to do justice to the potential impact of the Web on future forms of machine intelligence: by immersing intelligent systems in a linguistically-rich environment, and by forcing such systems to assimilate linguaform representations deep into their cognitive processing routines, we potentially endow machines with the sorts of abilities and insights that only us language-using human agents are able to grasp.

VI. Child Machines

David: *Big things have small beginnings.*

—Prometheus, 20th Century Fox, 2012

In the Introduction to this paper (see Section I) we encountered the idea that issues of social embedding and social interaction play a crucial role in the development of human cognitive capabilities. Such claims are relevant to the present discussion in the sense that we can think of the Web as enabling human agents to participate in the socially-mediated development of machine-based cognitive capabilities. However, in considering the ways in which the Web can be used to scaffold and support the cognitive development of intelligent systems, it is easy to overlook the fact that human infants are not born with the same sorts of cognitive resources as their adult counterparts. It is here that we encounter a productive point of contact with work that shows how maturational shifts in cognitive, sensory and motor capabilities may be of crucial relevance to the emergence of advanced forms of cognitive competence [38]–[41]. Such ideas are typically encountered in the context of human language learning. Bjorklund [40], for example, suggests that by imposing constraints on the kinds of information that can be processed, maturational mechanisms can be seen as supporting the progressive reshaping of the 'effective' structure of a human infant's linguistic environment, transforming what might seem like an impossible language learning task into something a little more congenial. Similar ideas can be found in more recent work in developmental robotics [38][41]. Gómez et al. [38], for example, describe an intriguing set of results concerning the development of sensorimotor capabilities in a real-world robotic system. They report that a developmental profile characterized by progressive increments in the complexity of sensory, motor and neurocomputational subsystems results in a profile of task performance that is superior to that of a robot in which the relevant maturational processes are disabled. Commenting on this developmentally-grounded dissociation in 'adult' performance profiles, they suggest that:

> ...rather than being a problem, early morphological and cognitive limitations effectively decrease the amount of information that infants have to deal with, and may lead to an increase in the overall adaptivity of the organism. [38, p. 119]

Such findings intimate at the potential relevance of maturational parameters in the acquisition of advanced forms of cognitive competence. In particular, they suggest that various forms of cognitive immaturity may be of adaptive value in terms of a system's ability to achieve the sorts of cognitive success that mark the end of the developmental process (see [42]).

What implications do these insights have for our understanding of machine intelligence? In answering this question, it helps to consider the notion of *incremental learning* [43]. Incremental learning, as defined by Lungarella and Berthouze [41], is the "idea of some learning-related resource (e.g., memory, or attention span), starting at a low value, which then gradually increases while (but not necessarily because) the organism matures" (p. 1). In essence, the claim is that in our attempts to yield advanced forms of machine intelligence, we should attempt to emulate the developmental profile of human infants. We should, in other words, seek to create what Alan Turing [44] once referred to as "child machines"—machines whose cognitively-relevant processing capabilities emerge as the result of a particular form of artificial ontogenesis.

In the context of the present discussion, the notion of incremental learning helps to reveal an important research opportunity. This relates to the extent to which maturational shifts in computational parameters can assist with the task of pressing maximal cognitive benefit from Web-based forms of informational contact with the human social environment. There are a number of ways in which we might seek to explore this dynamic dovetailing of intrinsic information processing capabilities with the structure of the relevant learning environment. One possibility is for a machine learning system to exert some degree of control over the sorts of scaffolding that are supplied by the human social environment, in the manner, perhaps, of the active learning system described by Barrington et al. [26]. Alternatively, a system could be configured so as to process inputs of increasing complexity as learning progresses. One way of accomplishing this is to manipulate the computational and representational resources that are available to the system as it attempts to learn about a particular domain. Elman [39] provides a nice demonstration of this sort of intervention. By altering the configuration of a neural network, Elman was able to introduce a processing constraint that limited the network's ability to process complex natural language sentences. As a result of this limitation, the network was able to achieve a level of 'linguistic' performance that was otherwise difficult to attain.

What is important, here, is not the details of how incremental learning could be could be implemented by a machine learning system. Instead, what is important is that we appreciate the role of maturational processes in shaping the course of cognitive development. In the absence of such an awareness, it might be all too easy to think that only advanced forms of machine intelligence are able to benefit from the sorts of contact the Web provides with the human social environment, and this is especially so once we consider the complexity of the digital traces that mark our occasional forays into the online world. There is thus a danger that our reasoning becomes somewhat circular: only advanced forms of machine intelligence are able to press maximal cognitive benefit from the Web, and only machines that press maximal cognitive benefit from the Web are able to exhibit advanced intelligence. In this sense, the notion of incremental learning serves a useful prophylactic purpose: it helps to remind us that big things often have small beginnings. Indeed, it is perhaps by virtue of being small that certain kinds of big thing are ever able to exist.

VII. The Engineers

Elizabeth Shaw: *We call them Engineers.*
Fifield: *Engineers? Do you mind, um, telling us what they engineered?*

—Prometheus, 20th Century Fox, 2012

One of the characteristic features of the Social Web is that everyone can contribute to it: every time we edit a Wikipedia article, write a blog, or post a tweet, we are, in some sense, contributing to the totality of information that is available on the Web. This feature is, of course, so well-established as to be hardly worth mentioning. And yet the idea that the online environment emerges as a result of human contributions is an important one. In particular, inasmuch as we see the Web as a form of environment or ecology (see [1]), then our creative contributions to the online realm can perhaps be glossed as a form of *ecological engineering*. This helps to establish an interesting point of contact with work that goes under the heading of *niche construction*. Niche construction is a term used by evolutionary biologists to refer to the ways in which animals actively engineer their local environments (niches) so as to alter the sorts of selective pressure that apply to future generations [45]. The idea is relevant to the present discussion, because the notion of niche construction has been implicated in the evolutionary emergence of human intelligence [46]. The full details of this proposal need not detain us here; the main point, for present purposes, is simply the idea that humans have the potential to engineer their environments in ways that alter the evolutionary trajectory of future generations.

Issues of ecological engineering and niche construction are important when we consider the potential role of the Web in supporting the emergence of future forms of machine intelligence. Thus just as progressive alterations in the structure of the physical and social environment may help to establish the conditions that favor the evolutionary emergence of human intelligence (see [46]), so too, perhaps, our current forms of interaction and engagement with the Web can be seen to yield an ecological niche that is conducive to the emergence of advanced (perhaps human-like) forms of machine intelligence.

As a means of helping us get a better grip on what is being proposed here, it may help to focus our attention on the way in which the Global Positioning System (GPS) has contributed to the emergence of spatially-aware autonomous systems. The constant stream of data provided by GPS satellites has obviously impacted the way in which we humans navigate and locate ourselves in space. But it should also be clear that the *very same system* has had a significant impact on the development of a rich array of intelligent systems. The availability of GPS signals has thus transformed the kinds of approach that can be adopted with respect to the implementation of (e.g.) driverless cars and pilotless drones, enabling forms of navigational competence that may have been difficult, if not impossible, to achieve in the absence of such a suitably structured environment. Crucially, once we focus our attention on the sorts of capabilities that are exhibited by driverless cars and pilotless drones, the 'cognitive' relevance of the environment in which such systems are embedded starts to come into clearer view. Absent the constant stream of data provided by GPS satellites and the complexity of the navigational problem may become so severe as to stymie our best attempts at automation. The moral to emerge from all this is that we should not underestimate the transformative potential of an appropriately configured and suitably enriched environment. When it comes to issues of machine intelligence, the ability to engage in various forms of intelligent response may have as much to do with the environment in which a system is embedded as it does with the sophistication of the system's inner information processing mechanisms.

We can clearly think of GPS signals as establishing a particular kind of digital data ecology—one that has proved to be of value when it comes to the implementation of certain kinds of intelligent system. But much the same could be said of the digital data ecology that we encounter in the case of the Web. Consider, for example, one of the key exemplars of the emerging cognitive computing paradigm: IBM Watson. Watson's virtuoso performance in answering an array of difficult questions is undoubtedly an important demonstration of the growing sophistication of Artificial Intelligence (AI) algorithms, especially in the areas of natural language processing, machine learning and domain-specific reasoning. But, in the course of being awestruck by (at least some of) Watson's outputs, it is easy to overlook the simple fact that many of the inputs to the system—especially the information resources that Watson exploits in supplying its human interlocutors with answers—are ones that are, in general, developed by large numbers of human individuals. Such resources include online encyclopedias, dictionaries, thesauri, taxonomies, ontologies and so on [47]. None of these resources, it should be clear, were specifically intended to support Watson, or indeed any of the other cognitive computing systems that are the focus of current research efforts. Nevertheless, such resources play a crucial role in enabling Watson to exhibit capabilities that surpass those of the average human individual. Perhaps if Watson had emerged in an earlier era, we would have been astounded by its question/answering capabilities. And yet Watson is, at root, exactly the same kind of symbol manipulating machine that has long been the focus of philosophical theorizing and the primary instrument of cognitive scientific practice. Arguably, what has changed in recent times is not so much the underlying technologies as the nature of the environment in which such technologies are situated. The emergence of the Web has thus yielded an environment that has altered the 'evolutionary' landscape for intelligent systems. It is an environment that we humans have created, and it is one that we will bequeath to our biological progeny. But perhaps this particular form of niche construction is unlike those that preceded it. Perhaps it is no longer just the cognitive destiny of our own species that is affected by our attempts to create, configure and construct the informational ecology of the online digital world.

VIII. Conclusion

On the basis of the foregoing analysis, we are in a position to identify a number of ways in which the Web can be seen to provide access to the human social environment. One kind of access is captured by the notion of the human cloud (see Section II). In this case, we saw how the Web could be used to 'recruit' human agents into complex information processing tasks. A similar idea emerged in the discussion of active learning (see Section IV). Here, we saw how machine learning systems could actively shape their learning trajectories by soliciting particular kinds of input from the human social environment. Finally, in Section III, we saw how human contributions to the online environment could support the processes of social learning and experiential knowledge mining.

In addition to outlining the ways in which the Web provides access to the human social environment, the present paper also highlights a number of areas for future research. For example, in Section V, we touched on the idea that language has a supracommunicative function, helping to promote productive shifts in the cognitive capabilities of language-wielding agents. We also encountered the idea that maturational shifts in cognitively-relevant parameters may play a crucial role in enabling an intelligent system to acquire certain kinds of cognitive and behavioral competence (see Section VI). Such insights are relevant to the development of intelligent systems that are able to press maximal cognitive benefit from their contact with the human social environment.

The advent of the (Social) Web marks a potentially significant milestone in the development of advanced forms of machine intelligence. Traditionally, issues of social embedding, social interaction and enculturation have been discussed in relation to human intelligence. It is thus the nature of our contact with the human social environment that has been seen to underlie the kinds of cognitive capabilities that are the hallmark of our species. Prior to the advent of the Web, the opportunities for machines to be embedded within the human social environment were somewhat limited. Now, in an era where a significant proportion of humanity engages with the Web on a more-or-less daily basis, it is increasingly difficult for online forms of machine intelligence to ignore the vagaries of the social world. Inasmuch as we accept that human intelligence emerges as the result of our attempt to navigate the complexities of the social realm, then perhaps the online environment is the perfect place to look for machines whose capabilities enable them to reach those parts of the cognitive terrain that only our (human) minds are able to call their home.

Acknowledgment

This work is supported under SOCIAM: The Theory and Practice of Social Machines. The SOCIAM Project is funded by the UK Engineering and Physical Sciences Research Council

(EPSRC) under grant number EP/J017728/1 and comprises the Universities of Southampton, Oxford and Edinburgh.

REFERENCES

[1] P. R. Smart, R. Heersmink, and R. W. Clowes, "The cognitive ecology of the Internet," in *Cognition Beyond the Brain: Computation, Interactivity and Human Artifice*, 2nd ed., S. J. Cowley and F. Vallée-Tourangeau, Eds. London, England, UK: Springer-Verlag, in press.

[2] E. Law and L. von Ahn, "Human computation," *Synthesis Lectures on Artificial Intelligence and Machine Learning*, vol. 5, no. 3, pp. 1–121, 2011.

[3] R. I. M. Dunbar, "The social brain hypothesis," *Evolutionary Anthropology*, vol. 6, no. 5, pp. 178–190, 1998.

[4] R. W. Byrne and A. Whiten, *Machiavellian Intelligence: Social Expertise and the Evolution of Intellect in Monkeys, Apes, and Humans*. Oxford, UK: Oxford University Press, 1988.

[5] E. Herrmann, J. Call, M. V. Hernández-Lloreda, B. Hare, and M. Tomasello, "Humans have evolved specialized skills of social cognition: The cultural intelligence hypothesis," *Science*, vol. 317, no. 5843, pp. 1360–1366, 2007.

[6] H. Kummer, L. Daston, G. Gigerenzer, and J. B. Silk, "The social intelligence hypothesis," in *Human By Nature: Between Biology and the Social Sciences*, P. Weingart, S. D. Mitchell, P. J. Richerson, and S. Maasen, Eds. Mahwah, New Jersey, USA: Lawrence Erlbaum Associates, 1997.

[7] K. Dautenhahn and A. Billard, "Studying robot social cognition within a developmental psychology framework," in *Third European Workshop on Advanced Mobile Robots*, Zürich, Switzerland, 1999.

[8] J. Lindblom and T. Ziemke, "Social situatedness of natural and artificial intelligence: Vygotsky and beyond," *Adaptive Behavior*, vol. 11, no. 2, pp. 79–96, 2003.

[9] M. Tomasello, "Primate cognition: Introduction to the issue," *Cognitive Science*, vol. 24, no. 3, pp. 351–361, 2000.

[10] M. Strohmaier and C. Wagner, "Computational social science for the World Wide Web," *IEEE Intelligent Systems*, vol. 29, no. 5, pp. 84–88, 2014.

[11] P. R. Smart and N. R. Shadbolt, "Social machines," in *Encyclopedia of Information Science and Technology*, M. Khosrow-Pour, Ed. Hershey, Pennsylvania, USA: IGI Global, 2014.

[12] P. R. Smart, "Extended cognition and the Internet: A review of current issues and controversies," *Philosophy & Technology*, in press.

[13] E. Kaganer, E. Carmel, R. Hirschheim, and T. Olsen, "Managing the human cloud," *MIT Sloan Management Review*, vol. 54, no. 2, pp. 23–32, 2013.

[14] B. Hayes, "Cloud computing," *Communications of the ACM*, vol. 51, no. 7, pp. 9–10, 2008.

[15] D. Schall, "Service oriented protocols for human compuation," in *Handbook of Human Computation*, P. Michelucci, Ed. New York, New York, USA: Springer, 2013.

[16] P. Minder and A. Bernstein, "CrowdLang: A programming language for the systematic exploration of human computation systems," in *4th International Conference on Social Informatics*, Lausanne, Switzerland, 2012.

[17] J. Hendler and T. Berners-Lee, "From the Semantic Web to social machines: A research challenge for AI on the World Wide Web," *Artificial Intelligence*, vol. 174, pp. 156–161, 2010.

[18] R. J. Crouser, A. Ottley, and R. Chang, "Balancing human and machine contributions in human computation systems," in *Handbook of Human Computation*, P. Michelucci, Ed. New York, New York, USA: Springer, 2013.

[19] S. Dieleman, K. W. Willett, and J. Dambre, "Rotation-invariant convolutional neural networks for galaxy morphology prediction," *Monthly Notices of the Royal Astronomical Society*, vol. 450, no. 2, pp. 1441–1459, 2015.

[20] C. J. Lintott and J. Reed, "Human computation in citizen science," in *Handbook of Human Computation*, P. Michelucci, Ed. New York, New York, USA: Springer, 2013.

[21] L. von Ahn and L. Dabbish, "Designing games with a purpose," *Communications of the ACM*, vol. 51, no. 8, pp. 58–67, 2008.

[22] N. R. Shadbolt and P. R. Smart, "Knowledge elicitation: Methods, tools and techniques," in *Evaluation of Human Work*, 4th ed., J. R. Wilson and S. Sharples, Eds. Boca Raton, Florida, USA: CRC Press, 2015.

[23] S.-H. Myaeng, Y. Jeong, and Y. Jung, "Experiential knowledge mining," *Foundations and Trends in Web Science*, vol. 4, no. 1, pp. 1–102, 2012.

[24] B. Settles, "Active learning," *Synthesis Lectures on Artificial Intelligence and Machine Learning*, vol. 6, no. 1, pp. 1–114, 2012.

[25] A. Holub, P. Perona, and M. C. Burl, "Entropy-based active learning for object recognition," in *IEEE Online Learning for Classification Workshop*, Anchorage, Alaska, USA, 2008.

[26] L. Barrington, D. Turnbull, and G. Lanckriet, "Game-powered machine learning," *Proceedings of the National Academy of Sciences*, vol. 109, no. 17, pp. 6411–6416, 2012.

[27] F. Ciravegna, S. Chapman, A. Dingli, and Y. Wilks, "Learning to harvest information for the Semantic Web," in *First European Semantic Web Symposium*, Heraklion, Crete, Greece, 2004.

[28] S. Sarawagi, "Information extraction," *Foundations and Trends in Databases*, vol. 1, no. 3, pp. 261–377, 2008.

[29] B. Pang and L. Lee, "Opinion mining and sentiment analysis," *Foundations and Trends in Information Retrieval*, vol. 2, no. 1–2, pp. 1–135, 2008.

[30] E. Ferrara, O. Varol, C. Davis, F. Menczer, and A. Flammini, "The rise of social bots," *Communications of the ACM*, vol. 59, no. 7, pp. 96–104, 2016.

[31] R. Dale, "The return of the chatbots," *Natural Language Engineering*, vol. 22, no. 5, pp. 811–817, 2016.

[32] J. Lester, K. Branting, and B. Mott, "Conversational agents," in *The Practical Handbook of Internet Computing*, M. P. Singh, Ed. Boca Raton, Florida, USA: Chapman & Hall/CRC, 2004.

[33] A. Tumasjan, T. O. Sprenger, P. G. Sandner, and I. M. Welpe, "Predicting elections with Twitter: What 140 characters reveal about political sentiment," in *Fourth International AAAI Conference on Weblogs and Social Media*, Washington D.C., USA, 2010.

[34] M. Donald, *Origins of the Modern Mind: Three Stages in the Evolution of Culture and Cognition*. Cambridge, Massachussets, USA: Harvard University Press, 1991.

[35] A. Clark, "Magic words: How language augments human computation," in *Language and Thought: Interdisciplinary Themes*, P. Carruthers and J. Boucher, Eds. Cambridge, UK: Cambridge University Press, 1998.

[36] ——, "How to qualify for a cognitive upgrade: Executive control, glass ceilings and the limits of simian success," in *The Complex Mind: An Interdisciplinary Approach*, D. McFarland, K. Stenning, and M. McGonigle-Chalmers, Eds. Basingstoke, England, UK: Palgrave Macmillan, 2012.

[37] D. Dennett, *Conciousness Explained*. Boston, Massachusetts, USA: Little, Brown & Company, 1991.

[38] G. Gómez, M. Lungarella, P. Eggenberger Hotz, K. Matsushita, and R. Pfeifer, "Simulating development in a real robot: On the concurrent increase of sensory, motor, and neural complexity," in *Fourth International Workshop on Epigenetic Robotics*, Genoa, Italy, 2004.

[39] J. L. Elman, "Learning and development in neural networks: The importance of starting small," *Cognition*, vol. 48, no. 1, pp. 71–99, 1993.

[40] D. F. Bjorklund, "The role of immaturity in human development," *Psychological Bulletin*, vol. 122, no. 2, pp. 153–169, 1997.

[41] M. Lungarella and L. Berthouze, "Adaptivity through physical immaturity," in *2nd International Workshop on Epigenetic Robotics: Modeling Cognitive Development in Robotic Systems*, Edinburgh, Scotland, 2002.

[42] D. F. Bjorklund and B. L. Green, "The adaptive nature of cognitive immaturity," *American Psychologist*, vol. 47, no. 1, pp. 46–54, 1992.

[43] S. K. Chalup, "Incremental learning in biological and machine learning systems," *International Journal of Neural Systems*, vol. 12, no. 6, pp. 447–465, 2002.

[44] A. M. Turing, "Computing machinery and intelligence," *Mind*, vol. 59, no. 236, pp. 433–460, 1950.

[45] K. N. Laland, J. Odling-Smee, and M. W. Feldman, "Niche construction, biological evolution, and cultural change," *Behavioral and Brain Sciences*, vol. 23, no. 1, pp. 131–146, 2000.

[46] K. Sterelny, "Social intelligence, human intelligence and niche construction," *Philosophical Transactions of the Royal Society B: Biological Sciences*, vol. 362, no. 1480, pp. 719–730, 2007.

[47] D. Ferrucci *et al.*, "Building Watson: An overview of the DeepQA project," *AI Magazine*, vol. 31, no. 3, pp. 59–79, 2010.